Fast Muscle

Alex Gabbard & Squire Gabbard

Published by Gabbard Publications
Rt. 1, Box 76
Lenoir City, TN 37771
Copyright 1990, Gabbard Publications
Printed in USA
1st Printing
by Viking Press

Distributed by:
Motorbooks International
729 Prospect Ave.
Osceola, WI 54020

NOTICE: The information and historical accounts contained in this book are true and accurate to the best of our knowledge. The authors/publisher disclaim all liability incurred in connection with the use of the information contained in this work. However, should an error in historical accuracy appear, it is solely the responsibility of the authors and will be corrected in later editions of this book.

Library of Congress Cataloging-in-Publication Data
Gabbard, Alex & Squire
   Fast Muscle: America's Fastest Muscle Cars

Includes index.
1. Automobile history - History - Pictorial works.
2. American automobile manufacturers - History -
   Pictorial works.
I. Title.
1990
ISBN 0-9622608-1-9

Cover design and photos by Alex Gabbard.
Gallery of Fast Muscle design and photos by Alex Gabbard.
Book layout and design by Alex Gabbard.
Black and white photos by Squire Gabbard unless noted otherwise.
Feature sections by Squire Gabbard.

CONTENTS

Fast times remembered: The cars of my youth.

Alex Gabbard

The late '50s and early '60s were indeed exciting times. I saw my first drag race in 1957 as a tagalong with my older brother and his friend. The location was an outlaw drag strip near North Wilkesboro, N.C. It was in a valley wooded on one side with a sloping hill on the other for spectators to sit and watch.

The booming announcer's voice blared one phenomenal speed after another. At that time, elapsed times were not as important as they would later become. Speed was far more widely recognized as more descriptive of a car's performance. The fastest "car" that Saturday was a '40 Ford stripped of everything. It was nothing more than a running chassis and wooden chair strapped in place behind the steering wheel! Those days were "run whatcha brung".

As the driver blasted down the quartermile, the noise from that Ford's stubby exhaust pipes reverberated through the trees with the whap-whap-whapping sound characteristic of flathead engines. Following that run, the announcer bellowed a fantastic speed of over 128 mph. For a short run, just one-fourth of a mile, that was really something in those days. For comparison, Buddy Sampson's Olds-powered dragster that won NHRA's Top Eliminator at the US Nationals that year turned an impressive 141.5 mph in 10.49 seconds as the best in the country.

Enthusiasm for drag racing grew like mad. It was the "in" thing to do for us high schoolers and produced innumerable arguments that heightened make loyalties. Whatever we drove was fastest, except for my 6-cylinder Studebaker. A few weekend dollars provided thrills aplenty just to watch, but the itch to race was too much. Later, my wife and I raced, too, and made many passes in a 17-second flat, 4-cylinder Sunbeam Alpine.

Several local drag strips drew weekend racers and fans by the droves: Farmington, East Bend, Greensboro in addition to North Wilkesboro. Every town of any size had a strip, and some like Farmington had no town at all. It was just a converted field, but we packed the stands every weekend anyway.

In the late '50s, North Carolina was known more for stock car racing than drag racing. That was because so much of it was centered in Charlotte. If you wanted a fast car, somebody in Charlotte could build it. By 1961 and '62, many top league quartermilers also got their start in that part of the country. Ronnie Sox in Burlington became a factory Comet driver in '65 and a legend at 25. Paul Norris worked as a pit crew member for Holman-Moody, then went drag racing with the Holman-Moody Mustang that year.

There were many national caliber drivers touring the country, and Farmington, just west of Winston-Salem, attracted the best. Richard Petty added his name to the greats of drag racing that year with a light blue number 43-Jr hemi-powered 'Cuda. National champion Jack Chrisman ran his blown A/FX Comet there. Shirl Greer piloted his A/FX hemi Dodge, TENSION, to many thrilling passes against HEMI HANNA, Sox in the Gate City Plymouth and many other cars and drivers long forgotten. Hubert Platt and his GEORGIA SHAKER was one not forgotten. Back then, big-time match racing went on all around us. You name the strip, somebody big was going to be there. And there were always many exciting cars of all types. How about a blown and injected 4-4-2 Olds? That was some machine, but I don't recall any names associated with it.

Racing was a way of life in my part of North Carolina, stock car racers, drag racers and bootleggers. Just up the road from my home lived Junior Johnson. Like many other men in the area who were trying to get ahead in a rural economy, he had been in trouble with the feds for running "corn squeezin's", otherwise known as "moonshine". After a stint in the "pen" in 1957, Junior returned to racing and became a big name. In 1960, he won the Daytona 500 in a 348-powered '59 Chevy and invented drafting to get around the faster Pontiacs. When he retired from driving in 1965, Junior had racked up 50 Grand National victories. He was a local hero for us kids. His future wife, Flossie, worked at the telephone office in Elkin where my future wife worked. Since then, he and Flossie have become greats in stock car racing history.

Farther down the road at Randleman lived the Petty family. Their farm didn't look much different from many others in the area, although it was the home of three-time NASCAR champion Lee Petty and future seven-time champ Richard. Young Richard was the idol of aspiring high schoolers who wanted to race, but he hadn't quite reached Elvis status among the girls.

Through the spring of 1964 at Surry Central High School in Dobson, the main topic of discussion among us boys was always cars. How fast? What new and faster car was coming to a dealer nearby? Did you see that red 409 in the showroom in Elkin? What marvelous and powerful engine was coming out next? Who won what race? Wow! Were those Pontiacs fast at Charlotte ('61). Did you go to the drags Sunday? Some guy named Chrisman smoked'em ALL the way through the traps! Didja hear, Junior won another race. Betcha Petty coulda got by Fireball at Daytona ('62) if he had another lap. Son! How those Fords ran at Daytona ('63), and what happened to those superfast "Mystery" engine Chevys, pal? Fireball set *another* record at Darlington? Have you seen the fabulous new super stock hemi Dodge? What's a "hemi" anyway? Petty did what at Daytona? A blistering new record! What'd you say: The hemis cleaned house and Ford is going to quit? That new hemi is a cheater, buddy-boy! On and on.

The Southern 500 at Darlington in September opened the school year with debate. The Daytona 500 fired us with wintertime disputes. The World 600 at Charlotte in May was the final round as the school year ended. They were the top three races in our schooltime conversations, then came summertime drag racing. It was racing, all year long.

Those were great times. Not only did we have fast cars, we had the excitement of our own rock 'n' roll music about cars and good times. And we thought it would never end. Throw in the movies that were made in our area, *Thunder in Carolina* and *Thunder Road*. They were favorites (and still not out on video). Drive-in restaurants flourished and catered to the automobile. Waitresses learned about us car nuts out having a good time at their expense. "Could I have a sauerkraut sandwich and prune milkshake, pleez?"

The major stock car races were infrequent, but drag racing was all the time. If not on strips, on the highway. North Wilkesboro, East Bend and that super quartermile strip at Farmington were within easy driving distance. It drew the big names on the national tour, the Super Stocks and later A/FX cars. By the time I was in college in Winston-Salem (1964), the first of Super Experimental Stocks, later called Funny Cars, began appearing. A little further afield were the Greensboro and Charlotte drag strips, and in Bristol, Tennessee, was awesome "Thunder Valley" with some of the best drag racing and biggest names in the country, so much so that NHRA held its first Springnationals at Bristol in 1965. Lexington, Kentucky, also had an excellent strip that attracted many top cars and drivers. Good drag strips were literally everywhere.

Regardless of how fast a car might look, or how big an engine it might have, bragging was just bragging until decided on the line. Along with an occasional new car, some of the fastest cars at school were the older police "Interceptor" Fords owned by a few of the students. A 352-powered '58 with 3-speed and overdrive might have been a plain car, but it was scintillating when the roar of a full throttle 4-bbl lit up those narrow rear tires. Those ex-Highway Patrol cars weren't quick, but they definitely had top end. They also had the best suspensions. Most cars back then were "three on the tree", and a quick full-power shift to second was a work of art. The linkage mechanisms had a tendency to hang up between gears. Results? A blown clutch. Conversions for putting the shifter in the floor quickly became common, and if you had a few coins, you could brag about YOUR Hurst shifter. Hurst was not yet the giant in the industry.

My introduction to fast cars was brother Johnny's '51 flathead Ford coupe, and Uncle Ben's Studebaker Hawk. That old Ford was another police "Interceptor" with overdrive. It couldn't take power shifts either. Johnny blew a clutch three times. It wasn't rare to see that car parked on the side of the road for days at a time. When Uncle Ben came to visit, a ride in that fabulous Hawk was a treat of lasting memory.

Working boys didn't usually go around blowing clutches and wasting tires, but my brother's move into building a Ford pickup with an Olds 88 engine produced a local legend that could do both. It became legendary not so much for racing exploits, but for its electric fuel pump that whined like a supercharger, an unplanned benefit caused by the stock pump not fitting. Even the guys standing around the pool room trying to look James Dean cool became enthused when this "supercharged" Ford came by, and NOBODY got to look under the hood of that pickup. A little intrigue never hurt a good thing!

There wasn't another car or truck around that sounded like that pickup when under power, so the "supercharged" stories flourished. That faded green truck could lay down dual black marks for a hundred yards up hill. Peeling off a set of 900s, the largest tires available at the time, was to the tune of that big Olds howling with power as Johnny left another cloud of smoked rubber. Those who saw it went away to tell the story bigger each time it was repeated. During the summer for several years, that old pickup hauled many loads of drag racing fanatics to Farmington, North Wilkesboro and East Bend. It also "dragged town" creating all sorts of stories that were amplified by the few of us who kept the tales flying. Tail gate down - wanna drag? Tail gate up - no draggin'.

The fastest new cars back then weren't the Fords or Chevys or Pontiacs or Oldsmobiles, although they were the cars seen in stock car racing and on drag strips. The fastest car in 1961, though perhaps not the quickest, was widely recognized to be the Studebaker Hawk. Uncle Ben's earlier model Hawk was the first I had seen. Its smooth and rapid acceleration pushed me firmly back in a contoured bucket seat. Studebaker had them years before other makes.

When the 1961 Hawk GT was introduced, not only was it the first production GT car built in America (GT meaning Grand Touring personal-size coupe), it was also recognized as the fastest car on the road. None of my friends seemed to care. It didn't matter that the bigger engine cars from the big three tended to run out of breath around 120-mph while the Hawk was good for 140. Hawks were lighter, smaller and more sleek, the sort of car that muscle cars would become in the mid-60s. But they were so rare that they had no impact.

The sensational Avanti of '63 caused a lot of heads to turn. It was in a class by itself, exclusive in sight, sound and speed, truly an exotic car. It was without doubt THE fastest car built in this country. Take your pick from 140- to 170-mph models! They set so many high-speed records at Bonneville that their "fastest" title was uncontested, but nobody cared because they were so expensive and also too rare to matter. Still, when a local shopping center put one on display and added a sign about giving it away to the holder of the chosen raffle ticket, everybody jumped at the chance to own an Avanti for 50 cents. They were highly desirable cars.

In 1964, just when the "baby boomers" were telling the big three that they wanted cars with Hawk and Avanti features, Studebaker died. My father had been a Studebaker dealer, and they have always been a part of my life. Soon, each manufacturer had GT models in their lines, the GTO for instance, and later long hood, short deck, personal-size cars.

I don't remember seeing a single Studebaker drag racing. Generally, they were cars that admirers aspired to own and drive, something of an exclusive. In those days, new cars were not common at drag strips. Although great stories were told about all sorts of cars, by 1960, fast cars were still mostly homebuilt pre-war bodied gassers and altereds or older model "Interceptors". Enthusiasts built the most exciting cars for themselves and dominated the strip scene until the coming of the factory-built Super Stock and FX cars, and later Pro Stocks. The Super Experimental Stock cars (early day Funny Cars) quickly became favorites. "Slingshot" (engine in front of the driver) rail dragsters were fairly common and were regarded as the ultimate homebuilt. When a big name such as Connie Kalitta or "Sneaky Pete" Robinson came to town, huge throngs of fans poured into the strip wherever the star was performing.

When my future wife and I went to the drags during that time, we had the fortunate opportunity to meet several of the drivers who have since become legends. One was World Champion Jack Chrisman who made the tour with his '65 SOHC Mercury Comet. While at Farmington one Sunday, I helped unload and load that car, then had the honor of looking over the mechanic's shoulder while the wrenching was done. Jack laid down tire-smoking blasts through the quarter-mile that had everyone on their feet. That beautiful car was an immense thriller, and Jack and his mechanic were superstars. Later, Mary and I had the honor of having dinner with the two of them at Staley's in Winston-Salem.

By this time, high performers that would later be termed "muscle cars" began rolling, and fan turnout increased as their numbers grew. Make loyalty produced heated rivalries and resulted in grudge race after grudge race among locals. Whose car was really fastest was no brag, just fact. The second driver through the traps lost.

Although most "real" racing was done within the safer confines of drag strips, the urge to run some top speeds was hard to resist. Back then, traffic was thin by late evening, and open stretches of straight road occasionally became the sites for seeing "what she'll do". Unmodified cars could usually top 110 mph, but with '50s style suspensions and the skinny tires of the time, they were unsafe. A few of my friends were killed in those cars, three at one time, so I have a little different perspective than most modern muscle car fans.

At that time, seat belts in a car were sure signs that the driver was a racer. Belts were not factory standard equipment, and people who installed them usually did so because ads showed them endorsed by a famous racing driver. Seat belts were for racing, not safety. Few cars had them.

Then there were the braggers, those proud new car owners who were torn between not "hurting" their new car by running it hard and racing. Repairs cost a lot, and the embarrassment of being known to have blown an engine was hard to live with. If your car blew the rear end, that was bragworthy as testimony to having a very powerful engine. But strangely, when the Detroit Lockers came along, the clunking sound produced when they "locked up" was regarded as a bad differential by friends who knew no better. For fear of break-ing something, owners didn't run their cars hard or had the Locker removed. In fact, Lockers were among the strongest performance differentials ever built. In a time of high opinions, opinions prevailed over believing that factory engineers knew what they were doing. But then, consider that so many new products were coming along so fast that confusion over just what was what could not be sorted out before something better came along.

Whose car was fastest? With so many fast cars around, including modified older cars and new factory hot rods, it didn't take long for a few to pair off for a challenge. Occasionally, the Highway Patrol got wind of some of those empty-stretch showdowns along newly constructed Interstate 40, and that caused some problems. They drove fast 427 Fords with good suspensions and fat tires, and had top end galore.

As a high schooler in 1961, I recall the thrill of a tri-power Ford Starliner at North Wilkesboro with the number "401" stenciled on its light blue flanks. It drew me like a magnet. After a little tuning to correct some low-end spitting, that car laid down run after run ahead of similar size cars. Back then, class differences were corrected by spotting two car lengths per class. That was a time before "Christmas Tree" lights and dial ins. A flagman highlighted the drama of each contest as he first signaled each driver to check readiness, then flagged them away for quartermiles of high-speed gear snatching.

Then came the 409s. There were three of them at school. A couple of '63-1/2 fastback Galaxies were also in the parking lot. In Elkin was a Holman-Moody modified street 427 fastback that was faster than anything from anywhere. A few 413 and 426 wedge Dodges and Plymouths turned heads as they rolled around town. Hemis were seen at Sunday drags. There was the occasional Corvette, but never a Cobra until Zac Reynolds rolled into Farmington one Saturday with a one-day-old 427SC. He blew away a 427 'Vette and everything else, and quickly became known as a "gunfighter" with that Cobra: "Have Cobra, Will Race". At a real 170 mph top, he was king.

"Draggin' town" in Elkin was a Saturday night "have to" while in high school. As a college guy, cruisin' Winston-Salem with my favorite lady, now my wife, was the scene. There was Zac and his Cobra, Dickie Smith and his svelt E-Jag roadster, Ronnie Joyner and his 409 (and GTO, a 426 Dodge and who knows what else). Home town best friend R.J. Cummings was there with his red and swoopy 383 Dodge Charger. Friday and Saturday nights brought out the fast muscle. They were everywhere!

This book is a product of that time. It is a look back through my memories: the people I've met, the cars I've known, the cars I've owned, the engines I've built, the racing I've done, the racing I've seen, all are parts of this book. To the many people at Ford, GM and Chrysler, to everyone whose cars I've photographed for the many hundreds of magazine articles I've done, especially to Bob Costanzo at Daytona and to Bonnie Nestor for her proofing labors, I extend many thanks. The features were written by my son, Squire, whose enthusiasm for cars of all types parallels my own. This is our book about muscle cars, yesterday and today.

Bill Humphrey in a factory-sponsored 427 A/FX 427 Fairlane versus a fuel injected A/Sports Production 'Vette, 1963.

Early Rumblings

Muscle cars, those awesome big cubic inch cars of the 1960s, were the result of product promotion wars between the manufacturers. The decade began with Ford, GM and Chrysler in an expanding cubic inch and horsepower war. When the rapid growth in performance cars was recognized, the "kids" crashed through the gates of the new decade into what has become recognized as the automobile's most flamboyant era, the age of muscle cars.

The market for new high-performance cars began with the overhead valve V-8 engines from GM in 1949. Ford launched its line of overhead valve engines when the "Y-block" V-8s were introduced in the 1954 models. The next year, Chevrolet hit the market with the revolutionary small block V-8, and the heated Ford versus Chevrolet rivalry has grown ever since. By the late '50s, Ford's first FE series and Chevrolet's W-engine big blocks had caught up to the big Pontiac, Olds and Chrysler engines in capacity, almost 400 cubic inches, and soon matched them in horsepower. By 1963, an entire generation of high-performance enthusiasts was both responsible for and indulged in the widest selection of big cubic inch engines the industry had ever seen. Then came the hemi engines from Chrysler and Ford, and rapid escalation in the horsepower war begun in the mid-'50s.

All three of the major manufacturers built hard running machines that made the '60s truly sensational. Add some very fast machines from Studebaker, out of business by '65, and a big splash from American Motors at the end of the decade to see the breadth of new car selection offered to '60s new car buyers. Along with indelible marks made by small firms such as Shelby American and Hurst, performance-minded dealers like Yenko, Baldwin and others offered buyers an enormous range of high-performing cars to fit any price range. Racing shops such as Holman-Moody in North Carolina, Bud Moore

in South Carolina, Bill Stroppe and Les Ritchey in California, Bill "Grumpy" Jenkins in Pennsylvania among many others throughout the nation made significant contributions to the muscle car age.

The greatest variety of muscle cars came in 1970, but then Ford withdrew from racing late in the year. Chevrolet's "back door" effort closed up even tighter, and Chrysler backed away from high-performance as did American Motors. MoPars of the early '70s were the last of the muscle cars, and were by then derelicts from a rapidly changed economy. The age of the muscle car came crashing to a close as insurance and emission regulations made muscle cars unsalable. In '68, manufacturers entered a new era of increasingly stringent government dictates on emission and safety standards. Also, "baby boomers" were growing up and some had families of their own. Muscle cars had places only in their memories. The excitement of the '60s was gone, and when the oil barons of the middle east tried to concentrate the world's wealth in their own hands, used muscle cars became cheap. They were gas-hungry dinosaurs of a past age when fuel prices were one-fourth of '70s prices.

The bleak '70s brought econoboxes and wistful glances back at the sensational '60s. The differences in the decades are remarkable. The 1950s turned into the '60s as a great time to be alive. Fueled by the exuberance of youth, America was having good times with cars and rock 'n' roll music. In contrast, the turn into the '70s was pitched as the "sizzling '70s" but it fizzled out when the economy entered a deep recession and manufacturers turned their backs on performance to survive. Chrysler Corporation almost collapsed and was saved by a billion dollar loan, Lee Iacocca and dynamic leadership.

The decade from 1973-83 is remembered more for the doubt and worry that replaced a once vibrant America. Our population's average age had increased, and '60s youthful values had passed. The influence of the Viet Nam war was pervasive and dire. The good times beat of rock 'n' roll had become ballads of philosophy. America had lost its spirit.

Muscle cars were for the kids. By 1962, a huge wave of young people began reaching driving age. They were what was known as the "baby boom" following World War II. The "boomers" created their own markets and their own cultures. Cars were their mobility and music with a dance beat was their statement. The kids of the '60s were the pulse and vitality of this country. Fast cars were their expression.

Second and third cars in the family became increasingly normal as the teenagers became drivers. They picked up friends on the way to and from high school and college. They took their dates to Friday night ball games and to sock hops on Saturday night after cruisin' the local "scenes". Sunday afternoon engine tuning or drag racing or going to the races to watch the stockers roar around the growing number of thunderdomes were summer pastimes. Good friends, a favorite girl and fast cars were the themes of the time, a golden era focused on America's youth.

Drive-in restaurants catered to the newly mobile youth. They were an outgrowth of the '30s-era "diners" that were usually made from surplus railway dining cars from which the sandwich mills got their generic name.

Cars were the medium of fun and provided inexpensive forays for friends into local drive-in movies at 50 cents a head, not including all the jokesters in the trunk who didn't get counted. Cars were also the medium of courtship where drive-in back row passion pits and secluded lover's lanes produced intimate moments surrounded by the voices of Elvis, Rickie, Buddy, the Beatles, the Beach Boys, Jan and Dean, and many others who were young people singing for young people, not today's forty-year-olds making music for the money in it. The forever infectious beat of rock 'n' roll rhythm was the heartbeat of the time.

It was an age of engines, later supplanted by audio systems in the '70s when cars didn't "go" and all that was left was "show." Cult symbols were 409, 413, 396, 427 and Hemi. GTO, 4-4-2, BOSS, Super Bee Six Pack were the rage, and every hot-blooded American boy wanted one. Fastbacks, ram air, two four-barrels, four-on-the-floor, and the roar of big inches bellowing through open pipes making low elapsed times and quartermile top speeds were the measure of cars, not stereos. Engines were the heartbeat of America. Drag racing was the sport invented by the kids, and it was drag racing that became the showcase of muscle cars. Back then, it was real flat out drag racing, not today's brackets and the art of "sandbagging" by braking hard at the end of the strip to keep from "breaking out" of your class index and losing. The quickest and fastest no longer win, just the driver who can run closest to his index.

With the 1970s' ever more stringent environmental controls on engines, emasculation of the brute power of what had become known as the muscle car produced big cubic inch low performers during mid-decade. Manufacturers responded to the issue of their environmental responsibility by spending a full ten years trying to learn how to make cars perform well with smaller engines. With modern electronics, exciting cars returned by the mid-1980s, but the muscular brutes seen and talked about ten to twenty years earlier were gone. The age of the muscle car was over. Today, the growing number of collectors who still dream of driving one of those fabled over 400 horsepower, big cubic inch muscle cars keeps them alive.

The following chapters illustrate muscle cars and their time, then end with a brief look at Jr. Muscle cars and Trans-Am racing. Perhaps the reader will get a sense of the tinny "vibes" from AM radios and small speakers tucked in the dash of an imaginary Galaxie 500 or Dodge Charger or 396 Chevelle of a quarter-century ago. Use a little imagination to put yourself behind the wheel and glide back to the '60s when fast Fords, Chevys and MoPars were everywhere. Twist the key of a Thunderbolt and feel the blast of 427 cubic inches coming instantly to life. Grasp the shifter and glance over at your adversary in the other lane, rev the engine to get his attention, catch the light to wring out a 12-second quartermile amid the deafening thunder of open pipes roaring through the bonds of time. That's what this book is all about.

Butch "Mr. 427 Ford" Leal and Dick "Mr. Chevrolet" Harrell, in the 427 wedge war of 1964. Gold Dust Classics photo.

The Johnny Beauchamp driven Holman-Moody built 430 Thunderbird in the fabled 1959 photo finish against NASCAR legend Lee Petty. Beauchamp was declared winner, but after 60 hours of deliberations, Bill France reversed that decision and awarded Petty the win. Daytona Speedway photo.

The Beginning:

Some historians argue that muscle cars were nothing more than the evolution of the type of car that American manufacturers built from 1955 through '57 when factory stock car racing was intense. Those years saw the "horsepower wars" flourish between Detroit's big three. One-up-manship advertising rivalries meant that each firm sought to market larger cubic inch and higher horsepower cars than the other.

That era laid the base for the over-400 cubic inch muscle cars of the '60s. Product planners and engineers were charged with the responsibility of producing cars to beat the competition in stock car racing, and that took increasingly larger and more powerful engines. Then, the explosive growth in popularity of drag racing brought the high drama of factory competition to the quartermile sprints with the super stocks. These cars were powered by engines largely developed for stock car racing. Still later, aerodynamics began to play an increasingly important part in stock car competition, but was only styling on the wild side for muscle cars.

The beginning of what later became the muscle cars is rooted as early as 1957. The '57 models with their tall fins were not just a styling exercise. Fins were claimed to give improved stability at high speeds, and that made speed an integral part of the overall automotive styling and marketing picture. Perhaps the most aggressive of the '57 styling jobs was the stunning Plymouth Fury, the work of Chrysler Corporation's Virgil Exner. The Fury's aggressive tilted-forward frontal lines accented long sweeping chrome along the sides that ended with "arrow fins". Such styling spoke of tall top speeds. The tilted-forward mode of styling was common to the big three and further illustrates that speed was the leading design theme of the time.

The factory decisions to go racing produced the big engines and cars capable of higher and higher speeds. That launched the muscle car era about ten years after Smokey Yunick, Ed Cole and several other Chevrolet people met on a hilltop overlooking a stock car race in the North Wilkesboro, N.C. area. (See *FAST CHEVYS*, pgs. 24-31.) They were there to discuss how Chevrolet could get into NASCAR racing with the new 1955 V-8s. That was the beginning.

When Ford learned of the plot, the movers and shakers at Dearborn set up a racing organization through Schwam Motors of Charlotte, N.C. Its purpose was to compete heads up with Chevrolet and everyone else. (See *FAST FORDS*, pgs. 33-42.) The factory "horsepower wars" began in a big way, and the major showcase was the Southern 500 at Darlington.

Radio broadcasts and newspaper accounts of the big races, especially the Southern 500, fired the imaginations of many young men to want to go racing. One was a mechanic by the name of Fred Lorenzen who was to become Ford's big gun and NASCAR's most popular driver in the early 1960s. He heard the announcer describe the tactics of hard charger Curtis Turner and Joe Weatherly along with Daytona Beach area stars Glenn "Fireball" Roberts, Herb Thomas and Marshall Teague. Later in 1959 and '60, the giant speedways at Daytona, Atlanta and Charlotte opened their gates, then Talladega at the end of the '60s decade. By then, a multimillion dollar sport had developed complete with heavy factory involvement and headline drivers. It hasn't stopped growing since.

When a particular car won, fans poured into local showrooms to see just what a winning stock car racer was like, and that produced sales. The "win on Sunday, sell on Monday"

9

In 1960, Joe Lee Johnson drove a 348 Chevrolet to win the World 600 at Charlotte. Rex White was NASCAR champion that year and won 6 races among Chevrolet's 13 wins.

The '60 Fords were not as fast as the Pontiacs, but won 15 NASCAR races anyway. Here, Jerry Titus of Trans-Am fame runs the Riverside road course in 1968 in a '60 Ford.

theme emerged during the mid-'50s era, and manufacturers responded to the public's feverish thirst for high-performance with all sorts of new products. Both Chrysler and Chevrolet had fuel-injected engines in 1957. When the 300B Chrysler set the passenger car speed record in its class, it was the fastest production car in the country. Options for the 300B produced a one horsepower per cubic inch hemispherical combustion chamber engine grown out of the first hemi of 1951. Chevrolet's 283 horsepower, 283 cubic inch V-8 was another one horsepower per cubic inch engine, but more compact than the Chrysler. By 1957, the 283 had a new 4-speed transmission, the first time for such equipment in a production American passenger car.

The year before, Ford had offered supercharging on its 312 cubic inch Thunderbird and adapted the huffer to the '57 line of full-size cars with the optional "racing kit". That bumped output to 285 advertised horsepower, two more than rival Chevrolet. In the low-priced field, Plymouth came equipped with 318 cubic inch engines, thus claiming a larger engine than either Chevrolet or Ford. Dodge cars came with the 354-inch version of the big Chrysler Fire Power hemi, and the 300s staked claim to being the largest in the industry with the 392 hemi.

On the race tracks, car hoods were emblazoned boldly with horsepower figures. That gave racing fans of 1957 more points to argue, right or wrong. Everybody "knew" that the 283 H.P. on Chevys was low and Ford's 300 H.P. couldn't be real, more like the 325 H.P. on Mercurys, they argued. The new 347-cid engine from Pontiac was another 325 H.P. powerplant while the much larger 371 from Oldsmobile was said to be underrated at 325 H.P. because the Dodge 354 was a 330 H.P. racer. Arguments among fans grew like mad.

Factory engineers at Dearborn and Warren were honing their high-performance designs, and their lighter cars captured all but 5 races that went to Olds and 2 taken by Pontiac that year. Fords and Chevys now had better power curves matched to racing weight. Ford won 27 NASCAR races, and Chevrolet took 18 and the championship. Buck Baker won 10 races that year, all in Chevys, to take the 1957 NASCAR crown.

Stock car racing had won an enormous following of fans

who increased sales of Chrysler products by 40% to 1,223,035 cars produced that calendar year. Ford fans gave FoMoCo an increase of 16% to 1,889,705. While Chevrolet production dropped 6% down to 1,522,549 cars, Olds production dropped by almost 10% as did Buick by nearly 24%. Pontiac, a new force on the competition scene, rose 3.3%.

Factory planners knew that it took about three years for a concept to find its way into production, and they were eyeing the coming surge in sales by the World War II "baby boomers". Spurred on by increased levels of factory competition and the projected huge increase in sales, they laid the foundation for another very exciting episode in American automobiles in the 1960s.

While the planners made plans for a bigger future, another "growing pain" was being felt in the automotive industry. More and more cars were traveling America's mostly two-lane highways, resulting in more and more deaths and injuries. The voting age public was becoming increasingly alarmed at the carnage, and rumblings of government intervention into the automotive industry grew louder. To ward off government controls, the moguls of Detroit threw an unsuspected curve.

During the waning minutes of the February 1957 meeting of the Automotive Manufacturers Association, GM boss Harlow "Red" Curtice cast a deft maneuver on his counterpart at Ford Motor Co., Robert McNamara. The idea was that manufacturers should not compete with their customers. McNamara was new at the top post of Ford, and while old Henry rolled over in his grave at having an outsider dictate Ford policy, McNamara accepted the proposal as a way to cut expenses. It matured into the AMA ban on factory participation in racing issued the following June. The ban was a radical change in policy. The key points said that manufacturers would no longer support racing competition; no horsepower figures or high-performance data, real or implied, were to be used in advertising; and each manufacturer was to delete all high-performance equipment from catalogs.

McNamara handed down the edict, and Ford was out of racing and high-performance in every way. Only heavy-duty equipment for police cars and taxi (fleet) use were allowed, and they could not be advertised. While high-performance

Pontiacs were the fastest cars in 1960. At Daytona, they won both 100-mile qualifiers and the 500. Glenn "Fireball" Roberts (shown here on left) won the first round and Jack Smith took the second. "Fireball" set a new record of 151.556-mph and led the first 19 laps of the 500, then went out with mechanical problems. The final laps were Bobby Johns (Pontiac) and Junior Johnson (Chevrolet) who won. Daytona Speedway photo.

lived on at Chevrolet and Pontiac, safety became the marketing theme for Ford.

Chevrolet? Things were a bit different over at the Tech Center in Warren. Insiders with strong personalities such as "Bunkie" Knudsen at Pontiac, Zora Arkus-Duntov at Chevrolet and Bill Mitchell of the Art and Color section of the Design Staff (Corvette) went ahead with their plans. Knudsen built Pontiac into a leader in innovation to rival Chevrolet. Mitchell funded his own racing with champion driver Dr. Dick Thompson at the wheel of his prototype Sting Ray Corvette. Thompson raced the car to SCCA's C/Modified national championship in 1960. This was the car that later spawned the Corvette Sting Ray introduced in 1963.

It was also Duntov who pursued the 348 "W-engine" development as a stock car racing engine. From 1958 through 1960, it was an unstated part of Chevrolet's marine engine development program contracted through Jim Rathman of Melbourne, Florida. That program came to fruition later with Junior Johnson's Daytona 500 victory of 1960 in a '59 Chevy along with Rex White's NASCAR championship that year.

The rise of Pontiac as a performance marque was due to Semon "Bunkie" Knudsen, who brought his maverick ideas to GM as a tool engineer in 1939. He was molded in the MIT intellectual atmosphere and was for Pontiac what Ed Cole was for Chevrolet. Both wanted a "young man's" car, and Cole's '55 Chevy with the new V-8 produced by project engineer Al Kolbe was on target. At 44, Knudsen became the youngest of GM's division chiefs when he assumed the helm at Pontiac. He reversed some of the styling trends that his father, "Big Bill" Knudsen, had established years earlier in an attempt to revitalize the staid Pontiac as a car to attract young buyers. He brought a new excitement to the old Indian line. His first impact was introducing the Bonneville marque to Pontiac in 1957. This line began as the new high-style convertible that first year. Soon to follow was a new engine that would prove to have enormous potential for future growth.

In preparation for increased stock car racing, each of the big three introduced big block engines in 1958. The three years from concept to product did not anticipate the AMA ban. The top Plymouth was the "special edition" Fury with the twin 4-bbl Dual Fury V-800 engine, but making the Fury even more special was a new engine, the optional fuel-injected Golden Commando 350 producing 315-hp. This was another version of the Chrysler B-block that was to see evolution through the 440-cid mills of the early '70s. Dodge retained the smaller 361-inch Chrysler hemi rated at 345-hp while the big Chryslers kept the 392 Fire Power hemi. In optional fuel-injected form, the 300D Chrysler hemi was rated at a whopping 390 horsepower, highest in the industry. These cars were fitted with a speedometer numbered to 150 mph! Although there was some advertising that Mercury would offer an optional 400-hp version of the 430-inch engine adapted from Lincoln, it didn't happen. Chrysler was king of the hill.

Ford's new FE series big blocks came with a maximum displacement of 352 cubic inches rated at 300-hp. The '58s began the line of FE engines that became the legendary 427, followed by the 428 and 429 engines of the '60s. Ford fans were able to maintain a cubic inch bragging advantage over the Chevy 348, initially a truck engine adapted to passenger car service. It was to prove an illustrious marriage, as shown by NASCAR racing championships in both forms, 348 and 409. The 409 became immortalized in drag racing before Ford's 427 rose to dominance.

Ford introduced the Edsel that year with available 361- or 410-cid engines, the latter rated at 345-hp in top form. Mercury shared the 430-inch Lincoln engine, but when these were installed in Thunderbirds in 1959, the 'Birds gave the debut of the new super-speedway at Daytona a decidedly Ford look. While controversy flew that the track was a "killer" (Marshall Teague had been killed there while attempting to set a new record) and that tires were not up to such speeds, unknown Johnny Beauchamp's Thunderbird crossed the line with Lee Petty's Olds in a photo finish. Beauchamp was declared winner, only to be dethroned after 60 hours of deliberation. France gave the win to Petty.

Putting a big engine in a smaller car was the theme of the muscle car era. Which car began the trend? The first muscle car was the 430 Thunderbird of 1959. Although pricey for young buyers and clearly a limited option, it was a car whose idea was ahead of its time.

Ford's stock car racing connection, Holman-Moody in Charlotte, marketed such cars through their advertised "T-

Bird Power Products" for going 150 mph in a complete race-ready stocker for $4,995. This was another feature of H-M's "Competition Proven" products during the lean times before Ford ventured into "Total Performance".

How the 430 'Bird came about was two-fold; the engines were available, and Holman-Moody had nothing to race because of the AMA ban. John Holman went to Ford and bought reject parts at junk prices to build six T-birds to race. As racing cars, no one would know that the parts were sub-quality for production Thunderbirds. And no one would know that they were not factory-built race cars, either.

These cars became the rub that further inflamed the Ford versus Chevrolet feud. Although Ford was not behind the effort at all, when Beauchamp and the other Thunderbird drivers put on a grand showing at Daytona, no one believed that Ford was holding to the AMA ban. "How could two stock car racers build winning cars without factory support?" asked competitors. After all, Chevrolet was clearly behind the spread of show cars and official cars at Daytona. And how about all those Chevrolet and Pontiac executives and engineers? And Ed Cole, too! If Chevrolet wasn't into performance, why were the boss and his staff having lunch in one of booths at the track?

Two of those box lunches went to George Merwin and Bob Graham, the only two Ford people allowed to attend the race, and only as observers to see what the other side was doing. They saw Everett "Cotton" Owens post a qualifying record of 143.198 in his '58 Pontiac during the first 100-mile qualifying race. Bob Welborn in his '59 Chevy won that race. Then "Shorty" Rollins put his '58 Ford in the winner's circle of the second qualifier but averaged 13.7-mph slower than Welborn. In at third overall in that second race was Richard Petty in another '58 Ford, his introduction to big-time stock car racing. For the last 51 laps, Beauchamp and Petty swapped the lead ten times only to finish in a dead heat. Then France decided that Petty won the first Daytona 500. Petty averaged 135.521 mph, then went on to drive Oldsmobiles and Plymouths to capture his second NASCAR championship in a row.

During the '59 season, the Ford men saw Chevrolet win 14 races. Ford diehards took 10 wins, but none were major victories after the Daytona 500. Merwin and Graham drew two conclusions from the Daytona Speed Week that year; the AMA ban wasn't working the way McNamara envisioned the agreement, and Ford was clearly at the bottom end of the performance ladder with cars more than 10 miles per hour slower than Chevys and Plymouths, Ford's low-priced competitors.

Chevrolet wasn't actually racing as a factory effort like they had in the mid-'50s, but Duntov had clearly thought out his performance parts development programs for easy application by independents. The factory backed up the hardware with manuals on how to order racing cars and how to prepare them for competition. That was the origin of the Chevrolet Power manuals of later years through to modern times. Chevrolet had the hardware for enthusiasts to race and win, Ford didn't.

Ford had planned to release the 390 cubic inch version of the FE engine in 1958 expressly for NASCAR competition, but McNamara squelched it according to the AMA ban. It had to wait until 1961. He also did away with performance parts development. Unlike Chevrolet, Ford had no high-performance parts or development programs to offer racers. That would change in time, and the roles would reverse as Ford emerged as the performance leader when GM management restated the AMA ban in 1963.

Over at Pontiac, Knudsen had pushed the growth of the overhead valve Indian to 370 inches, later to become the famous 389 and 421. In final form, it became the massively powerful 455 over ten years later. The speed of Pontiacs was legendary, as was shown at Daytona in 1960 when Glenn "Fireball" Roberts won the first 100-mile qualifier followed by Jack Smith winning the other, both in Pontiacs. Roberts set a new record in the first round, 151.556-mph, while newcomer to the highbanks, Fred Lorenzen, was the highest Ford finisher at 3rd in a '60 model. He was followed by Joe Weatherly (Ford) and Junior Johnson ('59 Chevrolet). Although Johnson's Chevy was well underpowered compared to Pontiacs, he went on to win the 500 that year by drafting faster cars as a setup move to pass, a maneuver he discovered during practice. The next year, David Pearson won the World 600, the Firecracker 250 and the Atlanta 400, all in Pontiacs. The Indians proved to be winners at the 500 through 1962, Marvin Panch winning in 1961, Roberts in 1962. Each set a new race record.

Looking back at these cars and engines says that the fuse that lit the explosive growth of muscle cars was actually touched off during 1958. The following year, the Chrysler hemi and fuel injection were gone. In their place was the new 413-inch B-block boasting 380-hp in the 300E Chrysler. A new Sport Fury received the 361 cubic inch engine while Dodge (and DeSoto) got a new version, the 383. The building blocks of the muscle car era had been laid.

For 1959, Chevrolet restyled its cars with giant horizontal rear wings. That made the earlier claims of high-speed stability from vertical fins just so much more hype. The Corvette 4-speed was now an available option in full-size Chevys behind the top 348. It was rated at 335-hp. Then there was the 401-inch Buick, another over-400 inch production engine.

That year, new car sales rallied, but the public liked Fords more than Chevys. Ford production surged ahead 37.5% to 1,427,835, while buyers took home 7.5% more Chevrolets at 1,349,562 passenger cars. Plymouth found 7.2% more buyers with 393,213 cars. Dodge was also more successful with an increase of 68% to 192,798 buying customers.

For 1960, Ford allowed the 352 "Interceptor" police engine to be fitted to regular production cars. Rated at 360-hp, it was a small offering of performance and not advertised in that vein at all. Sales plummeted by almost 30% while Chevrolet was up 19.6%. Plymouth sales were also down, by 35.8%. However, Chrysler gained a huge measure of public appeal with the cross-ram, dual 4-bbl Golden Commando 413. This was the beginning of the "cult" engines, those that the kids talked about because they were so visually impressive.

The "baby boomers" were now becoming car crazy and made cult symbols out of engine displacement such as 413, 409, 421 and 406. The age of the over-400 cubic inch muscle car had arrived, and the kids were ready for it.

Plymouth had its best showing in the Daytona 500 of 1960 in the hands of young Richard Petty who finished a solid 3rd and on the same lap as Junior Johnson's winning Chevrolet. Petty went on to win 3 races that year and finished 2nd in the NASCAR season-long points race. Daytona Speedway photo.

Ned Jarrett was Ford's leading winnner of 1960 with 5 wins. He finished 5th in the standings. Eight of Ford's 15 wins were on dirt tracks, far removed from the publicity Ford Motor Co. was seeking. Daytona Speedway photo.

409 Chevys were tough A/Stock drag racers and became Super Stock with additional power equipment offered through Chevrolet. This is the Gardner-Waldman 409 that made it to the A/S final round of the US Nationals in '63 only to lose to 16-year old Don Gay's 421 Pontiac. Gold Dust Classics photo.

The Roar of Power

Before the muscle cars came the Grand Touring cars. The blending of European GT ideas with American big cars was the basis of the GT tradition in this country. Luxury cars such as the 1958 and later Thunderbirds have sometimes been confused with GT cars. The European cars that originated the concept were smaller, personal-size sports model coupes with the addition of back seats for two more passengers. Throughout the '50s and especially the '60s, a growing number of European manufacturers produced such cars. By the early '60s, there were was one American GT car, the Studebaker Hawk GT. There were other luxury cars, but all of them were large and heavy cruisers of America's smooth and wide highways.

When the GT concept was applied to American cars, became four- or five-passenger cars. The Pontiac Grand Prix introduced in 1962 is a good example. Buick and Oldsmobile also had their versions as did Ford with the Thunderbird. Only Chevrolet's Corvette remained a two-seater of small dimensions. Knudsen's youth movement at Pontiac had produced the Bonneville in 1958, thus tying the make to America's high-speed namesake, but naming a big American car "Grand Prix" was sheer blasphemy. The term came from the top form of European racing with small, lithe, high-powered open wheel cars regarded as racing's best, not a 4,400 pound "tank".

The origin of the name didn't matter. Americans loved the new Pontiac and bought 30,195 that first year. Production more than doubled to 72,959 the next year. The Grand Prix was a beautiful car with an alluring name. In a *Motor Trend* road test, the judgement was that "style-wise and price-wise, it competes directly with the Thunderbird."

However, unlike expensive European GT models that offered leather interiors and were virtually devoid of chrome, the new Grand Prix was strictly American in execution; big, chrome plated and heavy. The tach was positioned on a console of bright work in an unusable position. Most cars were automatics, although an all-synchro 4-speed was optional from the beginning. In some Grand Prix Pontiacs, under the hood throbbed the soon to be legendary Super Duty 389 rated at 385-hp in 4-bbl form. The base 389 was a 303-hp engine. Others had the 313-hp tri-power, the three Rochester carb setup that lasted through the 1966 GTO models. When this engine and 4-speed combination went into the GTO in 1964, a new love affair was ignited, and a new muscle car was born.

Pontiac engineers had to design engines with enough torque to push around heavy cars. The Super Duty 389 delivered 395 ft-lb while the 421 was a real stump puller at 451 ft-lb. Unlike Ford's big car engines, the Pontiacs produced their torque at relatively high rpm - the 389 at 4000 rpm, the 421 at 4400. That gave excellent low- and mid-range pulling power, the sort that made Pontiacs among the quickest accelerating cars on the market. The proof of that was Jim Wangers who raced his Super Stock Pontiac to the Stock Eliminator title (14.14 @ 102.04) at Detroit during the NHRA US Nationals in 1960.

The GTO did not receive the Super Duty 421, Pontiac's heavy hitter. A total of 1,521 GPs received this dual 4-bbl engine, a 405-hp stormer, and drag racers, notably Mickey Thompson, saw the combination of the big Indian in the small Tempest to be an ideal match. That Tempest became a Factory Experimental Stock combination, the beginning of the trend that led to Funny Cars.

Ford's answer to escalating performance in full-size cars

Pontiacs were the big guns at Daytona in 1961, winning 1-2-3. Marvin Panch won and "Fireball" Roberts set a new record, 155.709-mph. Daytona Speedway photo.

Fred Lorenzen was highest Ford finisher at 4th with Ned Jarrett in at 7th in Chevrolet's highest finish. Nobody could compete with the Pontiac drivers. Daytona Speedway photo.

was not the 5,000-pound Thunderbird, but the stylish and lighter Starliner. New for 1961 was a bored and stroked 352, the FE series 390. "GT" had not yet reached mainline Fords, and although a tri-power version of the 390 (340-hp) was a Thunderbird engine, it was cammed to be a low-rpm, high-torque engine. Top form was the 375-hp 390 build from a new, reinforced block engineered for stock car racing. Under a single 4-bbl carb on that engine was a cast aluminum intake, Ford's first move into saving weight.

The 375-hp 390 was a solid lifter engine with cast iron exhaust manifolds and came only with a 3-speed transmission. Overdrive was an option. When geared for high speeds, such a Starliner was capable of more than 150-mph. Ford engineers reached almost 159-mph in testing for the Daytona 500, and

Don White set a new 159.32-mph flying mile class record on the beach at Daytona.

On the highbanks in '61, Banjo Matthews was the highest placed Ford in either of the 100-mile qualifiers when he finished 4th in the 2nd race. The Pontiacs were faster, but Ford diehard Fred Lorenzen charged on in the 500. At the finish, Marvin Panch, Joe Weatherly and Paul Goldsmith in three Pontiacs took the checkered flag in that order. Panch set a new record, 149.601-mph, almost 15-mph higher than the '60 500. Lorenzen's lone Ford finished 4th two laps down. "Cotton" Owens and Jack Smith rounded out the top six in Pontiacs followed by Ned Jarrett and Johnny Allen in Chevrolets. If anyone was to beat the Pontiacs, they had to have more power. Ford, Chevrolet and Chrysler had big plans.

1961 Studebaker Hawk GT

"The Hawk prescribes motoring pleasures as no other American car can. Think of its powerful V-8 engine, its smooth 4-speed gearbox, its contoured bucket seats and best of all, its soul-satisfying performance and controllability." A Studebaker ad.

Studebaker offered many performance options in the Hawk line for buyers to equip cars to order, including a tach.

With 225 horsepower, a 4-bbl, 4-speed and Posi-traction in 1961, the 289 cubic inch V-8 Hawk GT was quite a car.

"This is motoring in the modern manner: High average cruising speeds in Continental Gran Turismo fashion, with luxurious accommodations for five. Every Hawk has its owner's name and the car number engraved on a special instrument panel plaque.

"Visit your Studebaker Dealer and place your order now."

So read the lines of a Studebaker penman upon the announcement of the new Studebaker Hawk GT, a limited edition car introduced in 1961.

Hawk GT advertising placed the car squarely in the midst of the high-class, fast-paced world of refined automobiles. Actor James Mason added Hawk GT #12 to his stable of cars that included a Rolls Royce and an Alvis roadster, both expensive British cars, and Mason was pictured with all three cars in full-page advertising in 1961. In another ad, Lucius Beebe was shown with Hawk GT #15 along with a Jaguar XK-120 and a Bentley from his collection in the background.

Clearly, the appeal of Studebaker's Hawk GT was to the man of taste, the successful man who didn't mind expressing himself in the automobile he drove. And like expensive suits, the Hawk GT was a statement of class, a statement of image, a statement that ordinary was unacceptable. Hawk GT buyers received personalized and numbered engraved plaques for the dash of their car, as stated in advertising.

In 1961, the Hawk GT was small, very sporting and handsomely styled with an aggressive, high-speed look. It offered refinements like no other car built in America. There certainly was no other car that looked like the Hawk; thus it offered exclusive grand touring motoring. Its spacious interior easily accommodated four although it was advertised as a five-place car.

Behind the wheel, drivers saw the best equipped instrument panel of the time. A 4-speed transmission with floor mounted shifter was to become a main feature in cars a few years later. Its 4-bbl equipped 289 cubic inch V-8 engine provided for motoring in the highest order of the day. (The owner of the Hawk shown on page 15 reports seeing 120-mph in 3rd gear.) Here was a refined car for the gentleman and his lady, the sportsman and his companion, the man with zest for life, "Just the best of everything..." said Lucius Beebe.

Not only did each buyer of a new GT Hawk receive a personalized car, he also received a letter from Studebaker-

Packard Corporation vice-president, Lewis E. Minkel.

In part, letters to this elite group of buyers read:

"Each Hawk has been produced with care by a Studebaker craftsman. As America's first Gran Turismo Car your Hawk represents motoring in its proudest tradition. We at Studebaker-Packard are proud of the Hawk. We know you will share our pride, and will enjoy many miles of pleasant driving in your new Hawk."

Distinctive styling was one aspect of the Hawk GT that was definitely Studebaker. The rakish Starliner coupe of 1953 was one such car. It has become a certified milestone of American automotive design and was the basis of all Hawks. This sensational coupe of European influence was penned by famed designer, Raymond Loewy, and was a stunningly bold venture into volume manufacturing by an American firm. The Hawk evolved from the Starliner to carry the tradition of distinctive styling through the end of Studebaker as a US manufacturer in 1964.

The "best of everything" Hawk GT meant a long hood, short rear deck design in a 3200-pound, low-slung coupe with full instrumentation and more than enough power to cruise at 100-mph. No other manufacturer offered such a combination. It can be said that the Hawk GT was the first of the line of muscle cars that later included the Pontiac GTO, Olds 4-4-2 and Mustang GT. That makes Studebaker the muscle car innovator a full three years before other manufacturers had similar products on the market. The legacy of the Hawk GT of 1961 was further refined in the Gran Turismo Hawks of 1963 and '64.

Road & Track reviewers said of their Hawk GT test car (March 1961), "to the potential buyer who is accustomed to the size, performance and handling of most domestic cars, the Hawk will be a refreshing change." They concluded their road test with, "A family man who covets a sports or GT car, but who can afford only one, would do well to examine the Hawk."

Motor Life said in its 1961 road test, "The Studebaker Hawk with four-speed stick shift and Twin Traction differential should not be overlooked as a car that can put some fun back into everyday motoring."

Hawk of '61 netted just 346 GT buyers out of 3,117 sales. Bill Cheek's GT, shown here, is thought to be the finest surviving example of South Bend's American GT car of 1961.

Ford's top driver in 1962 was newcomer Fred Lorenzen. In a 406-powered Holman-Moody Ford, "Fast Freddie" won 2 of Ford's 6 wins that year. Daytona Speedway photo.

Ned Jarrett drove 409 Chevys to the winner's circle just once during his 46 starts in '61. He finished in the top 5 22 times and won the NASCAR crown. Dayotona Speedway photo.

'60-'61:

What all the stock car racing meant did not show up in new car showrooms for a while. Chevy's 348 had not caught on with hot rodders, who favored the much more versatile small block. Then came the optional 409 in 1961, the strongest "bowtie" engine up to that time. It came in a single high-performance version rated at 360-hp, the RPO-580 (Regular Production Order). With cowl induction, power was pegged at around 380-hp. While the engine was showing promise as a stock car racing engine in the hands of Rex White and Ned Jarrett, it was recognized by factory engineers to be near the end of its development.

However, the 409/409 was proving to be a big winner in NHRA's A/Stock class. Chevrolet offered the 409/409 in many models, and the number of them showing up at drag races, and the speeds they ran, caused NHRA to create Super Stock class. When the RPO-Z11 427/409 came along in 1962, Chevrolet had a hard-to-beat Super Stock drag racer.

The RPO-Z11 was a special package car, not just an engine. With similar valve covers, the engine looked like the 409 but displaced 427 cubic inches. While the dual quad 409 was rated at 409-hp in 1962, the Z11 was a 427-hp drag strip thumper.

Because of the W-series engine combustion chamber shape, canted 16-degrees in the block rather than in the heads, factory engineers soon realized that the 409 and Z11 were at the limit of their development. By a directive from "Bunkie" Knudsen and under the direction of Dick Keinath, a completely new big block engine, the Mk II "Mystery" engine, was under design as the 409's replacement. It began by displacing 409 cubic inches, but was bumped to 427 on a phone call that caused many in-process changes. (See *FAST CHEVYS*, pgs. 129-167.) This version became known as the Mk IIS (S for Stroked) and became THE fastest running stocker anywhere in 1963. It was then yanked off the tracks by GM top management in a restatement of the AMA ban.

In 1962, no one outside of the Tech Center in Warren knew of the "Mystery" engine, and Chevrolet fans lauded the many quartermile wins the 409 was racking up as Chevy's best effort yet. Fans mistakenly viewed the Z11 as another dual 4-bbl 409 with cowl induction. It was, in fact, a very different engine.

The 409 block was slightly different from the 348 and was recored for larger bores, 4.312-inches versus 4.125. Sides of the webs were machined to accommodate the engine's larger crankshaft counterweights needed for its 1/4-inch longer stroke. Chevrolet engineers specified "impact extruded" (forged) aluminum pistons with an 11:1 compression ratio and a single Carter 4-bbl carburetor on an aluminum intake manifold.

The 409 and Z11 did very well on the nation's top drag strips. Among many tough racers, Don Nicholson nailed down a class win and then scored Stock Eliminator at Pomona during the 1961 Winternationals. His '61 Super Stock Chevy (409) turned a 13.59 @ 105.88 mph. The next year, he captured the title again with a '62 Z11 running 12.84 @ 109.22-mph. Hayden "Mr. 409" Proffitt won the season finale, the US Nationals at Indianapolis, with very similar Z11 stats of 12.83 @ 113.92. The '62 racing season was against Ford's new, improved 406 and Chrysler's 413.

The bottom ends of both the 409 and Z11 engines were similar, and both used the same size valves, 2.023-inch intakes and 1.734-inch exhausts. Valve actuation hardware was also the same. The complete RPO-Z11 package was specified by Chevrolet engineers and offered through Chevy's racing man, Vince Piggins, and drag racing contact, Paul Prior. Those who needed to know about the Z11 knew about it.

RPO-Z11 specifications by part number were: crankshaft 3838396; connecting rods 3837686; pistons 4 each 3837682 and 3837683; cylinder heads 3837730; intake manifold 3830623; camshaft (.511-inch lift) 3837735.

During 1962, a total of 55 RPO-Z11 Chevys were built, and the first one went to Ammon R. Smith Auto Co. for Bill "Grumpy" Jenkins to build for drag racer Dave Strickler. The RPO specification listed aluminum bumpers, special sheet metal, a 427-cid "W-series" engine, special cowl induction, vented metallic brakes, 4-speed transmission, Posi-traction, tach and deleted sound proofing and insulation. According to Bill Jenkins, Strickler won about 90% of his races in that car.

Although built in late 1962, the Z11s were in '63 model cars. At a list price of just over $4,000, including $1,237 for the RPO-Z11 option, such a Super Stock Impala could be the terror of the strip. With the preparation of Jenkins, who never drove the car until after acquiring it in the mid-1980s, the "Old Reliable" Chevrolet became perhaps the winningest Super Stocker in the nation. Strickler handled the driving, and in some 200 races during the '63 season, Jenkins estimates that he won right at 180. Some record!

Lightweight components brought the weight of "Old Reliable" to around 3,400 pounds. Lighter light front end components gave a weight transfer of about 62% to the rear wheels. With that much rearward weight bias, the car was known for fantsastic launches. Compression ratio of 13.5:1 produced 430-hp at 6000 rpm, and with a close ratio Muncie 4-speed and 4.11:1 rear gears, trips down the quartermile came up quickly; sensational 12.10 second blasts at around 126-mph! The Z11 was a drag strip bruiser.

These cars were developed by Vince Piggins' group at Chevrolet and handled by Paul Prior as Chevrolet's drag racing inside contact. 1962 was the last year Chevrolet was into racing, though not acknowledged. The AMA ban was restated in February, '63.

1962 409 Chevrolet

In 1961, Chevrolet created a legend when it introduced the new 409 cubic inch W-series engine. The 409 is still revered today as perhaps the best performing engine of its time. The engine was based on Chevrolet's 348-cid truck engine that was introduced in 1958 as an option in the new Impala. Later, the 348 proved itself as a winning NASCAR engine and spawned both the 409 and another NASCAR winner.

Due to its thin wall casting, enlarging the bore of the 348 was limited. To alleviate this problem, Chevy engineers redesigned the internals of the 348 and relocated bore-centers, allowing the bore to be increased to 4.3125 inches. The bottom of the block was ground and milled so the quarter-inch stroker crankshaft and its heavier counter-weights would fit. That increased the stroke by .25 inches to 3.50 inches to produce 409 cubic inches.

Along with the 409 cubes came improved race shop goodies. Inside was a forged steel crank shaft spinning shortened connecting rods and high-quality, impact-extruded aluminum pistons with milled valve reliefs. The compression

produced was a healthy 11.25:1. The heads were basically the same as those used on the 348 and retained the same valves as the 350 horsepower engine, except they had been modified to handle the 409's longer push rods. Another change was made in the valve seats, which were modified to accept single, instead of dual, valve springs.

The 409's rumpity-rump idle was provided by a high-performance solid lifter cam with .4396 inches of lift against 273-285 pound valve springs. The aluminum intake manifold was a carryover from the 348. Its only modification was enlarged throttle bores to accommodate a larger carb. Since it was rumored that NASCAR was going to outlaw multiple carburetors, a single 3720S Carter AFB was chosen because it had nearly the same CFM capacity as the three deuce setup. That was the RPO-580 rated at 360-hp at 5800 rpm and torque at 409 lb-ft at 3600 rpm.

Along with the new engine, Chevrolet redesigned the Impala making it smaller overall than the previous year's model. Also in 1961, Chevy introduced the legendary Super Sport, or SS, option. The option included special external

Hayden "Mr. 409" Proffitt sat in an office like this when he won Stock Eliminator at the 1962 US Nationals with a winning 12.83 second pass at 113.92-mph.

The dual quad 409-hp 409, top, became a drag racing legend in 1962. Then came the 425-hp, 427 cubic inch RPO-Z11 in 1963 that looked like another 409. Looks were deceiving!

dress-up items such as SS emblems for the quarter panels and the center of the trunk, and wheel covers with distinctive tri-blade spinners. The interior received a special "dressed up" instrument panel with passenger assist bar with the SS logo, a padded instrument panel, a floor-mounted Hurst 4-speed shifter with a trim plate, and a column-mounted 7000 rpm Sun tachometer.

Underneath, the Super Sport option included the LPO (Limited Production Option) 1108 police handling package for a firmer, more controlled suspension. This package contributed heavy-duty springs and shocks along with 8.00 x 14 inch four-ply nylon whitewall tires. Power steering and power brakes with sintered metallic break linings and honed drums completed the SS option.

The 409's massive low-end torque was transmitted to the rear by a heavy-duty four-speed gearbox with a 2.45:1 low gear. Backing it up was a very necessary Positraction unit which came standard with 3.36:1 cogs. For quicker performance there were 4.11, 4.56, and even higher gear sets available through any Chevy dealer.

As well as looking good, the '61 SS 409 Impala was quite a performer. When *Motor Trend* magazine tested one on a quartermile drag strip, they got some very impressive results. Running the standard 3.36:1 rear, they found that the engine was not producing full power at the end of the quarter. They were able to run a 15.31 second pass at 94.24-mph with the car still in third gear and the engine taching only 5300 when they broke the lights at the end of the track. When the rear was changed to an over-the-counter Chevy 4.56:1 unit, elapsed times dropped to an amazing 14.02 seconds with a final speed

of 98.14-mph. What is even more incredible is that the run was made on narrow 8.00 x 14 inch tires.

"Dyno Don" Nicholson, soon to become a legend, warmed over a 409 with a complete balance job and performance valve grind. He opened up carburetor secondaries and adjusted the primary metering rods. After replacing the stock exhaust manifolds with a set of Jardine headers, recurving the distributor, reworking the car's springs for better weight transfer, and adding a set of 8.50 x 14 inch Firestones to the rear, he won the 1961 Winternationals in Pomona. Nicholson won his class with a 13.9 second pass at 103-mph. In practice he had run an incredible 13.19 second blast at 109.48-mph!

In 1962 the Impala was redesigned again, and the Super Sport package became a regular production option designated RPO-240. The 409 was retained but with several changes. The engine could be ordered with two Carter four-barrels connected by progressive linkage. Cylinder heads were improved by increasing the intake valve size to 2.20 inches and enlarging both the intake and exhaust ports for better breathing. The cam from the earlier engine was not changed but aided by stiffer valve springs. The horsepower rose dramatically to 409 over the previous top of 360.

In '62, *Motor Trend* magazine again tested a 409. This car came with a Muncie 2.20:1 close ratio 4-speed and a 4.56:1 rear. In zero-to-60 tests the car showed itself to be a true thoroughbred by posting a fastest time of 6.3 seconds. The stock '62 was also quick through the quarter, running a 13.9 second pass at 98-mph.

In the hands of engine builders like Bill "Grumpy" Jenkins and Bill Thomas, the 409 could be turned into a real fire breather. In full Super Stock form, the cars were capable of running 0-to-60 in 4 seconds flat and could reach 100-mph in just 9.5 seconds. The quartermile was where these cars were at home, and the best of them could run deep into the 12 second range at speeds over 112-mph!

Just the mention of 409 raises eyebrows and conjures up stories of old stoplight races and Sunday drags. Today, things are very different. The kids talk about stereo power, not horsepower. But, the old times still live on "oldies but goodies" radio. You can just about hear the roar of those big cubes when the Beach Boys sing their famous "She's real fine, my 409" one more time, even if the kids don't know what it all means.

On the highbanks in '62, Pontiacs were the fastest cars. "Fireball" Roberts bettered his previous year's record by over 3-mph to 158.744-mph. In the 500, the final 50 laps were all "Fireball". Daytona Speedway photo.

Big Cubic Inches

For 1961, Ford's highest performer was the dealer option 401-hp tri-power 390 or the factory-built single 4-bbl, 375-hp version. These engines began with a new stronger block with thicker webs and reinforcing ribs. Main bearing journals were also wider to compensate for high rpm loads on crank journals. Oil galleries were enlarged for increased oil passage, and a new center oiling gallery running the length of the block was cast in. The blocks were drilled differently for head bolts. The crank, rods and most other hardware in the HiPo 390 engines were the same as standard engines except for much higher quality control that insured that only the best parts were used. Small chamber heads were selected for these engines to maintain the desired high compression, 10.6:1, and stiffer valve springs provided valve control for up to 6500 rpm. A larger passageway aluminum intake manifold was part of the package. Standard exhaust manifolds came from Ford's 1960 High Performance 390.

Only three men were allowed to pursue high-performance parts development at Ford. It was McNamara's "limited re-entry". They did a lot with so little. The 6-V tri-power was a contender in drag racing while the 4-V was a middle marker in stock car racing. Both engines had the same over-square configuration of 4.05-inch bore by 3.825-inch stroke. A radical solid lifter camshaft worked 2.030-inch intake and 1.560-inch exhaust valves, but high rpm breathing seemed to have evaded the engineers. Fords tended to run out of breath toward the end of the quartermile.

Chrysler Corporation had a few strong-running engines when the '60s decade opened. All those first efforts were surpassed when the special order, 350-hp, 413 cubic inch Golden Lion V-8 was introduced in 1961. It was available in most Dodge, Plymouth and Chrysler full-size passenger cars. However, the 413 was not a true high-performance engine. Power and torque curves peaked at low rpm and indicated that the engine was really no more than Chrysler's big and heavy car engine. With 470 ft-lb of torque produced at 2800 rpm, it couldn't help but be a tremendous puller. This was another case for "there is no replacement for cubic inches".

The 300G Chrysler benefitted from this dictum when its 413 received a little hotter cam. With dual 4-bbl carbs, power reached 375-hp. Torque improved to 495 ft-lb! However, of the 18 Chrysler products entered at Daytona from 1959 through 1962, only Richard Petty's 1962 2nd place finish (Plymouth) was notable. Chrysler was not yet in the running.

Contrasting Chrysler's lack of equipment was Pontiac's vast array of high-performance hardware. Pontiac advertisers capitalized on stock car racing successes, and rapidly escalating sales allowed continued development of new heavy-duty parts. Pontiac production jumped almost 16% during 1960 (450,206 cars), then fell by 29% the next year, only to rise 51.9% in 1962 to 547,350 units, second largest since the 1955 models.

Pontiac offered only one engine displacement, the 389, in ten different configurations. As many as four more versions could be built from parts offered through Pontiac dealers. The top factory engine, the Trophy 425-A, was rated at 333-hp with a single 4-bbl carburetor and 348-hp with optional tri-power. These engines were built from regular production parts, but the high-performance versions were assembled using special blocks and heads. Where the Trophy engine differed from other versions of the 389 was that engineers

The '63 "swiss cheese" Pontiacs got the name from holed frames to reduce weight. Aluminum body pieces dropped weight to 3,325 pounds. Bill Blair, owner and restorer, counts 15 "swiss cheese" cars in Pontiac records.

This famous drag racer was the factory "mule" car, the first "off-road only" Catalina. The factory supplied all the info and hardware to make an 11-second stripper like the 421-powered "Passionate Poncho III".

designed it with stronger low-end webs and used more durable 4-bolt main bearing caps on the 2, 3 and 4 bearings. The upper end of each cylinder was chamfered to clear larger diameter valves used on the Trophy engine.

These engines were available in any full-size Pontiac. However, each factory-built engine received a cast iron crankshaft. A special heavy-duty forged steel crank was available over-the-counter. Bore and stroke (4.06 x by 3.75 inches) remained the same. A standard set of rods went into factory-assembled engines, while the over-the-counter set was a higher quality and stronger heat-treated version. Both types were forged steel. The bolt boss on the high-strength rods was 1/16-inch longer than standard, while the cap was also a stronger variety.

Standard pistons were flat top, slipper-type cast aluminum with a highest compression ratio of 10.25:1. Tin plating was applied to reduce skirt scuffing. Like other over-the-counter parts, there were heavy-duty pistons, forged aluminum flat tops that bumped compression up to 10.50:1. With special shallow chamber heavy-duty heads, compression

was 10.75:1. Each chamber was fully machined to insure that each one did its share of work. These heads were considerably different from standard 1961 Pontiac heads and looked more like earlier heads. Breathing was also improved in these heads by using 1.920-inch intake valves (versus 1.880-inch standard) and 1.660-inch exhausts (versus 1.600). Enlarged ports helped improve high rpm breathing.

Two versions of the racing-only heavy-duty intake manifolds were over-the-counter parts. Both were cast aluminum alloy, one a 4-bbl, the other the tri-power. 4-bbl carbs were all Carter while the deuces were Rochesters. The Trophy-A engines received improved exhaust manifolds instead of standard versions, and once again, cast iron "headers" were over-the-counter parts. These "headers" were much longer and heavier than stock, and ended in flanges for mounting dual exhaust pipes to each "header". The thinking behind dual "header" pipes was to separate the exhaust charges from combustion chambers that produced back pressure, and loss of power, from the next firing cylinder.

Pontiac offered every part needed to build a winning

21

Mickey Thompson was the first to run an A/FX Tempest, a car he built in '62 with the 421 engine. The Tempest 326 V-8 had the same dimensions as the 421. Swapping out was easy. Lots of body strengthening was required to handle the power.

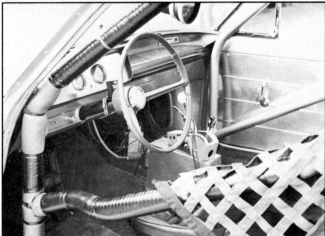

Aluminum front sheet metal brought weight down. GM banned racing in 1963, and that ended A/FX Tempest production at 9 with 5 more station wagons. This is another of Bill Blair's restored original drag racers, the 1st Tempest.

high-performance engine including camshaft kits with stronger springs, push rods, solid lifters and heat-treated rocker arms of 1.65:1 ratio rather than 1.50:1 used in standard engines. These cams were the product of the Pontiac engineer, McKeller, whose name appeared on the cams along with numbers 7 and 8. The #7 cam was for drag racing, #8 for stock car racing and other high speed applications.

Aftermarket suppliers offered lighter aluminum rods, roller tappet cams, superchargers, fuel injection, dual 4-bbl intakes, 3, 4 and 6 deuce intakes, hot ignition systems and many other high-performance pieces that fueled the rapid growth of interest in Detroit iron.

Getting the power to the drive train was the job of transmissions. As early as 1958, Chrysler engineers began designing two new 3-speed synchromesh boxes that had a great impact in the '60s. The Warner Gear Co., later to become Borg-Warner, produced manual transmissions for Chrysler, but with the 1961 models came Chrysler's own stick shift. It was 13 pounds lighter than the Warner box and weighed 81 pounds. Ford had its own 3-speed transmission, some with

overdrive, and was soon laying the groundwork for a new 4-speed. Chevrolet was well ahead with the Corvette 4-speed introduced in 1957. Other GM divisions relied mostly on the Hydra-Matic autoshifter.

Prior to 1961, all Hydra-Matics were 4-speed, but new that year were 3-speed units for Olds and Pontiac. They did not prove satisfactory for high-performance, especially drag racing, and that opened the door for a booming aftermarket transmission business. B&M Automotive of Van Nuys, California, stepped in. B&M was the home of the fabulous Hydra-Stick, and reworked Hydra-Matics for any high-performance application. Hydra-Sticks came in several versions up to those capable of sustaining the load from 750 horsepower. They were extremely strong.

A transmission controversy broiled over the Hydra-Stick. It wasn't stock, but modified stock as were most components of any drag racing car. While they were widely used by gasser, altered and dragster builders, Super Stock cars could not run them. Stock meant stock. Consequently, there was a need for stronger 4-speed transmissions or stronger autoshifters for

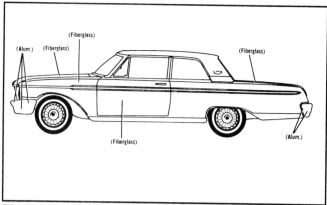

The lightweight Fords were introduced in 1962 and were built from 9-piece sets of parts that reduced weight 164 lbs. A new 4-speed and the tough 406 made a lightweight a fast Ford.

Ford's top FE-series big blocks grew from the 401-hp HiPo 390 of 1961 to become the tri-power 406 of '62, then the awesome 425-hp 427 in '63. Ford Motor Co. photo.

the type of car that everyone could see was going to be very popular, muscle cars. Each manufacturer responded to the fast growing market with excellent equipment. Ford's was the top-loader 4-speed introduced in 1961.

A huge turnout of top class stock cars were on hand for the opening of the 1961 drag racing season at Pomona. The NHRA Winternationals has always been the "Big Go West", and "Dyno Don" Nicholson raced his 409 Chevy to both a class win and the Stock Eliminator victory, as mentioned earlier. It was to be a very good year as the tuner/driver from California went on to win the US Nationals, only to be disqualified.

At the US Nationals, fan appeal was greatest for NHRA's Optional/Super Stock class of factory-type cars. Hayden Proffitt was really hauling in Mickey Thompson's big block Tempest. He went through the lights at the new Indianapolis Raceway Park with a best of 12.55 seconds at 110.29-mph. Crowd response was enormous for under 12 second passes, but he missed a shift during Stock Elimination and had to put the car on the trailer.

In Super Stock, "Dyno Don" Nicholson and his 409 Chevy turned 13.25 @ 110.29 followed by twenty Fords, Pontiacs, Dodges and Plymouths that were all capable of taking the win. In Super Stock class, Arnie "The Farmer" Beswick lost a squeaker to Nicholson. He drove the torrid '61 Pontiac sponsored by Iowa's Johnson Pontiac, "Home of the Passionate Ponchos". Nicholson came away with the class win and went up against Al Eckstrand in the "Ramchargers" Dodge in the final round of Stock Eliminator. Eckstrand had trouble with the factory's push-button autoshifter and lost to Nicholson. However, "Dyno Don" was later disqualified after teardown, and no Stock Eliminator was awarded.

The following year, Chevrolet's 409 received larger valve heads and two new choices of high-performance cast aluminum intakes. New cast iron "headers" similar to Pontiac's improved breathing. During mid-year, a "Service Package" (part number 3822953) offered improved performance, but increased output was not quoted. The package consisted of a new cam and spring kit with sturdier exhaust valve push rods, a new 360-degree low restriction intake, the "headers" mentioned, and associated hardware. Properly dialed in, this equipment was good for a few tenths lower ET. Chevrolet wasn't racing, right?

There was a huge amount of drag racing going on by then, but more of everything was yet to come. Jack Chrisman handled the Howard Cam Special to the Drag Racing World Championship that year, 1961. His AA/Dragster was powered by twin supercharged small block Chevys. For his championship, Chrisman won a Thunderbird hardtop presented by George Hurst. Ford Motor Company wanted the top drag racer to be seen driving a Ford product. World Stock Point Champion that year was Bruce Morgan, who piloted his fuel-injected '57 Chevy to the Stock title. His season-long points chase was rewarded by Hurst who presented him with a Hurst-equipped Pontiac Catalina. Pontiac sought identification with fans of stock class drag racing.

The following year, 1962, was a year of transition. Ford was moving up, Chevrolet was moving out, and Pontiac was still king of Daytona. The 16 Ford entries in the 500 of 1959 increased to 24 in '60, dropped to 21 in '61 and remained at 21 the next year. Chevrolet entries dropped each year from 25 to 21 to 14 to 5 in 1962, even though the latter two years were run with 427 cubic inch "409s", the famed RPO-Z11 engine. Junior Johnson's win in 1960 was the only Chevrolet finish in the top four during Daytona's first decade, and that was with a 348.

Ford presented buyers with a hot new engine in 1962. The HiPo 390 was bored .080-inch to produce the 406. Two versions were offered, the single 600-cfm Holley 4-bbl rated at 385-hp and the 900-cfm triple Holley turning up 405-hp. 406 blocks were cast from different castings than the HiPo 390 to increase main web thickness and strengthen ribs. The purpose for the improved block was for survival during stock car races, particularly Daytona, Darlington and Charlotte.

At 265 pounds, "Tiny" Lund wasn't so tiny, but when he and four others helped save Marvin Panch from a burning wreck, he proved to be a big man indeed. Panch, whose back was burned, gave this Wood brothers '63 fastback Ford to "Tiny" for the Daytona 500 that year. Lund went on to win the race, averaging 151.566-mph, and led a Ford 1-2-3-4-5 sweep. Daytona Speedway photo.

'62-'63

One problem the Ford engineers found during long-distance races was that the number 2, 3 and 4 main bearing caps worked loose. Factory engineers corrected this problem by cross-bolting the caps from the outside of the block just above the oil pan rails. The cross-bolt main technique was to carry on into the legendary 427 introduced in 1963. All 406 engines ran solid lifters. Oil galleries to the hydraulic lifters in other engines had to be blocked off. Oil pressure was controlled by a relief valve set at 75 psi. A second relief valve was built into the full-flow filter assembly and released at 105 psi to prevent blowing out the filter gasket.

Ford's cast nodular iron crankshafts had proven so durable that 406 cranks were fabricated of the same material. However, connecting rods were much stronger, and slightly heavier, than previous equipment. 406 cylinder heads were also different from earlier heads because of larger 1.625-inch diameter exhaust valves that required a change in combustion chamber shape. Unlike Pontiac, chambers were cast rather than machined. Intake valves remained 2.030-inch diameter. Nominal compression ratio was advertised to be 10.9:1, although it could have been as high as 11.4:1 given design tolerances. Improved breathing and a gain of 30-hp were provided by cast iron "headers" similar to those of other other manufacturers. Steel tube headers were a thing of the future.

The factory was interested in stock car racing. At Daytona during the 100-mile qualifiers, sports car racer Dan Gurney made his first foray into southern-style highbanks racing and brought his '62 406 Ford in 4th in the first qualifier. Nelson Stacy posted a 2nd overall in the second race with his 406. Chevrolet's 1960 NASCAR champion, Rex White, put his '62 Z11 Chevy into 4th position in that race. But, both qualifiers were Pontiac races won by "Fireball" Roberts and Joe Weatherly. Roberts went on to win the 500 at record speed, 152.529-mph.

It was Pontiac's second Daytona 500 win in a row. Richard Petty in one of four starting Plymouths rolled in 2nd place that year and was the only other car on the winning lap with Roberts. There had not been a Plymouth entry in 1961, and a single Dodge carried the banner for Chrysler's low-priced cars that year and finished 52nd out of 58 entries. In '62 there were two Dodge entries. Larry Thomas was highest finisher at 31st. Chrysler Corporation was not in the running, and factory engineers began looking at the ancient hemi as an idea for a new engine.

Pontiac engineers were beating the Indian's 421 cubic inch drum in '62. A .030-inch bore of the 389 along with a stroke increase of .625-inches produced the 421. With an 11:1 compression ratio, the engine was rated at 405-hp with dual 4-bbl Carter carburetors. However, for stock car racing, Pontiac developed a cast aluminum intake for a single 4-bbl.

The 421 also received new heads (part number 544124) with .100-inch larger diameter valves, 2.020-inch intakes and 1.760-inch exhausts. Slightly larger ports and much larger passages improved flow dynamics considerably. These heads were easily identified by a steel plate bolted to the upper portion of the head that acted as a push rod guide. Other engines didn't receive this piece. The 421 also received a McKeller #10 cam with solid lifters. As optional competition use equipment, Pontiac offered a set of low-restriction cast aluminum "headers" (part numbers 543053 and 543054) for $45 each. Not only did these pieces improve performance, they reduced weight by about half the burden of the similar

Johnny Rutherford drove Smokey Yunick's Mk IIS "Mystery" engine Chevrolet to victory in the second 100-mile qualifier for the 1963 Daytona 500. He averaged 162.969-mph, then set the fastest qualifying lap for the 500, a record 165.183-mph. The Chevys were around 10-mph faster than other cars, and that aroused a great deal of attention. Chevrolet wasn't racing, right? Daytona Speedway photo.

cast iron manifolds. However, the engineers also specified a special starter motor to provide clearance for the "headers".

Pontiac considered all its 421 engines to be competition versions. Consequently, the engines received all the goodies assembled at the factory. Unlike the 389 owner who had to buy the hardware over-the-counter and build his own engine, the 421 buyer received the best hardware Pontiac offered in showroom models. Pontiac engineers meant for their products to work, and work they did. Mickey Thompson took a stock 421-powered Catalina to the Bonneville Salt Flats and set a bunch of new records, including a new American Class B mark (305 to 488 cubic inches) of 150.666-mph in the flying kilometer and 150.552 in the flying mile.

Although Plymouth and Dodge fans watched from the sidelines as Fords and Pontiacs led stock car racing in 1961, '62 was a new year. Chrysler released two new versions of the high-performance 413-cid engine that year. They differed only in compression ratio. In lightweight Plymouths and Dodges, the 413 proved to be stiff competition. The 13.5:1 engine was rated at 420-hp while the 11:1 came in at 410. In the continuing horsepower war among enthusiasts, 413-powered cars had bragging rights as the most powerful of America's stock engines.

The major difference between the 413 and Chrysler's 361 and 383 engines was its higher deck to accommodate a longer stroke. It was another over-square engine with bore of 4.188-inches and stroke of 3.75-inches. Another small difference included chamfering the tops of the cylinder bores to clear larger diameter exhaust valves, a feature the other blocks did not receive. The engine's forged steel crankshaft was flame hardened and shotpeened to improve durability. The high-performance engines received heads machined from special castings that increased port and passage cross section by 25%. HP and standard engines received 2.080-inch diameter intake

valves and 1.880-inch exhausts. Forged aluminum pistons and forged steel connecting rods made for a tough engine.

Gone were those magnificent, long cross-ram intake manifolds, replaced by a compact short-ram intake that positioned dual 4-bbl carbs diagonally across the top of the engine. Valve covers could not be removed when the long manifolds were in place, and that made for difficult tuning in racing situations. The short-ram intake engine quickly rose to the top in drag racing. NASCAR and USAC cars ran a single 4-bbl on another cast aluminum intake but were not as successful. Both competition engines received the swept upward style exhaust headers for low restriction.

This was the Ramcharger 413 engine, a formidable drag racer. They were built by Chrysler's Marine and Industrial Division to supply racers with winning hardware. Not only was there now stiff competition from Chrysler Corporation, the M&I Division was charged with making parts available to anyone who wanted to buy them.

To put the power to the ground, Chrysler gave its Torque-flite automatic the full treatment. Factory engineers tested the improved autoshifter and determined that it was very capable of handling full-throttle, high-rpm shifts from the 413. This combination was what it took for Chrysler's re-entry into competition.

The Ramcharger 413 was the Dodge version while Plymouth labeled its similar B-block engine the Super Stock. Both Plymouth and Dodge cars were about 200 pounds lighter than the previous year, and with such newfound power on tap, the 413 was bound to be a tough competitor.

Instantly, they were record holders. In 1962, Dick Ladeen of Portland, Oregon, established the Super Super/Stock record of 12.71 seconds in a Ramchargers Dodge. Bill "Maverick" Golden in another Ramchargers Dodge Super Super/Stock Automatic nailed down a win with a strong 12.50

The famous Super Stock Dodge Ramchargers from 1963 were thrilling 426 wedge powered drag racers. Here, Bill Blair relives the old days in a vintage blast.

Dave Strickler handling Bill "Grumpy" Jenkins' 12-second, 126-mph Z11 Impala puts down a Super Stock Plymouth in 1963. Gold Dust Classics photo.

second pass at 112.40-mph. Note that Golden's ET was lower with an automatic than Ladeen's in a floorshift 3-speed car. That showed the advantage of the Torqueflite in competition. Chrysler did not offer a 4-speed with either the Ramcharger or the Super Stock engines because the Torqueflite was extremely efficient.

A new class emerged in drag racing. Factory Experimental class was set up for non-production but optional engines such as the 413 Chrysler or 421 Pontiac installed into small cars like a Dodge Dart or Pontiac Tempest. The 413-powered Dragmaster Dart, built by Jim Nelson and Dode Martin, and Mickey Thompson's 421 (actually 434-cid with legal .060-inch overbore) Tempest were two of the first. They built their cars in response to rule changes by NHRA and NASCAR for 1962 that established a stock displacement limit of 7-liters (427 cubic inches). Racers could combine any sort of factory-produced equipment into any sort of car. And the war in Factory Experimental was on.

Cars were broken down into classes by the ratio of advertised horsepower and weight. A/Factory Experimental was the 8.99 pounds per cubic inch class. B/FX were cars weighing 9 to 12.99 pounds per cubic inch. C/FX cars weighed in at over 13 pounds per cubic inch. Nelson and Martin set an early A/FX record with their "Golden Lancer" powered by a 413. Top quartermile figures were 12.26 seconds and 116.53-mph which was really hauling in 1962. The Thompson Tempest lowered the ET record to 12.22 seconds and consistently notched 117-mph blasts.

By 1962, 4-speed transmissions had finally been included on options lists for about every type of car a high-performance enthusiast could want. Still, the Torqueflite practically owned Super Super Stock class and made it tough on the 4-speeds during SS eliminations. It didn't always work out that way, though, as the NHRA US Nationals proved.

Over 50,000 fans jammed Indianapolis Raceway Park for the US Nationals of 1962. What they saw were over 70 Super Super/Stock cars and 24 SS/AAutomatic entries have a showdown. The SS/S battle between Nicholson, Strickler and Proffitt during the 1961 US Nationals revived in '62, but there were a few other drivers intent on capturing the wins. One was Al Eckstrand in the Ramchargers SS/SA Dodge.

When the Super Stock field was called to the staging lanes, fans of all makes had several to cheer on. When Arlen Vanke of Akron hammered down the S/S class victory in his '62 Pontiac (13.40 @ 108.43), it looked like the Pontiacs were on the warpath. The A/Stock final round was a Chevy versus Ford classic with the Dearborn Steel Tubing 406 Ford taking the win, but later disqualified. In Super Super/Stock, it was all Chevrolet 409s in the final. Strickler in the Jenkins-prepared "Old Reliable" pulled a hole shot on Proffitt that looked like "Mr. 409" had gone to sleep. A quick 12.97 ET put away Proffitt.

A/Factory Experimental was another Pontiac showcase. Mickey Thompson and his Tempest shut down Ace Wilson in the Royal Oak small Pontiac with a 12.66 @ 115.68-mph pass. That brought up the B/FX cars and it was another all-Chevy 409 contest. "Dyno Don", at the time just relocated to Atlanta, edged out Strickler in a close 12.93 @ 113.63 against Dave's 12.96 @ 114.06-mph. The C/FX class title was grabbed by Tom Sturm, who also won the World Points Stock Championship.

When the call went out for the Super Super/Stock Automatic rounds, it looked like a Dodge festival with a few Plymouths invited. In the SS/SA final round, it was Al Eckstrand in the Ramchargers Dodge putting away Bud Faubel with a 12.72 @ 113.35.

Fifty class winners earned the right to face off against each other for Super Stock Eliminator. Nicholson and Strickler worked their way up through the field only to lose in the ever-tightening field of remaining cars. The final round was for all the marbles and pitted the Ramcharger Dodge of Jim Thornton against Proffitt's SS/S Chevrolet. Proffitt added another trophy to his shelf with a 12.83 second, 113.92-mph blast versus Thornton's 13.12 @ 111.52.

When all the smoke cleared in NHRA's world points championship chase of 1962, Chevrolet drivers had won both the Competition and Stock titles. The Competition World Points Champion was Jess Van Deventer of California in his B/Modified Roadster. Stock World Points Champion was Tom Sturm, also of California, who piloted his '62 C/Factory Experimental Chevy to the title and received a Hurst prepared Pontiac Grand Prix. Runners-up were two Pontiacs followed by two more Chevrolets. In the 27 categories open to stock class cars, only three were taken by non-GM cars. One was a Ford win. As with stock car racing, General Motors "owned" stock class drag racing. From then until now, the majority of drag racing entries at any given event remains mostly Chevrolet. But then, in 1964, you couldn't find a top competitive GM car in NASCAR racing anywhere.

The change was swift. A news conference question after the Daytona 500 left GM Chairman Frederic Donner and President John Gordon without an answer to the sudden appearance of the faster than everything "Mystery" engine. Afterwards, they restated the 1957 AMA ban on factory racing, and GM was suddenly no longer competitive.

1963 427 Ford Galaxie

During the early 1960s, the big three were competing in a game of one-up-manship and continually tried to maintain a performance edge on each other. Nearly every model year, new, bigger and better performing engines emerged from the auto makers. This set the stage for the development of Ford's legendary 427 cubic inch, cross bolt main FE-series engine introduced in the 1963-1/2 fastback Fords.

In developing the new engine, Ford pulled out all the stops. NASCAR racing was intense, and to win the top events, Ford engineers set to designing and building a winning NAS-CAR engine first and a street engine second. They started with the highly successful High Performance and tri-power Super High Performance 406 cubic inch big block as the base engine. In order to get the 21 cubic inch increase in displacement, the bore was enlarged .110 inches. A larger port, lightweight aluminum intake manifold feeding through .060-inch larger intake valves was used to improve the engine's breathing. The compression ratio was raised to 10.9:1, a special long duration, high lift cam, new high rev valve train, and streamlined, cast iron exhaust headers finished off the new engine. There were many small internal modifications to the block and bottom end of the engine to take the higher stresses and rpms.

There were two versions of the 427 available. A single four-barrel equipped engine rated at 410 horsepower at 5600 rpm complied with NASCAR regulations, and a dual four-barrel engine rated at 425 horses at 6000 rpm was offered for drag racing. Both engines could only be ordered with a close ratio 4-speed. There was no automatic transmission option. Rear axle ratios included 3.50:1, 3.80:1, and 4.11:1, but there were many others available through the factory. Eight different part number gear sets ranging from 4.29:1 up to 5.83:1 were available across the counter from Ford dealers.

Ford redesigned the Galaxie for 1963-1/2, creating what was called the fastback. It was perhaps the most beautiful styling job of that year. The sole reason for the body change was to gain an aerodynamic advantage over the competition on NASCAR's high-speed tracks. The theme of "Win on Sunday, sell on Monday" was very much alive in the early sixties. Ford engineers beefed up the Galaxie to handle the increased stresses of the new engine. The modifications included a high-capacity clutch, heavy duty 4-speed trans, larger drive shaft and heavy-duty U-joints, and heavy-duty springs and shocks. Also, the cars received a heavy-duty rear axle assembly with 4-pinion differential and 15-inch diameter wheels, and high-performance nylon tires, along with half-inch wider front brake drums with fade resistant linings for added strength and safety.

According to a Ford salesman's handbook, the 427 Galaxie equipped with the standard 3.50:1 axle and full street trim could produce 0-60 mph times somewhere between 6.5 seconds and 7.0 seconds. Top speeds were around 130-mph.

Ford styling reached new highs with the mid-year 1963 fastbacks. A floor shifter in the car's spacious interior was a dead giveaway, this was a 427 Total Performance Ford.

Ford engineers were so confident of their new cross-bolt main 427 that 4,978 were installed in full-size cars. Dual 4-bbls were rated at 425 horsepower, singles at 410-hp.

Quartermile times were in the low 15 second range, in showroom trim, with terminal speeds between 95 to 100-mph. With some minor tweaking and the addition of a set of headers, high rearend ratio, and a set of drag racing slicks, the cars were capable of 0-60 times as low as 4.5 seconds and quartermiles in the low 12s with trap speeds above 110-mph.

Ford was actively campaigning the 1963-1/2 fastbacks even before they were announced to the public. On January 20, 1963, one of the new 427 Fords won the first 500 mile NASCAR race held at the Riverside International Raceway in California. With road racing star driver Dan Gurney at the wheel, 52,500 fans saw the new fastback Ford lead for 120 of the 185 total laps around the tricky 2.7-mile course. A Ford factory brochure stated that, "The winning Ford finished 30 seconds ahead of the second-best car, a Pontiac. The nearest Chevrolet was nine laps behind, trailing by more than twenty-four miles. And Plymouth, which claimed great performance victories over all its competitors in a private Riverside contest a week earlier, failed to finish." Only 20 of the starting 44 cars finished.

Later, on February 24, Fords posted an all-conquering win, taking the top five places in the Daytona 500. Of the 50 cars that started the race, only 23 finished and 10 of them were Fords. Fords went on to win more races than any other marque that year, 23, and Joe Weatherly clinched the NASCAR Manufacturer's Championship in 1963. Most popular driver, "Fast Freddie" Lorenzen, drove Holman-Moody Fords to become NASCAR's first over-$100,000 winner that year. Leading Ford winner was Ned Jarrett with 8 trips to the winner's circle followed by Lorenzen, who took 4. "Fireball" Roberts added 4 more. The biggest win was "Tiny" Lund's Daytona 500 victory. He coasted most of the final lap out of gas and crossed the line with an empty tank.

Ford was aiming its new car at a new market, the "hot rodders", and began advertisements oriented toward performance. Ford salesmen were issued handbooks telling how to recognize the new type of buyer and what their interests were. One such book described the "hot rod" market as, "These are the young fellows who buy cars strictly for fun driving! Their wants are simple: They want brutal, neck-snapping acceleration - preferably accompanied by a throaty roar from the engine and quick snap-shifting with a floor-shift, 4-speed

A brutal combo, a 425-hp 8-V 427 and a lightweight Galaxie.

transmission... They want to go, go, go!"

The 427 option was offered in three body styles, fastback, formal roof, and convertible. The '63-1/2 427 Galaxie was an expensive car in its day, with a typically equipped 500XL body package costing just over $4000. This is one of the reasons so few were made. Total production for the 1963 model year numbered just 4,978 units with only 413 of them being convertibles. All the 427s came with Ford's new mid-year top-loader 4-speed transmission. Due to low production numbers, the 427 Galaxies have become highly sought after collector cars. They remain one of the rarest, and most desirable, Ford "hot rod" street cars ever built.

1963 Studebaker Avanti

Today, Studebaker is a nearly forgotten marque, and Avanti was the best of the breed. What the Avanti was has mostly slipped beyond the memories of most performance car fans. But make no mistake, a choice Avanti could stomp your favorite 409! Or any other car of their era for that matter.

Names like ponycar or muscle car are widely used these days but are rather ambiguous and seem to describe a certain type of car. Some say the ponycar era began with the '64 Mustang. Others give the nod to the Pontiac GTO of '64 or perhaps the 427 Ford of '63. But that may be because most people just don't know that Studebaker offered stunning performance in nicely styled cars of modest weight before the big three put such cars on showroom floors.

Studebaker offered supercharged cars in the '50s. Put this in your muscle car memory banks: a track test of a supercharged Starliner coupe gave quarter-mile stats of 14.6 seconds and a top speed of 107 mph - in 1953! And when the Avanti came out ten years later, *Hot Rod* magazine did a drag test with one fitted with a supercharged prototype 299-cid engine called the R/3 and shot the traps in 13.71 seconds at 107.78-mph on its first run. Bigger tires were sure to produce quarter-mile runs in the low 13 second range.

Those stats put the Avanti in at 10th overall in *Car Review Magazine*'s "50 Fastest Musclecars" list, and the Avanti wasn't even on the list. All other top tenners were over 400 cubic inches and in cars of the late '60s and into the '70s. Thus, the figures show that Studebaker was half a decade ahead of other cars in the performance category. But who thinks of Studebakers as muscle cars?

The Avanti was a very advanced car and one of America's most exciting cars, ever! When they were first shown, their appeal was overwhelming and even by today's standards, Avanti (which means "forward") is still of modern design. In styling, Avanti set another high mark for Studebaker and became another milestone design along with the 1953 Starliner coupe.

An Avanti was not a large car. In size, they most closely approximated the contemporary Ford Falcon, although their rakish body was almost a foot longer. Wheelbase was 1/2-inch shorter, while overall width and height were the same as the Falcon.

All Avantis were four-passenger sports coupes. Wide doors gave excellent access to their spacious interior, composed essentially of four firm bucket seats with contour shaping for lateral support. The dash layout was a superbly functional set of gauges in an aircraft-like panel immediately in front of the driver. Console shifter in either automatic or 4-speed fitted in nicely with the sports styling of the interior. Centered above the windshield inside was another aircraft-like panel of rocker switches.

Although they were really in a class by themselves, by comparison, the only other car built in America that came even close to Avanti styling and features was the Corvette. Studebaker was years ahead of other American manufacturers in recognizing the appeal of European styling. Notice that there is no exterior body chrome other than bumpers.

Studebaker launched the Avanti in the spring of 1962. The body of the cars was of fiberglass and composed of over 100 precision pieces. Joints were filled and ground smooth. The manufacturer of the bodies, Molded Fiber Glass Co. of Ohio, developed some manufacturing problems and curtailed Avanti production in favor of their big customer, Chevrolet. The Sting Ray body change was underway, and Avanti production became very limited. Only a few Avantis reached Studebaker showrooms in the '62 model year.

The delay was wisely used by Studebaker engineers to improve overall quality of their product. When the cars began reaching the public during 1963, although they were always

The 4-bbl equipped R/1 was the base engine for the Avanti. At around 240-hp, it was a healthy performer.

Full instrumentation was a Studebaker Avanti feature. The magnificent cockpit made other cars look plain.

few in number, Avanti set quality standards beyond anything seen before.

Ray Brock, Technical Editor of *Hot Rod* (June, 1963): "Those of you who have inspected an Avanti body closely have probably noticed the finish is excellent, better than anything being produced in steel in this country and far better than the Sting Ray, which somehow inherited a bundle of wrinkles during the model changeover."

Because fiberglass was used in the body, above the frame weight was lower and that gave a lower center of gravity, thus better handling. The complete Avanti body with integral steel reinforcement weighed only 510 pounds. And one feature designed in was a roll-bar nicely contoured and padded inside. Shelby Mustangs are generally regarded as the first production cars so equipped, but Studebaker was there first.

The visual impact of the Avanti was distinctive, and its feel was certainly exclusive. The cars were solid and gave the "let's go fast" feeling characteristic of a sports car. Steering was a sensitive 3-1/2 turns lock-to-lock, and the ride was firm by any standard.

Studebaker was a leader in offering heavy-duty suspensions. The company was also years ahead of other American car builders in offering front disc brakes. On the Avanti they were a modest $97.95 option. Heavy-duty 11-inch drums on the rear made for a healthy stopping package, among the very best in America, and produced no fade or erratic behavior in *Hot Rod*'s track test of both 1/4- and 1/2-mile runs. Their Avanti 1/2-mile stats of 128.94-mph in 21.3 seconds raised the class record by almost 6-mph!

As for engines, four types were offered. They were the R/1, Studebaker's 289 cid; the R/2, the 289 with a Paxton supercharger producing about 5 pounds of boost; the R/3, a special Granatelli-built 304.5 cid engine with a Paxton and pressure box around a single 4-bbl (later adopted by Shelby); and the R/4, the same 304.5 but with two 4-bbls without supercharging.

The R/1 was the standard Avanti engine. It was fitted with a mechanical cam and 10.25:1 compression heads and produced around 240 horsepower with a single 4-bbl. The supercharged R/2 was a lower compression engine at 9:1 and was a $210 option producing about 285 horsepower. The R/3 was THE engine! Studebaker didn't advertise horsepower

ratings, so figures given are educated guesses, but a good guess was at least 340-hp. The R/3s were built by Paxton Products of Santa Monica, California, and received all the goodies, 9.5:1 compression pistons, a blower delivering a minimum of 6 pounds of boost and possibly as high as 12 pounds at 6500 rpm.

The R/3 was fitted with forged pistons, a forged steel crank, special head castings with larger port areas, larger valves, CCed chambers and clearanced decks, polished ports and chambers, just some of the Granatelli goodies. The engine also received a large runner aluminum intake under the cast aluminum pressure box.

Avanti was intended to be a smooth, quiet and docile high performer, and Andy Granatelli proved it. He and Studebaker became heavily involved in United States Auto Club (USAC) record setting and produced an astounding set of records. The first attempt with standard R/2 engines with 4-speeds in a Lark, a Hawk and an Avanti produced flying mile two-way averages of 132.04 for the Lark, 140.24-mph with the Hawk and a remarkable 158.14-mph in the super-slick Avanti. With similar engines, superior aerodynamics of the Avanti showed remarkable results. Its smooth shape made the Avanti a very quiet cruiser.

Later on, Granatelli took another set of Studebakers to the salt and captured 372 speed records without a single breakdown! No other manufacturer came anywhere close. Avanti set 29 new records and repeatedly reached more than 170-mph. However, Granatelli was disappointed that a specially equipped Avanti did not exceed 200-mph as hoped. Its best was just 197!

Excellent handling was another virtue of the Avanti. They were not lightweights at 3590 pounds, but front/rear weight distribution was very good at 56/44. Because the cockpit was displaced rearward, passenger weight tended to produce an even better distribution and improved handling still further.

Ray Brock: "...Avanti handling is great...Just pour the power on and you can direct the car anyplace you want to go in the corner. The oversteer gives the front end a light, easily controllable feel and the throttle takes care of the rear...The Avanti has a handling style all its own but with just a little practice, driving one on twisting roads can be thrilling."

An R/3 Avanti would be a rocket by today's standards,

Studebaker Challenger was the low-buck Lark. A complete set of gauges kept track of a supercharged engine. At around $2100, this was the Super Lark, a 409 killer.

R/2 was a supercharged 289 cubic inch engine producing upwards of 300-hp. Andy Granatelli drove one of these cars at Bonneville to 140.24-mph in 1963.

and put owners in the still exclusive 150-mph club with a factory-built car more than 25 years old.

Road & Track road testers summed up their review of an Avanti with, "It is not a copy of anything, and it is mercifully free of excrescent ornamentation. At night the instruments are illuminated by soft red lighting, which we found to our liking. To the Avanti's everlasting credit, it should be noted that it has absolutely the best seats we have sat in..."

For under $5,000, the beautiful Avanti put buyers as far advanced in American automotive design and innovation as they could get in 1963. With the supercharged R/3 package, Avanti owners also had the fastest car built in this country. Indy 500 winner Rodger Ward became the first Avanti owner, and of the 4,600 or so Avantis built, very few of them were R/3 equipped. Even fewer have survived. Those that have remain in a exclusive class of a true American milestone car.

Tucked under the hood of an otherwise docile-looking Challenger was a fire-breathing supercharged engine. One of these could dust off many performance cars in its day.

Road racing star Dave MacDonald moved from driving Cobras for Shelby American to this Bud Moore built 427 Mercury Marauder, the second car to Darel Dieringer. Atlanta, 1964. Ford Motor Co. photo.

Horsepower War

Automotive production for 1963 was the best year on record. Chrysler was back up to within 23.5% of the Corporation's 1955 high (1,047,722 cars produced) and soared past 1962 figures by 46.2%. A lot of Dodge and Plymouth sales were because of the fabulous successes the cars had been showing on drag strips around the country. These were the cars that fans could identify with. They were showroom cars, and many of the Super Stock, A/Factory Experimental and A/Modified Production car owners left the window sticker in their cars. Fans could see for themselves what they could buy, and $4,000 for a top-running street machine wasn't all that far out of line. Many drag racing fanatics could imagine themselves behind the wheels of these cars, and that was just what the factory sales people wanted.

Ford Division production reached 1,638,066 cars that year, up just 4.6%. However, Ford production had been holding around 1.5 million for 4 years, and 1963 was the first year since 1955 to exceed that figure. Improved sales brought increased racing budgets, and Ford was looking better all the time.

Chevrolet production sailed past the 2 million mark in 1962 and was further increased by 6.6% in '63 to 2,303,315 cars. Total General Motors production was over 4 million cars for the first time in the firm's history, 4,077,272 that year.

These statistics indicate that the "baby boomers" were coming on strong as car buyers, as anticipated by product planners. Racing was for the kids, to get them enthused about buying new cars. Enthused they were. On any summer weekend, if the total attendance at drag races throughout the country were known, it would probably have been in the millions. Drag racing was big-time publicity for the manufacturers. Even though Chevrolet totally dominated all but the top classes, most publicity for full-bodied cars was given Super Stock and A/Factory Experimental. A few A/Modified Production and B/MP cars received some notice, but very few. Publicity was what Ford and Chrysler were after, so it didn't matter that more Chevys turned out. What mattered was having winning S/S and A/FX cars in front of writers and cameramen. Product exposure was the name of the game, and while GM was out of the picture in '63, Ford and Chrysler were heavily re-arming with hemi engines.

In 1964, car production was even better for Chrysler and Ford, while Chevrolet Division and General Motors overall lost sales. The restatement of the AMA ban by GM top brass in early 1963 completely ended the glamour and prestige earned by the fast Chevys. Chevrolet production dropped 8.2%, while Ford's "Total Performance" commitment netted a 7.9% gain. That boost meant a 3.6 billion dollar increase in Ford Motor Co. sales.

At General Motors, jobs were on the line. Factory engineers had to back off or else. Dick Keinath, Chevrolet Chief Engine Engineer and designer of the Mk II "Mystery" engine that fathered all of Chevy's big block engines has commented, "We had an entire engineering department and an entire shop geared to machine cylinder heads, manifolds, exhaust manifolds, blocks and everything. And we had the pattern shops working, the foundry working, the different machine shops in the Detroit area making camshafts and crankshafts. So, there were a lot of people involved very intensely.

"It was a tremendous undertaking with a lot of esprit de corps. People would work nights, Saturdays and Sundays, anything just to get the job done...The "Mystery" engine time was a tremendous time. I don't think you'll ever see it again,

Junior Johnson called his "Mystery" engine Chevy of 1963, "The most superior car the sport has ever seen." He won the 1st 100-mile qualifier at 164.083. Daytona Speedway photo.

The final year of the 409 was 1964; 400 horsepower in 4-V form, 425 in 8-V. Chevrolet photo.

not in the auto industry."

The older iron was still around in '64. A 421-powered Pontiac could haul down the quarter-mile as Don Gay proved when he returned to the NHRA Winternationals and repeated his A/Stock victory from the year before. At the time, Gay held the A/Stock record with a 12.53 second elapsed time. The teenage Dickinson, Texas, terror added the Drag News Invitational shootout to his list of winnings by shutting down all A/Stockers to take the win with a 13.21/109.35.

The Drag News Invitational attracted the top names in the business and was a showcase for new 1964 model cars, especially the new hemi Dodge and Plymouth racers. Len Richter raced his 427 Thunderbolt to the Super Stock title by turning 12.22 seconds at 122.78-mph, then faced off against Bill "Professor" Shirey in a 426 wedge Dodge and lost. Shirey's winning 12.79/118.73 was rewarded with a new Mustang!

Wild action erupted at that meet when the A/FXers were called up. Jim Thornton's Ramchargers hemi Dodge battled Bud Faubel's Honker to win with an 11.85/124.13 pass. Burlington, North Carolina's Ronnie Sox rolled up to the line with his 427 Comet and nailed Phil Bonner's 427 Fairlane by posting a sizzling 11.80/121.13. Thornton matched Roger Lindamood in another hemi Dodge. Lindamood's Color Me Gone put a hole shot on Thornton's Ramcharger, and took the win with a slower 12.34/120.60 compared to a quicker but losing 12.23/122.73. That round matched Sox and Lindamood for the A/FX title. Sox launched well ahead of Lindamood, but earlier transmission problems returned and Sox missed 2nd gear as Color Me Gone went by to win at 12.29/120.00.

Len Richter avenged his loss in the AHRA Summer Nationals held at the U.S. 30 drag strip near Chicago. It was against Thornton again. Both of them had waded through a huge turnout of Super Stocks, and more rain than anyone imagined, and made the final round a feature. The Ford Thunderbolt had not been turning the elapsed times of the big Dodges, and Richter went for broke with a hole shot and scored an upset victory. His 11.49/121.62 took Mr. Stock Eliminator. Thornton's attempt at a triple play was nipped. His 11.04/130.05 win in SS/AOptional followed by his

11.08/128.57 Top Stock Eliminator victory in the wet showed the Dodge to be the superior machine, but Richter's win was a win just the same. Some say it was in the lights.

Among lots of drag racing going on around the country, NHRA held a big money meet at Riverside. As expected, it drew a huge turnout of top drag racers during the same weekend as a major UDRA event at Long Beach. The list of hemi MoPars was impressive; Dick Landy (Dodge), Tommy Grove (Melrose Missile Plymouth) and Al Eckstrand (Lawman Plymouth), to name just three. Gas Ronda (Thunderbolt) won Super Stock while Grove took Super Stock/Automatic. For Stock Eliminator, it was Eckstrand against Ronda for all the marbles, and Ronda laid down a 12.08/119.68 winner against the Lawman's 12.20/114.21. Landy's hemi was the only Dodge in the A/Modified Production ranks and he scored with a 12.01/121.11 victory.

A/FX was a thriller. The 427 Comets of Bill Shrewsberry and "Dyno Don" Nicholson made the MoPar field thin and gave the final round an all-Comet showing. Shrewsberry and the Sachs & Sons Merc scored by edging out Nicholson on a 11.72/122.11 blast.

Bill "Maverick" Golden's ride was a 426 wedge powered Super Stock/Automatic Dodge. He quickly became the scourge of western drag racing in his class by setting records at five drag strips. He was consistently in the 11.34 second range and turned in six consecutive runs between 127.50- and 127.85-mph at one strip.

To further illustrate the potential of the Super Stock MoPar, Hayden Proffitt moved over from Chevrolet to the driver's seat of the Yeakel Plymouth Center SS/A machine in 1964. He was a factory driver with four cars strategically located around the country. The fastest and quickest was his home based Long Beach ride. At the Long Beach quarter-mile, Proffitt shattered the class speed and ET records, and made 12 runs under 11.18 seconds. His best was a record-setting 10.97 at 128.38, perhaps the very first 10-second pass by a legal Super Stock/Automatic car.

For the right people with the inside track, plenty of performance equipment was available from the manufacturers. Ford and Chrysler made their efforts known. Lee

Thunderbolts were Ford Division factory drag racers of 1964. The high rise 427 turned out nearly 500-hp and required the "bubble" hood to clear the carbs. Bill Lawton lays down a win at Pomona.

A/Factory Experimental final round of the '64 Winternationals came down to the Lincoln-Mercury Division Comets of Ronnie Sox and "Dyno" Don Nicholson. Sox won; a 11.49/123.45-mph blast.

Iacocca at Ford had made good his corporate commitment of Total Performance in every phase of motorsport. Soon, Ford would be challenging Ferrari, Jaguar, Porsche and the rest of the world, then beating them in long-distance endurance racing to win the 24-Hours of Le Mans four times in a row (1966-69) and twice winning the World Sports Car Championship (1967-68). Ronnie Householder, the mid-'30s midget racing king, was boss of Chrysler's stock car racing and built the Pentastar into a champion with everything a stock car racer or drag racer could want. The superiority of the 426 hemi was obvious, and the Ford men had to go one better.

All the performance fights were in the background away from public scrutiny. NHRA did not require filing of homologation specifications until November, and NASCAR did not require them until December 10. Thus, public announcement of performance equipment was usually delayed until mid-year (recall the 427 engine and '63-1/2 fastback Ford). Car crazies were made even crazier by the factory's lack of publicity on the equipment of greatest interest. New model announcements did not have the latest equipment, so savvy enthusiasts kept calm about new models until the Daytona Speedweek and the NHRA Winternationals. These

34

Billy Cox won B/Factory Experimental in a lightweight Ford Galaxie at the '64 Winternationals. They are still quick.

426 Plymouths came in 3 versions in 1964, 8-V 415- and 425-hp Max Wedge engines and the 4-V 365-hp Commando.

were the events that drew the top drivers, and the latest and best high-performance cars and equipment.

According to the rules, competition engines had to bear some resemblance to production equipment. But when Junior Johnson and Ray Fox showed up at Daytona for testing in a Dodge, everyone wondered what had happened to the Ford connection. That car and the other hemi MoPars proved so superior that the "horsepower war" took a giant leap in escalation. Soon, skirting the rules was the trick, and cars began being cleverly cut down, weight was being shaved, weight distribution was being changed, noses dropped, profiles altered. Every mile per hour possible was searched out. It was belly-to-the-ground warfare.

Ford fought back at Daytona in the form of an answer to the Chrysler hemi. A week before the race, Ford officials petitioned NASCAR for approval of their latest engine, not just a hemi, but a single overhead cam hemi. First tests of the engine in Dearborn had shown 630-hp, a hundred more than the 427 wedge. Everyone was stunned. Householder's surefire hold on Daytona didn't look so surefire anymore. No one had even heard of the engine outside Ford engineering. Bill France turned down the request. Daytona was all MoPar.

Johnson (Dodge) won the first 100-mile qualifier and Paul Goldsmith (Plymouth) set a new record (174.910-mph) more than ten miles per hour faster than the year before. The nearest Ford was in 4th. Bobby Issac (Dodge) won the second 100-mile qualifier, and Richard Petty (Plymouth) was fastest qualifier at 174.418. The nearest Ford in that heat was A. J. Foyt who finished 4th.

The MoPars were untouchable and totally dominated the 500. Foyt was the only spoiler in a perfect MoPar day when he led the race for two laps. Otherwise, it was all Dodge and Plymouth with Petty easily winning in record fashion. He averaged 154.334-mph for the fastest 500 miles on record and was the only driver on the winning lap. It was a Plymouth 1-2-3 sweep, and Chrysler Corporation President Lynn Townsend was there to celebrate the crushing defeat of Ford. Henry Ford II was there, too, and no sooner was the race over than his crew knew what the boss wanted.

Chevrolet fans had nothing to cheer about. And neither did Pontiac. The top Chevy was Wendell Scott in 38th position. Scott gave Chevrolet its only win that year, at Jacksonville. That was the only non-Ford or Chrysler win of the year. The highest Pontiac at Daytona was G. C. Spencer at 33rd.

For Pontiac and Chevy fans, Daytona was no fun at all.

After that, Ford engineers produced an improved valve train for the 427 wedge that allowed reliable 7000 rpm. The engines were now up to 500 horsepower, but still shy of the hemi. Although Ford won the opening round at Riverside, it was due more to Dan Gurney's skill as a driver than to a superior car. The glory of that victory was darkened by the fatal crash of Joe Weatherly. The left front of his Mercury took a tremendous crushing, and the "clown prince" of stock car racing did not survive.

Daytona was a different kind of disaster. Ford drivers were whipped unmercifully, but as the season unfolded, they won 30 races, Mercury 5, Dodge 14 and Plymouth 12. The season was rather evenly split. Although the 427 wedge couldn't match the hemi in power, better overall preparation of the cars gave Ford its victories. Ned Jarrett was the biggest Ford winner with 15 victories, and Fred Lorenzen took three of the important races, Atlanta, the 300-miler at Darlington and the fall Charlotte race.

Disaster struck at Charlotte. The sport's most respected driver, Glenn "Fireball" Roberts, was fatally injured in a fiery crash. The largest crowd in the history of spectator sports, over 68,000, came to Charlotte for the World 600. On the 7th lap, a car spun coming out of turn 2 and stopped on the track midway down the back straight. Ned Jarrett glanced off the inside wall and clambered out of his Ford as it went up in flames. Roberts wasn't so fortunate. He hit the wall at over 100-mph backwards. The impact drove the fuel tank into the interior. It exploded. Jarrett helped pull Roberts, still conscious, from the wreck. When the race was resumed, veteran Jim Paschal won the 600 in the second Petty Plymouth, and everyone was wishing "Fireball" a quick recovery. For the next six weeks, he showed signs of improving from the burns over 75% of his body, then took a turn for the worse and died just before the Firecracker 400 in July. It was a sad day for a favorite driver, the man who did everything right.

The 1964 NASCAR season was Richard Petty's. He raced in 61 events, won 9, and finished in the top 5 a total of 37 times. He amassed such a point score that he won his first NASCAR championship by the widest margin in history.

For the high-performance enthusiast, the secrets from Detroit and Dearborn were slow in coming. It was usually in wintertime issues of auto magazines that fans learned of the new tricks. Although the magazine were usually two months behind the events, they provided more information than any other source.

Chevrolet was out of it, but the Mk II "Mystery" engine would spawn a new mass production big block in '65. The head bolt pattern was changed ("Mystery" engine heads are not replacements for later Mk IV engines) while bore and stroke were altered for lower cost production. The canted valve configuration was the source of the engine's "porcupine" moniker. This valve layout was patented by designer Dick Keinath. Note that the later Ford 351 Cleveland and BOSS 302 engines were widely acclaimed for their free breathing canted valve heads. Perhaps Keinath's "Mystery" engine that Bill France forced Chevrolet to sell to Ford before the Daytona 500 of 1963, as proof that the engine was available to the public, was the origin of Ford's design.

Chevrolet's Tonawanda, New York, assembly plant was the home of all the big blocks, including the W-engines. But for 1964, the mightiest Chevy was the dual 4-bbl 425-hp 409 that drew yawns. It was not competitive with either Ford's 427 or Chrysler's 426 hemi. When the Mk IV made it to production, it was in 6.5-liter form, 396 cubic inches. Not only did the GM front office edict of no racing carry weight, the ruling of no more than 396 cubic inches in A-bodied cars insured that Chevrolets (and other GM products) would not be competitive in that size cars.

Chrysler's hemi in 1964 was good for as much as 75 horsepower above the top running Ford 427 wedge and developed more than 600-hp in racing tune. It was an all cast iron engine, but aluminum heads for A/FX racing were in the works for '65. The superiority of the Comets, both their ram air hoods and better weight transfer, gave them the edge.

Ford's drag racing in 1964 was dual pronged; its engines had to be seen in both Top Fuel rail dragsters and full bodied cars. Fifty lightweight Galaxies had been scheduled in 1963, but 427-powered Thunderbolts were the stars of 1964. The cars were designed at Dearborn and built by Dearborn Steel Tubing, then finalized at Ford. The initial run of eight cars were tested and shown to be good for consistent 120-mph runs as A/FX cars, but afterwards, around 127 were built and qualified for Super Stock. The Thunderbolts ended up taking six of the seven NHRA divisional championships, and Gas Ronda tallied enough points to be National Champion.

Over at Mercury, veteran hot rodder Fran Hernandez was shaping up a low-budget drag racing effort. A run of 50 special A/FX Comets were scheduled, and four were kept as factory cars. (Some records show that 21 were actually built.) Don Nicholson, Tom Sturm, Ronnie Sox and Bill Shrewsberry were lined up as factory drivers for the NHRA Winternationals at Pomona in '64. Two days before the "Big Go West", Sox was dialing in 11.08 second quarters, and many competitors didn't even bother unloading their cars. Even factory sponsored Dodges and Plymouths were left in parking lots. The Comets easily went through the field, and as predicted, Nicholson and Sox lined up for final round of Factory Stock Eliminator. Sox won, 11.49/123.45. It was a Comet no-contest.

Proffitt, Landy, Lindamood, Eckstrand, Thornton and other MoPar pilots were tough on the Thunderbolts, but they were no match for the Comets. During the season, Nicholson and Sox lost only to each other. The overall win record of the Lincoln-Mercury Division Comets was unbeaten.

1964 Hemi Dodge

When early muscle cars and engines are considered, nearly everyone has a favorite. For Chevrolet people, it is probably the 409 or Z-11 427. For Ford lovers, the 406 tri-power and dual quad 427 rank high. For Poncho fans, the big Super Duty 421 stands out. For Dodge and Plymouth addicts, their's was rarely disputed king, the baddest of the early muscle, the Chrysler 426 hemi. The factory hemi cars, running in Super Stock/Automatic class, were just about unbeatable on the nation's drag strips. In the stoplight grand prixs that went on in nearly every American town, it was well known that

The highly controversial 426 hemi engine caused all sorts of factory squabbles in 1964, but on the the race tracks of America, it had no equal.

Jim Paschal was the highest hemi Dodge finisher at Daytona '64, 5th, in Cotton Owens' car. Daytona Speedway photo.

no matter what you were driving, you didn't mess with a hemi. On the high banked circle tracks, the hemi was a hammer, and Ford versus Chrysler battles thrilled race fans and caused intense bickering between officials and NASCAR.

From its conception, the Chrysler 426 hemi was designed to be a race-winning engine. In December of 1962, the Chrysler design staff was given the go-ahead to develop a new engine. *Hot Rod* magazine described Chrysler's executive criteria for the new engine as, "Develop an engine and vehicle that could win closed circuit stock car events throughout the country. Specifically, put together a power package that could dominate the glamour NASCAR races like Daytona, Charlotte, Atlanta ..." This directive was in line with the prevailing philosophy of the time, "win on Sunday, sell on Monday". One other stipulation was placed on the engine; it had to be competitive in organized drag racing.

The design for the new engine began in January of 1963 with a target completion date of February 23, 1964, the day of Daytona. From the very beginning, the hemispherical combustion chamber shape was considered an absolute necessity. Chrysler had produced highly successful hemis between 1949 and 1958, and consequently there was quite a lot of existing knowledge to draw upon. The 392 hemi was the premier engine in mainline AA/Fuel drag racing.

From this experience, the engineers knew that the hemi head with widely canted valves would provide the necessary power for future development. The fuel/air flow characteristics were such that the mixture had a straight shot from the intake manifold into the combustion chamber and then out the exhaust valve. For this reason, very little turbulence was generated. Consequently, the engine could breathe extremely well. Other benefits were high thermal efficiency of the hemispherical combustion chamber shape and the central location of the spark plug.

After experimenting with several designs, the engineers decided on a layout that was thought to encompass all the potential needs of a high-performance engine. There were to be two basic configurations for the engine, one for NASCAR with a single 4-barrel carburetor and one for drag racing with dual fours. The engines were hand built. With no assembly line, to keep costs down and maximize exposure, first plans were to build a few engines to race and place them in the

hands of the top teams. Under existing NASCAR rules, no minimum production numbers were required, and Chrysler had no showroom production cars with the hemi. The hemi was an eye-opener to everyone except the MoPar men.

The new engines showed up first at Daytona testing. They were immediately 10-mph superior to wedge engines, and Ford went away screaming, then pulled out an experimental engine and requested NASCAR approval for its own, and more radical hemi, the single overhead cam 427. Not a soul outside Dearborn knew of the engine until a week before the Daytona 500 (February, 1964), and although the cammer was not at all likely to be of any significance in the race, it was Ford's way of telling both Chrysler and NASCAR that Dearborn played hard ball, too. Bill France allowed the Chrysler hemi and turned down Ford's! For the next year, 1965, he wrote a new rule requiring at least 500 production car units to qualify an engine.

The first MoPar hemi engines were running on December 6, 1963, barely two months before Daytona. Though development time was short, the engine was ready on race day and performed extremely well. It powered the top three finishers in both 100-mile qualifiers and the top three finishers in the 500. Paul Goldsmith set a new qualifying record of 174.910-mph (9.7-mph faster than the year before), and winner Richard Petty set a new 500-mile speed record of 154.334-mph. The hemis were absolutely dominant, and throughout the 1964 season, the single 4-barrel engines had no equal.

The drag racing engines had considerable weight-saving modifications through the use of aluminum and magnesium components. In Super Stock, the hemi powered Dodges and Plymouths were just about unbeatable. There was also considerable use of the engine in AA/Fuel dragsters. A supercharged, fuel-injected hemi running nitromethane could develop over 1800 horsepower and run low 7 seconds and nearly 200-mph at will.

During this time, the full-bodied drag cars were extremely popular and received lots of press. Dodge and Plymouth Ramcharger and Max Wedge powered Super Stocks were already crowd favorites, and Chrysler upped the ante with factory-built drag cars powered by the hemi. Using inexpensive, plain jane, lightweight bodies such as the Plymouth Savoy and the Dodge 330, superfast straight line stockers brought a new era to drag racing. Typical modifications included lightening the body by replacing steel body panels with aluminum. Typically the front fenders, hood, hood scoop, doors, front bumper brackets, and radiator support panels were manufactured in aluminum. Further weight saving was done by replacing the glass side windows with clear plastic, with aluminum frames and hardware. Using cheap, lightweight, non-adjustable bucket seats and acid dipping the bumpers further reduced weight. These were not the types of cars to order if you wanted creature comforts. They were delivered without heaters, defrosters, radios, sound deadener, or back seats. For improved weight transfer, the battery was relocated to the trunk.

Under the hood was where the real magic resided, a full tilt, race hemi. The 12.5:1 compression ratio engines were equipped from the factory with headers and dual 4-barrels on an aluminum cross-ram intake manifold. Factory horsepower rating for the engine was 425, but NHRA, wise to factory underrating, refactored the engine at 550-hp. The driveline under the cars was all heavy duty with Super/Stock springs and shocks, Sure-Grip rear cogs, and a push-button operated Torqueflite 727 trans.

These cars were in every way factory-built race cars. Off the showroom floor, they were capable of running 12 second quarters at trap speeds exceeding 110-mph. At the NHRA US Nationals in '64, the Dodge of Roger Lindamood won S/SA and Top Stock Eliminator (11.38/127.84). A Super Stock Plymouth run by famed Jere Stahl set an A/Stock national record of 11.65 seconds at 122.44-mph in 1966. That year, the hemi was detuned and dropped into standard production cars to become the Street Hemi. The cars captured the imagination of America's youth and are now highly sought after by today's collectors.

The magic of the early hemi engines and the warfare they generated was the spark that exploded into new highs in the "horsepower war" between the big three. Chevrolet might have been out of the running, but France wrote the rules for 1965 to give the edge to wedge engines. The mighty hemi engine of Ronnie Householder's Chrysler men was vanquished, not by Ford or Chevrolet, but by Bill France and his pen. Among racing fans, the hemi was an instant legend.

1964 Oldsmobile 4-4-2

Oldsmobile added its image of "Rocket" power to the new muscle car movement of mid-size cars introduced in 1964. The 4-4-2 meant something special, but Olds marketing people missed the mark. The first ads to appear featured police cars. That marketing pitch was due to the impact that "Interceptors" had made on the youth sector. Old-model highway patrol cars were sought after by young buyers who got an inexpensive but fast and good handling ride. Back then, a plain-looking "sleeper" was a desirable car to own. They were the cars that didn't look like much, but could blow the doors off a lot of newer cars. The demise of the "sleeper" came with the factory-produced cars that were just as fast, but were new cars. The Olds 4-4-2 twist was all the straight line perfor-

mance you wanted plus something else, excellent handling.

Promotion was so lacking that the 4-4-2 of 1964 came and went with little attention. Were it not for auto magazine test reports, the 4-4-2 that year would be an obscure car indeed. Instead, magazines proclaimed it among the best of a new breed of cars because of the 4-4-2 twist. Different from most muscle cars that provided scintillating straight line sprints, the 4-4-2 combined an excellent handling suspension with a 4-speed, 4-barrel carburetor and dual exhausts. Those items were the source of its name.

Additional equipment that made the 4-4-2 package what it was centered on the intermediate F-85 with a heavy-duty suspension, high-speed tires and a special performance engine. Over the years, Olds had built all sorts of heavy-duty suspension hardware for police pursuit vehicles and simply applied the idea to their mid-year 1964 special edition.

Perhaps that was the source of confusion about just what the 4-4-2 was supposed to be, confusion on the part of Oldsmobile promotion people who headed off in the wrong direction at first. From today's perspective, it is clear that the 4-4-2 was the Olds answer to the new and exciting Pontiac GTO. The youth image of cars had exploded with popularity in the early 1960s. But, at the time, that image must not have been so clear because first 4-4-2 advertisements showed the car as a 4-door with two policemen inside. No young-at-heart car buyer wanted a 4-door sedan and certainly not a new car as austere as a police car. Clearly, Olds advertising was aimed at the wrong mark, although well intended.

Strangely enough, later 4-4-2 advertising recalled the introduction of the cars as 1965, not 1964, and it took some detective work on the part of Oldsmobile Club of America members a few years ago for the factory to acknowledge that 4-4-2s were actually built in '64. Perhaps that early confusion lingered longer than people realized.

However, there was no doubt in automobile magazines that 4-4-2s were alive and well. *Car&Driver* was so impressed with their road test 4-4-2 that they concluded it left them "downright breathless". Compared to other cars of its type, *Motor Trend* advised that 4-4-2 buyers should order the optional heavy-duty metallic brakes saying, "We found these (standard) brakes perfectly adequate for normal chores, but the Cutlass 4-4-2 isn't a normal car. It goes faster and handles better...and should have every advantage". *Motor Trend* also asked, "Why did they wait so long?" implying that the 4-4-2 was a very desirable car.

Even though internal disputes at Oldsmobile left the 4-4-2 without proper direction in its first year, the public who learned of the cars through magazines knew exactly what the cars were, 5-place mid-size cars with Oldsmobile class, exceptional handling and exhilarating performance.

Superb handling for a car of its size was what the 4-4-2 was all about. The package came on selected F-85 and Cutlass 2- and 4-door models and was called the "Police Apprehender Pursuit" package, Option #B09. Equipment consisted of a 310-hp, 330-cid V-8 equipped with a 4-bbl carburetor, a high-lift cam, a fully synchronized 4-speed transmission, and handling improvements brought by heavy-duty shocks and springs (410 lb-in in the front and 160 in the rear), a rear anti-sway bar, and larger size red-lined high-speed tires.

The 4-4-2 engine was a special item with extra high quality rod and main bearings and developed 355 ft-lb of torque at 3600 rpm. It was a premium fuel engine rated 20 horsepower higher than standard F-85 engines.

The new 4-4-2 Oldsmobiles were very stylish and appealing with a combination of equipment found in no other car. Their options list was long and allowed buyers to order a roll-your-own personal car to suit any taste. Their first year accounted for 2,999 sales in spite of very little marketing support. That low number makes the first year by far the rarest early 4-4-2 and adds interesting collector appeal.

A bone stock 4-4-2 of 1964 gave quartermile stats of 15.5 seconds at 90-mph with a test weight of 3,440 pounds. Top speed was around 116-mph and heavily optioned with air conditioning and power equipment, a 4-4-2 could be yours for about $3,600, quite a deal for what you got. Drag racing was big in those days, and proper preparation turned a 4-4-2 into a real hauler that posted 1/4-mile records of 12.68 seconds elapsed time at 109-mph. Clearly, those 330 cubic inches had a lot of punch.

As it turned out, the '64 model 4-4-2 proved to be an excellent launching for the '65 cars. That year, production leaped to over 25,000 cars that were well supported by a barrage of youth oriented advertising. But the big news was a larger engine, a 400-cid powerhouse turning out 345 horses. Still with a single 4-bbl, those big cubes, the theme of all muscle cars, increased torque to a whopping 440 ft-lb in a car of similar size as the 1964 models. A huge list of options made the '65 4-4-2 into a car offering something for everyone.

Convertibles, hardtops and coupes received 4-4-2 emblems, still small and inconspicuous, and came with 3-speed, 4-speed or automatic transmissions. The 4-4-2 was really coming into its own and received a distinctive grill and a standard equipment list of 14 heavy-duty items. Compared to the '64 model, the '65s offered improved performance to the tune of 1/4-miles at 98-mph in 14.15 seconds with only slicks added. Still, they were well-mannered and refined cars in the Oldsmobile tradition, but now the 4-4-2 was called "Olds' Hottest Number" in sales literature.

Hot Rod magazine agreed, saying, "Emphatically, the 4-4-2 remained one of the most likable machines we have ever had the pleasure to drive. At the going price of $2,799, this Olds is really a buyer's bargain; we wish there were more of them." Because of low quantities produced, early 4-4-2s are hard to find today. They recall a time when Oldsmobile marketed one of the best road cars built in this country.

4-4-2 for 1964 was a refined road handler with class.

That year, 330 4-4-2 horses were heavy-duty high winders.

Ronnie Sox handled this car, one of 4 factory sponsored A/FX 427 Comets, at Pomona during the NHRA Winternationals of 1964. The final round was all-Comet, Sox and Don Nicholson, with "Mr. 427" taking Factory Stock Eliminator. Photo courtesy Ronnie Sox.

'64-'65

What began in 1964 exploded into enormous change in 1965. The sales success of Pontiac's GTO opened the door to big profits in the muscle car market, and each manufacturer stepped into the fray with larger and more powerful engines. GM's A-body 330 cubic inch ruling was tossed out, and each division of the giant opted for 400 inchers. Even Chevrolet.

The new model Chevelle came equipped with a 396 cubic inch version of the Mk IV big block that traced its lineage, although a different engine, back to the Mk IIS "Mystery" engine and Daytona 1963. The 409 was well past its prime but carried on through the end of the model year. That engine, even the 8-V 425 horsepower version, was no longer talked about, nor was it a threat to either Ford's 427 or Chrysler's 426 wedge. Chevrolet and all of GM could only watch as the heated hemi war between these two makes was being waged. However, the Mk IV wedge engine had huge potential, and in the hands of a few bowtie diehards, the "porcupine" had many days in the sun to come.

With both Pontiac and Chevrolet gone, Bill France structured NASCAR rules to attract GM racers back. Following Ford's attempt to get its hemi cammer accepted in February '64, Chrysler engineers went to work on a double overhead cam hemi! In the spring of '64, company officials wrote to France requesting 1965 rules. Clearly, they were gearing up to do all-out battle. Given that much lead time to put Dodge and Plymouth hemi cars into production to meet the 500 rule, Chrysler was also sure to counter the cammer with an even better "stock" car. Stock car racing, and street cars by virtue

of the 500 rule, was headed for the stratosphere.

To stem the rapid escalation in horsepower, France put the ball back in the manufacturers' court by asking them what they would like the rules to read. While the fans were enjoying one of the best summers of racing, factory officials were responding. Leo Beebe, head of Ford's special vehicles, let it be known that Ford would not race the '65 season under the same rules as '64. Although Fords won the most races that year, on the super-speedways, the races that drew the most exposure, the hemi cars were long gone. Ford wins were due more to thorough preparation than to powerful engines. The hemis had at least a 60, if not 75, horsepower advantage, and that much power covered up a lot of sins. Once the Dodge and Plymouth teams sorted out their cars, they would steam roll right over Ford.

Beebe's alternatives were to legalize the cammer or return to real production engines, not engineering R&D products. Ronnie Householder wanted the '65 rules to remain the same as '64, and Chrysler VP Bob Anderson made it clear that if Ford's cammer was approved, Chrysler would not be back in '65. It was a stalemate, and France wasn't about to announce new regulations until after the final race of the season, Charlotte in October, to keep Chrysler from pulling out.

By the Firecracker 400 at Daytona on July 4, it was clear; the hemi teams were getting it together. The Fords and Mercurys had a tough go of it, and A. J. Foyt's Dodge took the win.

The debate of the hemis centered on both Ford and Chrysler acknowledging that neither of their engines would

Hemi Plymouths swept the 1964 Daytona 500 1-2-3. Richard Petty led the drubbing of Ford by setting a new 500-mile record of 154.334-mph. Paul Goldsmith, who finished 3rd, set the qualifying record at 174.910-mph. Petty was close at 174.418. In qualifying, Junior Johnson in a hemi Dodge set the fastest 100-miles ever run, 170.777-mph. The hemis were unstopable. Daytona Speedway photo.

be produced in large quantities. Ford wanted a return to stock block engines, but Chrysler had a trick up its sleeve; for 1965, Plymouth was going to a full-size, 119-inch wheelbase, up from 116 inches. Ford had been running 119-inch wheelbase Galaxies, and thus had a small aerodynamic advantage. An edge here or there can mean the difference between winning and losing, and Chrysler was backing Ford into an unacceptable corner.

Then, in the fall, word leaked that the cammer was not going to be permitted, and Chrysler canceled its double overhead cam work and went ahead with full-size hemi cars. When word came that France would rule against running the hemi in the larger cars, Chrysler President Lynn Townsend passed the word to France that his teams would not be at Daytona in 1965.

As fan turnout grew larger and larger, team owners, drivers and mechanics wanted to get on with racing, but all were mere pawns in the hands of corporate officials who were attempting to gain an unfair advantage for their side, and France, who was trying to work out an equitable set of rules that all manufacturers could race under.

Then came the rules: Non-production engines were ruled out. Ford's cammer was not allowed, nor was the high rise 427 wedge, and neither was Chrysler's hemi. Minimum wheelbase was 119-inches for super-speedways, while 116-inches was legal for all other races. Chrysler fumed and Ford cheered. Householder announced that Chrysler would not return to stock car racing unless the rules were changed. Not only did the new rules split the NASCAR house, they also caused USAC to break from its usual allegiance with NASCAR and continue the 1964 regulations.

France had stuck to his guns. Oldsmobile had a new 425-cid engine, as did Chevrolet with its February 1965 announcement of the 427-inch Mk IV. Ford's 427 cubic inch side-oiler was well proven, and Chrysler still had the equally well developed Ramcharger and Max Wedge 426 engines. France struck down the spiraling escalation of exotic engines

and put racing back within the scope of lower budget teams, and he responded to Chrysler's withdrawal by saying, "If Chrysler Corporation feels that its standard 426 cubic inch automobiles are not competitive with comparable size cars of other American makes, then I would be the last to criticize Chrysler on its withdrawal from NASCAR racing."

On the USAC trail, it was all hemi. NASCAR was all Ford. Chrysler would not cooperate with NASCAR, and Ford gave nothing to USAC. Everyone complained that France had given neither the manufacturers nor the teams sufficient notice to prepare for the new season.

The 1965 production year surpassed all previous records. Chrysler Corporation was up 18% to 1,467,553 cars. Ford Motor Co. reached 2,565,776 cars, up 19.6%. General Motors had its best year of the decade, rising 25.1% to 4,949,395 cars. GM wasn't spending a dime on racing, and Ford put millions into its racing, yet the General's production soared past Dearborn's by a sizable margin. And while racing fans watched Ford win 48 races, 13 each by Junior Johnson and Ned Jarrett (Jarrett was NASCAR champion), Richard Petty carried on the fight of the underdog and took all four Plymouth wins in his light blue Plymouth. David Pearson won both of the Dodge wins that year.

Just so he wouldn't get accused of waiting too long again, France announced the 1966 rules at Daytona '65, a year in advance. On the super-speedways of Daytona, Charlotte, Atlanta and Darlington, 119-inch wheelbase cars with 430 cubic engines were allowed. Short track cars of 115- to 119-inch wheelbase with a minimum of 3,500 pounds could run 430-inch engines, but all over 405-cid carried a weight penalty of 20 additional pounds. The new rules were the most confusing ever issued, but the racing went on.

Just as in stock car racing, drag racing fans saw a revolution on the nation's drag strips. Instead of one central rule maker, drag racing sanctioning bodies were overwhelmed with so many varieties of entries that they were kept busy just figuring out what the classes were. Where there had been a

Chevrolet's first muscle car was the 396 Chevelle of 1965. The 375-hp RPO-Z16 cost $1,500 more. 200 were built.

Rebirth of the Mk IIS "Mystery" engine of 1963 was the very different Mk IV of '65. It quickly went from 396 to 427 cubes.

few full-body cars of the type that became Funny Cars, there were now hundreds showing up at any one meet. Super stocks began losing their fan appeal, and top stock matches were used for trips to the burger stand and pits excursions.

Innovations of 1964 started the trend. The aluminum nose supercharged Dodge Chargers of Jim Nix and Jim Johnson performed exhibitions all around the country and help Dodge score its best sales year ever, but the 11-second Chargers were not competitive in the emerging Super/Factory Experimental class. Jack Chrisman in the Sachs & Sons supercharged cammer Comet faced off against the Chargers and beat them at their own game. His 10.13/156.25 B/Fuel Dragster attracted a lot of other builders to that style car. Chrisman's Comet was a factory machine sent out to beat the Chargers, which it easily did. Mercury sales were also up. For 1965, S/FX cars were everywhere.

The most important events of the 1965 season were NHRA's Winternationals at Pomona, the first Springnationals at Bristol and the US Nationals at Indianapolis. The Hot Rod Magazine Championships was another big draw, along with AHRA's Winter Championships.

The Winternationals had some 600 entries, and thousands of fans packed the stands for the eliminations. Although rain the previous days had cast a cloud over the event, the Sunday finals were fast and furious. In A/FX, 4 Comets, 2 Dodges, 2 Plymouths and 5 Mustangs composed a thrilling field for Factory Stock Eliminator. Semi-finals drew Len Richter (Mustang), George Delorian (Comet), Bill Lawton (Mustang) and Tommy Grove (Plymouth). Then Richter and Lawton squared off for the all-Ford Final. Richter's car broke an axle, but Lawton didn't make a bye, he blasted a 10.92/128.20 earth shaker.

Bill "Grumpy" Jenkins had moved over to wrench and drive a Super Stock/A Plymouth, leaving Chevrolet temporarily behind. This was Jenkins' first major event as a driver, and he nailed super stocker after super stocker on his way to the final round that pitted him against another Plymouth. Dick Housey bowed to "Da Grump" as Jenkins put a hole shot on Housey to take the round with a .02-second slower ET (11.39/126.76).

On the trek eastward toward warmer weather, the next big stop of the '65 drag racing season was Bee-Line Dragway

near Scottsdale, Arizona, for the AHRA Winter Championships. Connie Kalitta unveiled his "Bounty Hunter" slingshot rail dragster sporting the first SOHC 427 to leave Ford, and made a single qualifying pass at 7.67 seconds at 200.88-mph on the first try! His cammer engine failed after a few more passes, but the die was cast, Chrysler's hemi had a new threat.

With no place to go round racing in 1965, Richard Petty ventured into drag racing with a hemi Barracuda, number 43-Jr. Richard tested the car at Greensboro, North Carolina's Piedmont Drag Strip and immediately lowered both the ET and speed records for Super/Experimental Stock by running 10.50s at 140+ mph. At Bee-Line, he pushed the 'Cuda to 10.46.

Pontiac driving ace Arnie "The Farmer" Beswick parked his "Mystery Tornado" S/FX GTO and became Arnie "Tiger" Beswick at Scottsdale. His 10.23/145.16 blown "goat" had transmission problems, and he was offered the seat of the Gay Pontiac A/Sportsman machine. He capped off A/Sportsman class honors, then took Sportsman Eliminator with the dual quad tiger-striped Tempest cranking out an 11.70 ET at 102.27-mph. Top Stock Eliminator was in the hands of Mike Buckel and the Ramchargers Dodge running a super strong 11.02.

Bristol's brand new drag racing facility was host to NHRA's Springnationals and quickly became known as Thunder Valley. This beautiful facility has remained among the finest in the country, even though its mountain altitude is often cited as not conducive to record performances. Then Chris Karamesines with his blown Chrysler hemi blasted a 202-mph pass the first time out, and people weren't thinking altitude anymore. Kalitta had his Ford cammer AA/F dragster together and turned in a set of unbeatable runs, 207.84, 209.78 and 208.80 back-to-back. Records fell nearly every pass. For Top Fuel Eliminator, it was another Ford versus Chrysler round as Michigan pilots Kalitta and Maynard Rupp eased to the line. 426 hemi against 427 cammer; both had turned excellent times with the cammer given the edge. Both nitro burners launched well, then with everyone standing and holding their breaths, Rupp turned in a 7.59/203.16 to upset Kalitta's 7.82 at 205.94.

A star-studded field of A/FX, Super Stocks and AA/Stock cars was in for a surprise in Top Stock Eliminator.

Fred Lorenzen drove this Holman-Moody Ford in 1965. He won Daytona leading 12 more FoMoCo cars, and later won both races at Charlotte including the World 600.

"Competition Proven" was the logo of Holman-Moody. In this cockpit, Lorenzen kept track of the 427 medium riser under the hood. W.H.M.? What the Hell's the Matter?

1964 World Stock Points Champion Mike Schmitt brought his AA/Stock Desert Motors 427 high riser Ford Galaxie to the mountains and captured the title with a 12.32/117.18-mph. Another haulin' Ford was Bill Hoefer's C/FX Galaxie. Hoefer was the 1964 World Factory Experimental Points Champion and nailed down a shot at Junior Stock Eliminator against Doug Patterson's F/S Barracuda. It was a finish decided by electronic counters, Hoefer winning with a 14.32/84.98.

The big names brought the tour to Riverside for the Hot Rod Magazine Championships. Names like Dick Landy and his A/FX hemi Dodge were there. This car was another of the controversial drag racers of 1965. The car's body was shifted rearward for better weight transfer. Its wheelbase was also shortened from 116 to 111-inches by moving the front wheels forward 15-inches and the rear axle up 10-inches. Its hemi was fitted with aluminum heads and magnesium intake manifold. Landy was one of the first to use a fuel cooler, a device using dry ice to cool the fuel before entering the engine. Fiberglass doors, fenders, hood, front bumper and instrument panel saved weight, along with replacing all glass in the car with plexiglass. The car was not legal under NHRA rules but was under AHRA regs. Wherever it raced, Landy's Dodge was one of the quickest stock bodied cars in the country and laid down 10 second passes at 140-mph. His car was in the range of the blown S/FX cars but ran only dual 4-bbl carbs like the earlier Super Stock cars.

Butch "California Flash" Leal and Shirley "Dragon Lady" Shahan in MoPars; Mike Schmitt and Bill Hoefer in Fords; Gas (Gaspar) Ronda and Hayden Proffitt in Comets, and hundreds of other contestants rolled up pass after pass.

The "Big Go East" at Indianapolis Raceway park drew 130,000 spectators to watch 1,100 racers pit their skills and reaction times. The turnout for that event alone illustrates the huge appeal of drag racing in 1965. After a weekend at the drags, new car showroom traffic was tremendous and sale after sale was made.

The new generation personal-size car had enormous appeal, and with Ford's Mustang came the most popular car of its type in the history of the industry. The 1964-1/2 Mustang came in three versions, coupe, fastback and convertible, but it would be 1967 before the line received big block engines in production. On the drag strips, though, all sorts of Mustangs

Mustang replaced the Thunderbolts as Ford's mainline drag racer in 1965. Production models did not receive the 500-hp high riser 427, but the fast strippers did.

Pontiac GTO was a lean and mean street machine with the tri-power 389 and 4-speed transmission. They were extremely popular cars, selling 75,352 in 1965.

with carburetor 427s, fuel injected 427s, cammer 427s and blown 427s raced throughout the 1965 season and were a huge success. The muscle car war was in full tilt, and we couldn't wait to see what 1966 would bring.

1965 Pontiac GTO

An outgrowth of the emerging performance era of the early 1960s was legalized and organized drag racing. Thousands of people flocked to the numerous quartermile strips that dotted the nation to see the local hot rodders, tire burning dragsters, and the new Super Stock class cars from Detroit. Drag racing caught the attention of the manufacturers as an excellent way to showcase their new speed equipment. By '62, Ford had its hot 406, Chevy's 409s and Z-11s were tough, Chrysler came on strong with with the Ramcharger 426, and Pontiac with the Super Duty 421s put on impressive shows weekend after weekend.

As impressive as the Super Stockers were, their street counterparts made up very little of the the emerging youth market. For every Super Stock car sold, the manufacturer lost money. The few that were sold proved to be temperamental, loud, and hard to drive. Their radical cams were not suited for street driving, and their huge carburetors dropped fuel economy to the point of nonexistence. If you were drag racing, you didn't care, but for street use, the cost of gas mattered.

Pontiac solved the problem of combining high performance and roadability and made it profitable. Engineers followed the example set by the Mickey Thompson and Royal Pontiac V-8 Tempest A/FX drag cars. These cars illustrated one of the oldest performance principles - high power-to-weight ratio makes for exhilarating performance. With that basic philosophy, Pontiac stuffed a 389 cid full-size car engine into the intermediate-size Tempest for 1964 and gave birth to the GTO.

The fathers of the GTO are difficult to pinpoint. The two men generally credited are John DeLorean and Jim Wangers. At that time, DeLorean was chief engineer for Pontiac and had a great deal of influence on Pontiac's general manager, Pete Estes. Wangers was an account executive at MacManus, John & Adams, at that time Pontiac's advertising agency.

Both men possessed tremendous drive and were equally enthusiastic about furthering Pontiac's performance image. This is evident in the name that they chose, GTO, which was borrowed from the contemporary World Championship Ferrari 250 GTO.

There was nothing complicated about the concept. It involved using existing equipment combined in a different way to produce a totally new package. The platform that was chosen for the GTO project was the all-new Tempest that arrived for the 1964 model year. The car was a brand new design with little to no carryover from the 1961-'63 models. The '64 Tempest had a separate perimeter frame, four-wheel coil-sprung suspension with a four-link live rear axle, and a newly styled body shell instead of the earlier unit construction, swing axles, flexible drive shaft, and rear-mounted transmission. In place of the standard 4-cylinder engine, the new 326 cubic inch V-8 Tempest certainly offered a more stable platform on which to build a performance car.

The power plant that was chosen was the reliable four-bolt main 389 cubic inch big block. Its overall dimensions were identical to the 326 (and larger capacity 421), so going to the larger engine was a natural. The base engine with a single 4-barrel carb produced a healthy 325 horsepower. The optional high-output engine, sporting a trio of 2-barrel carbs and big valve heads borrowed from the mighty 421s, produced 348 horsepower.

Officially, putting a big cubic inch V-8 in an intermediate-size car was a no-no at General Motors. The rule makers at GM had placed a 330 cubic inch limit on V-8s in anything but full-size cars and the Corvette (note the 330-cid 4-4-2). DeLorean craftily outmaneuvered the edict by offering the GTO as an equipment option on the Tempest rather than a separate model. Before GM's top brass knew what was going on, the GTO was already in dealer showrooms. The positive response

Engines were the talk of '60s cars. Three deuces on the 389 GTO became a car cult symbol.

that the GTO received from the buying public turned it into an instant sensation which left little for GM's brass to complain about.

The GTO option was a performance bargain at a base price between $3200 and $3500. Different from the stripped down Super Stockers, the GTO could be optioned from an arm-long list. This list included choices between fancy interior packages, lighting groups, and body styles and could be ordered on the coupe, convertible, and hardtop. Also on the list were numerous performance goodies like three two-barrel carburetion, floor-mounted 4-speed close-ratio transmissions, tachometers, finned aluminum wheels, metallic brake linings, limited slip differentials, oversized tires, a wide choice of rear-end ratios, and extra tight suspension packages. The options increased the profit margin on every GTO sold making it a very lucrative car for Pontiac.

One of the major driving ideas behind the GTO was to produce a car that would keep Pontiac's performance image alive. And that it did. Recall the GM no-racing edict? New car sales had to offset lost prestige on racing circuits. Early road tests of the GTO showed it to be a tremendous performer. *Road & Track* tested both the 325-hp and 348 horse versions with 4-speed transmissions and 3.23:1 final drive ratios. The figures they reported were truly impressive. The 0-to-60 times were 6.9 seconds for the 325-hp car and 5.7 for the 348-hp. Quartermile times and speeds were 15.0 seconds at 91.5-mph and 14.1 seconds at 104.2-mph. *Car and Driver* performed tests on a Tri-Power car equipped with a 3.90:1 rear. The car was specially prepared at Royal Pontiac in Royal Oak, Michigan. The only modifications were advanced timing, richer carbs, blocked-off heat risers, thinner head gaskets and gasketless Champion J-10Y spark plugs, all of which were fairly simple changes. The stats that were recorded were incredible. The 0-to-60 time was 4.6 seconds

In "GTO", a Beach Boys song of the early '60s, the new Pontiac was immortalized. The cars were fast and beautiful inside and out, and became the car others were measured by.

with a quartermile time and speed of 13.1 seconds at 115.0-mph!

Car and Driver testers said this about the car, "It's almost worth stealing it for a few minutes of Omigod-we're-going-too-fast kind of automotive bliss." They went on to say, "One expects the acceleration to be spectacular in first and second but none of us were ready for the awful slamming back in the seat we got when we tromped on it at 80 in fourth."

Pontiac planned to build only 5,000 GTOs for 1964 just to test the market. This proved to be a classic example of underestimation. Just a few months into the model year, Pontiac received over 10,000 orders, and by the end of the model year over 32,000 had been sold, and there were still unfilled orders. Pontiac had discovered an untapped market with the GTO and provided the focus that shaped the American muscle car era which developed soon afterward.

1965 Skylark Gran Sport

By 1965 there were numerous big block powered mid-size cars on the market. Pontiac had its 389 in the GTO, Chevrolet offered a limited run of 396s in the Chevelle called the Z-16 option, and Oldsmobile offered a 400 in the 4-4-2, just to name a few. Ford had not introduced a mid-size car with a big block for the street; instead, it was building factory race cars. Ford sought exposure with the Super Stock Thunderbolts and A/FX Comets, and captured more press than a street car could. One marque that is missing from this list is Buick.

When most people think of Buick, they typically see the type of car that dad and mom would drive, a stately grocery getter, and certainly not a youth-oriented driving machine. The "Geritol generation" might not have the fire of youth, but Buick product planners were certainly not behind the times and produced their own high powered cars in the refined Buick tradition.

In 1965, Buick introduced a new option for the Skylark line called the Gran Sport. The basic idea behind the new package was to have a car that would be interesting to young people. The first criterion that had to be met was power, and the best answer to power was cubic inches. The heart of the Gran Sport option was the 401 cubic inch Wildcat V-8 which produced 325 horsepower at 4400 rpm and 445 ft-lb of torque at 2800 rpm. Backing up the engine there were three transmission options. Standard was a heavy-duty, all synchromesh 3-speed with floor-mounted shifter. Also there was a fully synchro 4-speed trans and a special, heavy-duty, Super Turbine 300, 2-speed, variable vane automatic, both with floor-mounted shifters.

Buick engineers realized that in order to have a well-balanced high-performance car, more than just a big V-8 would be needed. In order to handle the increased weight and power of the Wildcat engine, cars with the Gran Sport package were built on heavy-gauge, fully boxed convertible model frames. This added greater structural rigidity which resisted twisting much better than the standard frames. It was also an element of improved safety. Included in the GS package were high-rate springs and specially valved heavy-duty shocks at all four wheels. Up front a thicker, stiffer anti-roll bar was installed to control body roll during hard cornering. A four control arm rear suspension was used to handle the 325 horses being transmitted through the tranny. The layout of the four control-arms was such that the upper two prevented reverse torque or reverse spin of the differential, and all four worked together to prevent side-to-side movement of the entire rear-end assembly.

To complete the heavy-duty driveline, the rear-end was beefed up. For the manual transmission cars there was a standard 3.36 gear and for automatics a 3.08, neither being positive traction units. Buick included many optional gear ratios ranging from 3.09 to 4.30.

In the stopping department, Buick engineers used 9.5 inch diameter dual servo drum brakes. Inside, there was harder, tougher lining material which was thicker than standard shoes. Also, the front wheel cylinders were enlarged to improve stopping power. This was one of the few areas that needed improvement in the Gran Sport option. The front drums were shared with the Chevy II, and while they were larger than those on the standard Skylark, they were not large enough to dissipate heat quickly. For this reason, the brakes began to fade rapidly, and in panic stops, the rear brakes would tend to lock up due to increased loads.

Interiors of the cars were nicely appointed. *Hot Rod* magazine testers reported, "The dashboard layout is both pleasing and functional..." A tachometer was not standard but could be optioned. The tach was inconveniently placed at the head of the console that ran between the seats. Further

The new Skylark of 1964 was the Buick version of the GTO and 4-4-2. Gran Sport received the largest engine of the three, 401 cubic inches rated at 325-hp. It was called the "Superbird" in advertising. Dual 4-bbl carbs was a Riviera Wildcat option and gave around 20 more horespower.

interior appointments included bucket seats with expanded vinyl covers and full carpeting. Optional power brakes and air conditioning were also available for those who wanted a complete boulevard cruiser.

In full street trim, the Skylark Gran Sport weighed in at over 3,800 pounds, far from a lightweight in its size class. But even with all the tonnage to lug around, the engine performed admirably and even proved to be relatively quick. In a *Motor Trend* road test a Gran Sport was pushed from 0-to-60 in just 7.8 seconds and turned the quarter in 16.6 seconds at 86-mph. Just to see what one was capable of, a B-Stock prepared car was also tested. The only modifications to the car consisted of balancing and blueprinting the engine, adding a set of hooker headers leading into three-inch collectors, 4.30 Positraction rear cogs, and a set of super-bite Casler recaps. The quickest run the car made was a incredible 13.42 seconds at 104.46-mph!

The Gran Sport package with a three-speed trans cost only $252.86 above the regular Skylark. The automatic upped the price $457.11 and the four-speed $420.11. The base Skylark Gran Sport could be ordered for just over $3,100 including a radio. By the time air conditioning and power brakes were added the price rose to just over $3,800. At this price the car was certainly not for everyone, but one thing is for sure, Buick built more than just grocery getters and cars for the older set. There were some that fit very well into the youth market. These were the upscale cars for the young at heart, the people with taste who would rather drive a Buick.

The luxurious interior of the Skylark GS left only engine monitor gauges and tach relocation to be desired. Some owners installed gauge packages as shown in this car. On the rider's side visor mirror was, "Its a beauty, too."

The 426 hemi Belvederes of 1966 and '67 were awesome. Richard Petty put together two spectacular seasons on the NASCAR circuits, winning 8 races in 1966 and 27 in '67 with 404 cubic inch engines. His '67 year was the best individual season on record. One stretch consisted of 10 straight wins!

Street Fighters

The intensity of the factory men's desire to race and win in 1965 produced the fastest cars yet seen in '66. To meet NASCAR minimum production figures of 500 units, all sorts of high-performance cars were made available to the public. While there had been 207 hemi Plymouth and Dodge cars produced in 1965, the factory scheduled 1,800 each for both. The final combined production appears to be around 2,730 rather than 3,600, but even the lower figure put more factory-built street fighters on the street than ever before.

On the NASCAR rounds, Dodge won 18 races in '66, Plymouth took 16, and both makes exceeded Ford's total of 10. Richard Petty's Belvedere by Petty Plymouth won the February 27 Daytona 500, setting the fastest 500 miles on record, 160.627-mph (nobody could yet touch Junior Johnson's hemi Dodge lap record set in 1964, 170.777-mph). Paul Goldsmith brought his Belvedere into the winner's circle of the Rockingham 500 on March 13. The Jim Hurtubise Belvedere followed by winning the Atlanta 500 on March 27, and Petty took the second round Dixie 300 at Atlanta in record fashion (130.244-mph). Petty won the Darlington 400 on April 30, and USAC champion Norm Nelson took the Yankee 300 at Indianapolis on May 1. The "Toughest of Them All" World 600 at Charlotte went to Marvin Panch with relief driver Richard Petty. Jim Paschal won the Virginia 500 at Martinsville and the Staley 400 at North Wilkesboro. All were hemi Belvedere wins.

Sam McQuagg drove his hemi Charger into victory lane in the Firecracker 400 at Daytona. LeeRoy Yarbrough took the win in the fall 500-miler at Charlotte, and David Pearson won both rounds of the Richmond races. All were hemi Charger victories. Pearson was NASCAR champion with 15 wins in 42 starts, with 26 top five finishes with the hemi Chargers. James Hylton was 2nd (Dodge) followed by Petty (Plymouth). The hemis were untouchable.

The MoPar factory cars were run with 404 cubic inch engines in the shorter wheelbase Belvederes and were thought to sacrifice perhaps 30-hp. But with the new "throne" type single 4-bbl intake manifold and its plenum effect, factory engineers were getting almost as much power out of 404 cubic inches as the 426 produced with the older style intake. With Petty reaching 185-mph on the straights at Daytona, it became apparent to everyone that the smaller displacement hemi was developing around 575-hp. All the top Plymouths and Dodges were by far faster than any of the Fords, and most people considered the Ford 427 obsolete. The old wedge was good for little more than 500-hp.

What happened to the Ford racing machine? In the opening round of the '66 season, Dan Gurney drove away from everyone at Riverside for his 4th straight victory in the Western 500, and Darel Dieringer saved a little glory for FoMoCo by winning the Southern 500 at Darlington, but that was in a 427 Mercury Comet. Only five of FoMoCo's 10 wins were with '66 model cars, and only those noted were of significance. At Charlotte for the October race, kids were walking around with hand-scribbled signs reading, FORD IS DEAD.

Earlier in the season at Daytona, Fords had trouble

During 1966, NASCAR rules arguments raged over this engine, Ford's SOHC 427. If allowed, it would have killed Chrysler's hemi. It wasn't, but drag racers loved its box stock 640-hp. Blown and injected, it was a 1600-hp AA/FD winner.

Chevrolet wasn't left behind. Zora Duntov and his men worked quietly developing this, a single overhead cam 427. GM brass would not let it out, but Zora was ready. Tested to 660-hp, both Ford and Chrysler would have been in trouble.

Chrysler's toughest street and racing engine ever was the 426 hemi. Showroom models were rated at 425-hp. NASCAR racers got this version, over 600-hp with a single 4-bbl. Note the "throne" intake manifold, an off-road use only item. In blown, injected form, hemis were capable of over 1600-hp and 200+mph quartermiles in dragsters. It was the ultimate production car engine of the '60s. Chrysler photo.

retaining their windshields, and Cale Yarborough was heard to say, "Them hemis goin' by so fast, sucked them windshields out, I guess." Ford officials claimed it was the MoPars throwing tire chunks during the race. But the truth is that the leading edge of the roofs of both the Fairlanes and Comets had been altered to incline the windshields at a slightly reduced angle. That was a trick to improve aerodynamics, a growing new force in stock car racing, as was racing intermediate-size cars.

At Daytona, Smokey Yunick put a scare into everybody with his hand-built Chevelle powered by one of his own Chevrolet big block jobs. Old line driver Curtis Turner had been reinstated by Bill France (expelled earlier for trying to organize drivers), and with Yunick's preparation, that Chevelle was far more competitive than anyone expected. Then it was rolled into a wreck, and that was that. That car had the potential of beating both Ford and Chrysler factory teams without one cent from Chevrolet. When it was out, everyone sighed with relief.

Behind the NASCAR scenes that year, a war was being waged between Ford, Chrysler and Bill France. Leo Beebe at Ford announced early on that the official factory engine for the '66 season would be the SOHC 427. Its 600-to-800 higher rpm limit and 640-hp peak meant that Chrysler was in trouble. Ronnie Householder, and other top Chrysler officials, were careful to point out to France that his rules stated that, to be legal, engines had to be production in cars. They stated that Chrysler Corp. was going to build 3,600 hemi cars because of that rule, but Ford planned only to offer the cammer for sale, 500 of them, to anyone to install for themselves. It was not, according to Chrysler's interpretation of the regulations, a production engine.

Since the rules allowed a maximum of 430 cubic inches (to allow a .06-inch overbore of a 427) in full-size cars of 119-inch wheelbase, Ford planned to run the cammer in Galaxies. That was Ford's biggest seller, and it made

economic sense to race them. But when France announced that overhead cam engines would have to carry an additional weight penalty of 1 more pound per cubic inch rather than 9.36 of other cars, the cammer was instantly ruled noncompetitive. Beebe changed his plans and went to the 427 Fairlane.

Engineers calculated that the reduced frontal area of around 2 square feet and smaller overall dimension of the cars would give them an advantage of around 9% over-full size cars, and that translated into about 5 or 6 additional mph. That would be enough to be competitive in speed with the hemi Belvederes and Chargers. But France had thought that one out, too, and restricted engine displacement to 406 cubic inches in intermediates. That reduced the speed of Fairlanes and Comets to maybe 1- or 2-mph greater than a full-size sedan. That's not much, but with thorough preparation, the

One Ford Fairlane driver for Holman-Moody was Fred Lorenzen, shown here at Riverside, '67. These cars could run 406 cubic inch 427s and weigh 3,707 lb, or 371-inch 427s in 3,500 pound cars. Both were tough packages and won races.

Mercury raced a reduced budget schedule with Bud Moore handling the cars. At Darlington for the Southern 500, Darel Dieringer won. It was the first independent win in years.

Ford cars could be competitive if luck went against the Mo-Pars. As the season unfolded, luck had little to do with the winning MoPars, and the Ford teams resorted to tricks.

At Atlanta, Junior Johnson's Fairlane, driven by Lorenzen, was lowered so much in the front that half the lower headlight was hidden. The back end of the car was swept up into what amounted to a spoiler, and the car had many other modifications sure to disqualify it. Ford's Special Vehicles group had put together the car as a jab at France. It became known as Johnson's "Yellow Banana" and created all sorts of ill will.

On the 15th of April, 1966, Henry Ford II announced that "We are out of stock car racing. We don't like Mr. France's new rules, we think the rules are unfair to us, so we're out for the year." The remainder of the season was run only on a limited basis, mostly as preparation for the 1967 season. Dodge and Plymouth drivers won almost everything.

Prior to Atlanta and during the summer, there were no Fords or top Ford drivers running NASCAR. The "Yellow Banana" was so outrageous that ran as a factory car with Lorenzen driving, France would either embarrass the entire NASCAR organization by allowing this obviously illegal car to run (for the purpose of attracting more paying fans by advertising that Ford factory cars would be back) or kill the golden goose - Ford - that had been a staunch supporter until the '66 season. He let the car run, Cotton Owens loaded up his car and went home, and Lorenzen battled Petty out front until the halfway mark, then went out. If he had won, the rising storm of controversy would have caused enormous problems for Bill France and NASCAR. "Stock car" racing would have lost its meaning altogether.

In more sensible cars, the engineers thought out another scheme. If a 427 Fairlane were run as a 396, its weight would be 3,707 pounds, and that would reduce tire wear and gas consumption, resulting in one less pit stop. In practice at Rockingham, Lorenzen's 396 Fairlane showed such low wear on the high adhesion "gumballs" normally used just for qualifying that Ralph Moody and Lorenzen decided to race the tires. Keeping it a secret from everyone else meant that

they didn't go to the tire fitters until just before the race and were last on the lineup. When the ploy was discovered during the race, Lorenzen and Petty were dueling out front. When Petty went out after 320 laps, Lorenzen easily held on to the end and rolled up a remarkable average speed for a 1-mile oval of 104.3-mph, and led a Ford 1-2-3-4-5 finish.

No one could touch Lorenzen's Fairlane, and Ray Nichels wanted to know why. He put up the $100 protest fee to have the car checked by officials. John Holman was ready to prove publicly that all the leading Fords were legal, and put up $400 to have 2nd place finisher Don White's Fairlane, and Jarrett's, Yarborough's and Johnson's cars checked. It took hours to go through the cars, and by then almost everyone had left.

The reduced stroke 396 cubic inch 427 Fairlane won at Rockingham, the American 500, then won at Martinsville. With Dick Hutcherson's wins at Bristol and North Wilkes-boro, and Dieringer's Southern 500 win, Ford's tally of significant wins in 1966 was these five races. However, Dieringer's Southern 500 victory was in independent Bud Moore's Mercury who only had partial support. It should not be considered a Ford factory win and was the first major victory by an independent in years.

All the bickering over a few Fords late in the season was of no consequence. Petty had given Plymouth a magnificent year, as did Pearson with Dodge, and Chrysler Corporation had gotten more positive publicity than they could possibly use. As far as the public was concerned, the hemis were awesome. Fans poured into Plymouth and Dodge showrooms to see what the cars were like that destroyed Ford. The street hemis outsold Ford's 427 Fairlanes 10-to-1. Overall, 1966 was a season of controversy and was not a good year for Ford. For Dodge and Plymouth, it could have been improved only by winning the Southern 500, but since that was not a factory Ford win, so what, give Bud Moore and his team all the credit.

What the NASCAR squabbles did was to inflame the muscle car wars. Every manufacturer had its versions of high-performance cars, and that made for an exciting time. However, it also made for increased highway carnage, and public outcry by voters was reaching such proportions that the

Bruce Larson was one of few Chevrolet racers on the match racing circuit in 1967-68, the period known as the "Olympics of Drag Racing". His patriotic red, white and blue Chevelle ran a stroked 427 to produce 454 cubic inches. With fuel injection, the car set the NHRA 2400 pound class B/Experimental Stock record of 8.85 seconds at 159.29-mph. In 1968, Larson moved into a USA-1 Camaro and received "Mr. Chevrolet" honors when he won a major Funny Car shootout. Gold Dust Classics photo.

Chevelles were very popular in 1967. Production reached 375,831. With the 375-hp 396 engine, Super Sport Chevelles were stylish and fast muscle cars.

manufacturers were forced to listen. It was becoming increasingly clear that adverse public opinion was growing, and the car makers were described as irresponsible for making so many high-performance cars. Instead of faster and faster cars, they should make safer and safer cars.

The growing numbers of highway deaths and injuries had reached Senator Abraham Ribicoff. He was chairman of the Senate Subcommittee on Executive Reorganization. On his staff were Robert F. Kennedy and Ralph Nader, soon to be known as "unsafe at any speed" Nader.

At one of Ribicoff's hearings, GM chairman Frederic Donner, President James Roche and Chief Engineer Harry Barr testified. GM had shown a $1.7 billion dollar profit in 1965, and Ribicoff wanted know how much money GM was spending on making its cars safer. Perhaps overconfident from having done so well as a businessman, Donner came to the hearings ill-prepared and looked miserably inept throughout the proceedings. He also did not recognize the impact of the safety questions, and after consulting with Barr, he reported that GM spent about $1.25 million dollars on safety. In truth, that figure must have been grossly underes-

timated, but the testimony was given, and the revelation changed the automotive industry forever. The conclusion was clear: government controls on the automotive industry were needed because the manufacturers appeared incapable of regulating themselves. Safety hysteria was sweeping the nation, and while the kids wanted faster cars, parents were writing officials to do away with them. Highways were not for racing, and street racing among the kids had become an uncontrollable outrage.

It was in the Ribicoff climate that Ford officials decided not to put the SOHC 427 into a production car. This 700-hp engine was still being offered to drag racers, but it would not become a production engine beyond its demand for off-road use. For 1967, France changed the rules again allowing intermediate cars to run 427s with dual 4-bbls, and Ford engineers came up with the "tunnel port" intake and head system. This was a breakthrough for the old 427 wedge and added about 30-hp. The "tunnel port" was run first at Daytona, 1967. Dodge and Plymouth cars were already so superior that they needed only to run what they had and improve race preparation, the one edge that the Ford teams seemed to have.

'66 - '67

The NASCAR fights and rule changes brought the 427 Fairlanes, the 427 Comets, the 426 street hemi Plymouths and Dodges. There were lots more street fighters. Don't forget the 427 Cobra and 427 Corvette, nor the 427 Impala, 427 and 428 Galaxie, or the 426 wedge MoPars. Don't leave out the 421 Pontiac, 401 Skylark GS and 425 Riviera, the 400-inch Olds 4-4-2, or 396 Chevelle, and on and on. Street fighters were everywhere in 1966, and nighttime cruisin' was definitely "in". Organized drag racing had changed from the early '60s showcase of Super Stocks, and to show off the potential of their cars, the kids paired off at stop lights rather than wade through the hordes of cars at drag races to do one pass of grudge racing. There were plenty of spectators to settle whose car was fastest, if there was any doubt, and stoplight drags became the arena of muscle car battles, not drag strips.

Impala for 1967 was long and low slung. Five different 427s, 385- to 435-hp, were available. Chevrolet photo.

The face of drag racing had become one of hundreds of dragsters with stock-looking bodies. They came in every conceivable variation and gave stripper fans more thrills than they had ever seen before. No longer was A/FX the most exciting racing, Super/Factory Experimental was top. Match racing between top name drivers had become the big draw for promoters, and there were more match racers than you could count. There were so many match race cars that the business of touring the country on a circuit became more financially rewarding than trying to win points championships.

Drag racing had changed. It was more exciting than ever before, but stock classes were even more uninteresting, and forces were in motion that would split what had always been sportsman racing into professional and sportsman categories. The factories were deep into drag racing, and drivers for them had the best of everything. The little guy could not compete against factory engineering and development, especially when the cars were in the hands of factory drivers who raced for a living. Exhibition and match racing pitted these guys against each other, and to get them, promoters had to pay big bucks. That left paltry winnings for the sportsman racers, who were by far the largest segment of drag racing. That was and remains a source of contention that has never been adequately resolved. Even today, the argument continues that Pro Stock drivers earn far less than Top Fuel drivers, although it costs as much to race in Pro Stock as it does Top Fuel. And sportsman drag racers look forward to no more than paltry winnings.

For 1966, drag racing spectator turnouts were larger than ever before. The number of cars got so large that three-day Super Stock events had to be held to allow enough time to get through to eliminations on Sunday. Classes were invented to cover cars put together from anything imaginable, and the racing went on in high gear. Throughout that year of innovation, a few drivers maintained a closer association with truly factory-built cars modified for drag racing. One was Bill Jenkins. His Super Stock Nova proved the point at New York National Raceway on Long Island during the 1966 Super Stock Nationals. After three days of handicapping several hundred cars, Mr. Stock Eliminator was Bill Jenkins in his Nova, not Nicholson or Schartman or Landy or any of the multitudes of high-dollar "funny car" circuit riders.

Without doubt, the high-performance cars of 1966 were

Muscle cars like the 400 cubic inch Olds 4-4-2 were capable of ripping their rear tires to shreds.

a broader set than the '65s. And 1967 was even better. Ford entered the '67 NASCAR season with the smallest contingent of factory cars and drivers that it had fielded in years. Dan Gurney moved over to Mercury sponsorship with Bud Moore, who was running the new Trans-Am Cougar team with Gurney as lead driver. Holman-Moody brought on Parnelli Jones, and the two of them battled through the Riverside desert raceway, Gurney in a Comet and Jones in a Fairlane. Gurney was penalized a lap for passing under yellow, and Jones streaked on to win. It was Ford's 5th consecutive victory in the season opener at Riverside.

Then came Daytona, THE race of the season. Whoever won the 500 had publicity for the year. Win or lose all the others, Daytona was it. The factory teams were there in force, but who should be the No. 1 qualifier? Curtis Turner in Smokey Yunick's black and gold Chevelle! Chevrolet wasn't spending a cent on racing, and here were a couple of old '50s era racers putting the needle to all the high-buck factory teams and their glamour drivers.

In qualifying, the Fords raised the average speed to 177-mph. Beebe and his crews were confident. Then Petty went out in his concours quality Plymouth and went 179. Householder and his crews were smugly confident. Yunick sat back until late in the day, then sent Turner out. "We stuck her on the pole so easy," says Smokey.

The truth of that car was that it was a Chevrolet inside job, as suspected by a number of people. The chassis was

The Super Stocks and A/FX cars of the early '60s became Super/Experimental Stocks by 1966. They were really dragsters with stock-type fiberglass bodies. Here, "Dyno Don" Nicholson exposes the injected 427 cammer in his Comet.

Ed "The King" Schartman was one of the winningest S/FX drivers in '66 and '67. He won the AHRA Funny Car Nationals of 1967, turning 8.16/186.10 to beat Pat Minick's Chi-Town Hustler. He set the Milan Dragway and Michigan record in class at 7.73/184.48 while shutting down Larry Reyes' Super 'Cuda.

designed by Yunick and Chevrolet engineers and built at Chevrolet R&D at Warren, Michigan, under the direction of Frank Winchell and Jim Musser. "After they spent about a half a million dollars and run us out of time, we finally had to bring the car down here (to Smokey's Best Damn Garage in Town garage in Daytona Beach) with about ten of their guys. We finally got the thing finished and run it in the race," confirms Smokey.

In the pre-race 100-mile qualifiers, LeeRoy Yarbrough (Dodge) and A. J. Foyt (Ford) battled in the first round with Yarbrough winning. In the second race, the top four cars were Fairlanes with Lorenzen winning that round. Lorenzen also succeeded in breaking Junior Johnson's 1964 record of 170.777-mph by averaging 174.583-mph.

Out of 50 qualifying cars for the 500 that year, twelve of them were, surprisingly, Chevrolets. The rules France had written favoring wedge engines had indeed brought the bow-tie boys back, and Smokey was the leader of the pack.

In Friday testing, Turner streaked down the back straight at over 190-mph and around the highbanks lap after lap averaging more than 180-mph! Smokey waved the car in, parked it in an out-of-the-way location at the end of the garage area, covered it with a tarp, told his son not to let anyone near the car and went home. Saturday was a repeat of the day before. Turner was lapping almost 181-mph. The best Plymouth was Petty at 179.068 and Ford's top was Cale Yarborough at 178.660. Unofficially, Mario Andretti clocked over 182-mph with the new "tunnel port" 427 in a Fairlane, and Ford engineers were feeling a little more relaxed.

When Turner lapped at 180.831-mph, he was the fastest qualifier, and a Chevelle was on the pole of the Daytona 500! Everyone was shaking their heads and muttering to themselves. Chevrolets were not supposed to do that. GM was publicly saying that they were not involved in racing at all, but how could two old guys possibly put together one car that could show its tail lights to the finest factory engineering to come from both Ford and Chrysler? Then Smokey psyched everyone by saying he was going to install one of his better engines for the race!

More than 94,000 spectators were on hand for the 500. Turner streaked away with ten more cars tied to his bumper.

Lead changes occurred seemingly every lap, and it was clear that Smokey's Chevelle could win the race. Then Yarborough and Foyt went out. Turner, Dieringer and Lorenzen in Fairlanes and Pearson's Dodge were making a real race of the 500. With just 47 laps to go, Turner came into the pits. With a set of tires and a load of fuel, he would be at or near the front, but it was a bad pit stop, longer than planned, and it put Turner a lap down.

"I hollered at Turner," says Smokey. "Don't try to get it back in one lap! We'd agreed that he wouldn't turn it over 6600 or 6800, and I knew that it would turn about 400 more. Just what I was afraid of happened. He turned it loose, and if you'd go look at the lap speed, it would probably be about 184-mph. Broke a rod, and that took care of that."

Now that the Chevelle scare was behind them, the race settled down to a Fairlane versus Dodge Charger battle. But when Pearson went out, Andretti and Lorenzen made it a Fairlane showcase. With 54 laps under caution, including the last five miles, Andretti took the win with a slow overall average. Engineers had dyno tested his car's "tunnel port" 427 engine and found that it produced 583-hp at 6800-rpm before the race. Afterwards, it showed 575 at 6800. The old 427 wasn't so obsolete after all. Way down in 11th was Donnie Allison running two laps back at the finish. He was in a 427 Chevelle. It was the beginning; Chevrolet was coming back.

Despite the first two big wins of the season, Riverside and Daytona, the 1967 NASCAR season unfolded to be a spectacular Petty year. Nobody could touch Plymouth. His hemi Belvedere was winner in 27 races, 10 in one record-setting stretch, and finished in the top ten 41 times. It was the best individual year on record.

Although GM was not officially into factory racing, several engineers were participating privately in many areas of motorsport. Racers of Corvettes, Camaros and Chevelles benefitted from Vince Piggins' efforts at product promotion, and the factory men, of course, had inside connections. Zora Duntov was still developing high-performance equipment, and pieces found their way into a number of cars.

Production cars with the Mk IV big block 427 engines

Super Stock/B class was the domain of Chrysler's hemi cars and Ronnie Sox was baddest of the bad. Among many other wins, he took 4 NHRA Super Stock Eliminator titles in 1968 and '69 with this car, Lil Boss, and set the ET record, 10.23 seconds, in the '69 World Finals. Chrysler photo.

Don Nicholson unveiled this match race Cougar in 1968 and ran consistent 7.70/185 + quartermiles. Match racing had become more exciting than national championship meets.

included the SS Impalas, along with low-buck 427 Biscaynes. Three versions of the 396 were available (325-, 350- and 375-hp) along with four 427s (single 4-bbl 385-, and 390-hp and three tri-power 400- and 435-hp engines). There were others, too. Duntov's team had fully developed single overhead cam small blocks of 377 cubic inches that produced 545-hp @ 6000 rpm and 427 double overhead cam engines of 660-hp at 6800 rpm. They sat on the shelves, while an all aluminum Mk IV was being developed; the ZL-1 as a 430 cubic inch racing engine. Later in the decade, this engine would be taken to 494 cubic inches, producing 740-hp with fuel injection, and totally dominate Can-Am racing. Clearly, Chevrolet had the engines, but "we don't race" ruled.

Beside the intermediate Chevelle came the all-new personal size Camaro for 1967, and both got Chevy's 396 and 427 engines. Central Office Production Order (COPO) cars were Piggins' way of getting around official mandates. If you wanted to race a Chevrolet, he was the connection for the right stuff. "Grumpy" Jenkins went from his winning Nova to build a 427-powered Camaro and proceeded to become the 1967 National Champion, the SS/C national record holder and Super Stock Eliminator at the US Nationals that year! His winning 11.55/115.97 at Indianapolis was astounding, and proved that a 427 Camaro was one of the best muscle cars of that year. The exposure given by Jenkins and an entire cadre of Camaro racers, including Mark Donohue in the Trans-Am Sunoco Camaros, launched the new marque as a winning breed. Buyers went home with 315,323 new Camaros by the end of the year.

Fast running 427 COPO Camaros were quietly showing up all around the country. They came from Don Yenko's dealership, Baldwin Motion and other high-performance dealers who kept the COPO connection a secret. In fact, any dealer could order COPO cars if he knew the numbers. Piggins and Paul Prior were the factory connections.

From Oldsmobile in '66, the 4-4-2 line of super cars was being heralded by magazines as one of the best of the best. A new ram-air cold air induction system pushed output of the stock rated 400-cid from 350 to upwards of 390 in tri-power form. The tri-power option, coded L69, consisted of three 300-cfm carbs on a dual-plane intake manifold and cost

$264.54. A total of 2,129 tri-power 4-4-2s were produced in 1966. *Motor Trend* tested an L69 4-4-2 and praised it, saying "We would be hard put to find another car that does so many things so well." *Car&Driver* said of their 1967 test 4-4-2, "The 1966 version of the 4-4-2 won our six-way 'Super Car' test hands down, and the '67s are even better."

All GM divisions carried on their product lines with powertrains similar to those of 1965 or offered small improvements for '66, but sales were dropping. GM production was down over 500,000 in '66 (10%) and dropped another 331,000 in '67 (7.4%). From the high in '65, Chevrolet was down 25.8% to 1,920,665 cars.

Ford took a 33.9% beating from its 1965 high, even with Mustang being the biggest selling single marque in the industry. Chrysler Corporation was least affected by the slump, down just 7%. With decreasing profits, Ford was not as deeply committed to winning at any cost. The decision had been made to run Fairlanes and Comets with the awesome 427 wedge, instead of full-size cars with cammers, but an all-new fastback Fairlane for '68 was in the works, and so was a killer of an engine.

Because of the economic downturn, the battle for the NASCAR sweepstakes had lost some of its emphasis. After Andretti's win at Daytona, the remainder of the season didn't really matter for advertising purposes. Nearly all the publicity the factory men were after came out of that race. Dick Hutcherson and Cale Yarborough won the Atlanta super-speedway events, and Yarborough won the July 4th Firecracker 400 at Daytona. G.C. Spencer won the Southern 500 in the Petty Plymouth #42, and that split the eight super-speedway races, four for Ford and four for Chrysler. When Richard finished 2 laps ahead of everyone in the Wilkes 250, he had won 10 straight.

Chrysler's second year of near-total domination of stock car racing furthered the image that the Corporation was looking for. Plymouth crushed everything with 31 wins, Richard Petty won 27 races, and the street hemi cars had won the reputation as the strongest street machines available.

By mid-October at Charlotte for the final race of the season, Buddy Baker won the 500 in a Dodge averaging 130.317-mph. By then, for any fan who cared, Ford was indeed dead.

1966 Pontiac GTO

For the power-hungry youth market of the mid-1960s, Pontiac dropped the full-size Pontiac 389 cubic inch V-8 engine into the mid-size Tempest. For a razzle-dazzle name that had definite racing ties, GTO was borrowed from one of Ferrari's 250 series, sports-racing cars.

The 1964 and '65 GTO was the only car offered that was aimed squarely at the youth market. First year of production reached 32,450 units, far exceeding Pontiac's expectations. For the '65 model year, the GTO's exterior was slightly redesigned. The major change was placing the headlights on top of one another rather than side by side. The sales total for this year was more than double that of the previous year: 75,352 GTOs were sold.

In 1966, the GTO became a separate series rather than just an option on the Tempest line. Though the GTO was its own model, it was still tied to the Tempest in basic styling. For this reason it received the newly redesigned Tempest body that was introduced that year. The new body was quite different from those of the earlier cars, but several aspects, like the stacked headlights, were retained. The divided grill theme also remained but was redesigned so that each half started out narrow in the middle and gradually became wider as it approached the headlight moldings. The overall body was changed from the previous year's boxy look to one of graceful curves. The rear fenders took on the so-called upswept "coke bottle" styling that was characteristic of GM's cars in the mid-sixties. 1966 engine options remained unchanged with the single four-barrel 389 as base and the three 2-barrel 389 carrying top honors. In 1966 GTO sales peaked, with dealers moving 96,946 cars, proving yet again that the car had a huge market.

For the 1967 model year, the GTO was changed slightly on the outside. There were new chrome trim pieces on the front and others along the rocker panels. Also, the tail light treatment was redesigned. But the big news was the totally revised powertrain. The 389 was extensively retooled to improve performance and durability. The new engine boasted redesigned cylinder heads with larger ports. These new heads incorporated larger valves, 2.11-inch intake and 1.77-inch exhaust. New intake manifolds were cast to feed the free-flowing heads and to accommodate a 750-cfm Rochester Quadrajet carburetor that replaced the Carter AFB. In addition, the blocks were reinforced with beefier main webs and the camshafts were reconfigured. Engine displacement was increased from 389 cubic inches to an even 400 cubes by enlarging the bore to help low-end response for street driving. Sadly, the famous Tri-Power carburetion was dropped in favor of a single Quadrajet because it flowed nearly the same air volume without the complicated linkage and additional carbs.

The number of engine and transmission options was expanded in an attempt to encompass more of the market. The 3-speed Turbo-Hydramatic automatic with optional Hurst Dual Gate shifter replaced the unpopular two-speed Powerglide. The Hurst unit gave the driver the option of leaving the trans in drive, or locking a plate on the console and going through the gears manually. There was a new low-performance 225 horsepower, 2-barrel 400 for the faint-hearted economy-minded buyer who wanted the GTO image without the go. The standard engine was the 335 horsepower 4-barrel 400. Then there was the H.O. (High Output) 400 rated at 360 horsepower at 5100 rpm.

The top performance option was the ram-air engine. This equipment was similar to the Cold Air package of '65 and '66. Ram-Air equipped cars had a functional hood scoop, and a shroud was installed around the air cleaner to direct cold, outside air into the carburetor. The engines used the same carburetion as the H.O. engines but received different, completely new camshafts. Pontiac rated the Ram-Air engines at the same horsepower as the H.O. engines, but it was known that the company underrated its engines in order to give its cars an advantage in drag racing and to protect its customers from high insurance premiums.

1967 advertisements called the GTO, "The Great One." One such ad that appeared in *Road & Track* read: "A 360-hp

GTO styling and accommodations reached new highs with the 1966 model. They were beautiful cars inside and out.

Under the hood was the 389 cubic inch, triple carburetor powerplant that sparked the muscle car generation.

Quadra-Power Four Hundred option is big news in the GTO this year. New heads. New combustion chamber design. Bigger intake and exhaust valves. New valve location. Enlarged ports. New intake manifold with smoother, more efficient runners. New free-flow header type exhaust manifold. New Quadrajet 4-bbl carburetor. If you know what we're talking about, you can order all this with the Ram-Air induction hood scoop option and new high output cam to replace The Great One's standard 335-hp 400 cubic incher... If you don't know what we're talking about, you're excused."

Like the first cars, second-generation GTO styling also lasted for two years. For 1968, a new shape became GTO. It was shared by other GM divisions, and some of the exclusivity of the first four years was lost.

1967 Oldsmobile 4-4-2

Oldsmobile advertised its 4-4-2 for 1965 as "Olds' Hottest Number", and *Hot Rod* magazine claimed it to be one of the "most likeable machines we have ever had the pleasure to drive." Oldsmobile marketeers offered the 4-4-2 as an option (W29) on the F-85 Cutlass line. That option package lasted until 1968 when the 4-4-2 became an Oldsmobile line of its own. It survived that way through 1971, when 4-4-2 became the W29 option again on the 1972 models.

The 4-4-2 was known as the gentleman's express. The early models had plenty of power, and more muscle came in 1966. The single 4-bbl version 4-4-2 was rated as 350 horsepower, but the neat trick was ram-air tri-power that boosted output to around 390 horses at speed. The tri-power option consisted of three 300-cfm carbs on a dual-plane intake. A total of 2,129 tri-power 4-4-2s were produced in '66 among 21,997 4-4-2s built.

The 1966 and '67 4-4-2s were styled differently than the two earlier years. They were bigger, heavier and more luxurious and were offered with more options. Good handling high-performance was still their trademark. *Motor Trend*

Oldsmobile 4-4-2 performance was second to none. The '67 models were among the best muscle cars of their time.

A 4-4-2 convertible of 1967 was a rare sight; only 3,080 were built. This triple black beauty was loaded with options.

magazine testers singled out the car, saying "The 4-4-2 is the best handling car of its type we've ever tested." *Hot Rod* lauded the new cars as "...probably the most sophisticated volume produced machine on the market today. Tops in the handling department since their inception, 4-4-2s' straight-line performance is now the equal of any." The "W" designation for performance options soon became a 4-4-2 legend. The cars were known as the "W-machines", and even though the tri-power option was dropped for '67, the W-30 ram-air setup with a single 4-bbl (offered only on the Cutlass Supreme 4-4-2) included special engine preparation for more performance. Today they are rare; only 492 W-30 4-4-2s were built in 1967 among a total production of 24,829 cars.

The '67s were Oldsmobiles of exceptionally high style. But even at 3,700 pounds, they could whisk along at 130-mph and run the traps in 15.8 seconds at 91-mph. With preparation, a '67 4-4-2 became a B/Pure Stock record holder, an achievement claimed by very few cars.

Although Olds was not officially sponsoring racing, the special products people at the factory contracted George Hurst to specially prepare even hotter 4-4-2s. The results were really tall; 12.61 seconds at 110.42-mph through the quartermile. That was hot stuff by any standards and contributed to the growing reputation of Hurst as a major performance brand. His shifters had become THE performance equipment to have, and a number of manufacturers were installing his equipment on their high-performance models, both manual and automatic.

With such beginnings, Hurst and Olds grew into a partnership that produced the most formidable Oldsmobiles ever built. The first year of the special edition Hurst/Olds was 1968, and 515 were built. Beginning with the already highly developed 4-4-2, the Hurst people opted for the Oldsmobile big car engine, the 455 cubic inch monster rather than the plenty powerful 400. These 455-inch boulevard cruisers became the executive supercars of the late '60s.

1967 427 Fairlane

Fairlane styling for 1967 continued the '66 line and came with big block engines. These mid-size cars were a big hit.

The 427 Fairlane was one of the few cars ever built whose origin is traced directly to NASCAR racing.

One of the greatest influences on the types of cars that came out of Detroit during the mid-60s was NASCAR boss Bill France. NASCAR races drew hundreds of thousands of spectators, and America's major automobile builders saw this as a tremendous opportunity for mass market advertising. They had noticed that following a big NASCAR win, the popularity of the street version of the winning car increased. In order to ensure that their cars won, Ford and Chrysler Corporation spent huge sums of money creating new cars, engines, and speed equipment just to win races. That is how NASCAR influenced production cars and created headaches for the factories. Thriller street cars were the result of NASCAR's required minimum production of 500 similar units. NASCAR stipulated that for any equipment to be eligible to race, it had to be offered on production cars in that number. Therefore, most of the speed and high-performance parts that went into building the mid-'60s muscle cars were direct results of NASCAR.

In early 1963, Chevrolet had pulled out of racing with the restatement of the 1957 corporate policy of, "We don't race". With Chevy more or less out of the picture, the major forces in NASCAR were Ford and Chrysler. When Chrysler introduced its 426 cubic inch, hemispherical combustion chamber V-8 in 1964 it instantly raised Ford's hackles. The biggest threat the engine posed to Ford was on the highbanks, as shown at Daytona in '64. The hemi cars flew by Ford in both qualifying races. Paul Goldsmith's Plymouth set a new record of 174.910-mph. During the 500, the hemi cars proved equally unstoppable. When the checkered flag fell after 500 miles, it was Chrysler hemis finishing 1-2-3.

After the defeat at Daytona, Ford went to NASCAR's officials and complained. They argued that their wedge 427 side oiler couldn't compete with the hemi and threatened to boycott NASCAR if the rules weren't changed. Immediately following the race, Ford engineers were testing a mid-size Fairlane with the 427 engine. Such a smaller dimension and lighter car with that engine would give Ford a competitive edge. With the heavier engine, the car didn't work well at first, but it showed promise.

The controversy between Ford, Chrysler and NASCAR was further inflamed when the hemi was not allowed for 1965, Chrysler quit, and Fords won about everything there was, 34 in a row in one stretch. It was not fun to watch a Ford beat another Ford, and the fans went away. Competition was a must to have paying fans.

With everyone mad at everyone else, in mid-season, Bill France changed the rules again and allowed the hemi in mid-size cars like the Plymouth Belvedere and Dodge Coronet for all tracks except the major speedways. Chrysler had no big cars in production with the hemi and predictably announced that factory competition would be limited to shorter tracks.

Ford made the SOHC 427 available in 1966 as a regular production engine (for $1,963 compared to the Chrysler hemi at $900) and planned to build 500. France said it was allowed only in 119-inch wheelbase cars weighing 10.36 pounds per cubic inch, but two 4-bbls on the 427 wedge was now legal in cars weighing 9.36 pounds per cubic inch. This weight rule meant that a 396 cubic inch car could weigh 3,707 pounds. The Ford men thought about that. A Fairlane with a dual 4-bbl 396-inch engine would be competitive. It would be easier on tires and fuel, and could beat the hemi MoPars. Enter the 427 Fairlane.

The new rules meant that Ford could run the 427 wedge in a Fairlane body rather than in a Galaxie. But there was a problem; Ford didn't offer the 427 in the Fairlane from the factory. In order to comply with NASCAR production regs, there was a new option for the 1966 Fairlane, the 427 wedge.

The 427 Fairlane was produced in very low volume, with many being placed selectively in the hands of Ford racers. The big engine was available mainly in the two-door hardtop and sedan body styles. A grey area exists as to whether or not there were any GT 427 Fairlanes produced by the factory. This matter is not totally clear, but there are numerous magazine articles to substantiate the claim. The cheaper, two-door sedan bodies were built mainly for racers because they were more structurally sound.

The cars that made it to the street were some of the hottest runners Ford had ever made. The engines could be ordered with dual 715-cfm Holley four-barrels on an aluminum medium-riser intake. To help the engines breath, the factory installed a set of cast iron headers. The engines were so large that the header bolts were just about impossible to get to, so holes were drilled on the inside of the shock towers for access. Supposedly, the only transmission available was the 1-3/8-inch by 10-inch spline NASCAR four-speed gear box, but some C6 automatic equipped cars have surfaced. Completing the driveline was a nodular iron case 9-inch rear-end with a Traction-Lok differential. Rear gear ratios could be picked from numerous options. There was also an optional fiberglass hood with a functional scoop to reduce weight.

Running 11.1:1 compression ratio pistons and dual quads, the engines were rated by the factory to deliver 425 horses at 6000 rpm and 480 ft-lb of torque at 3700 rpm. These figures were no doubt quite conservative for insurance reasons. Without the optional fiberglass hood, the cars looked nearly identical to the 390-powered Fairlanes. This meant that many muscle car owners failed to notice the little chrome 427 emblems on the front fenders. But this was a mistake only made once, because after getting their doors blown off they became much more careful as to what they picked on.

The 427 Fairlanes were very fast not only on the street, but also on the strip. Super/Stock B prepared cars were capable of running the quarter in around 11.5 seconds at speeds over 120-mph. In SS/A class, they could run as low as the high tens. "Dyno Don" Nicholson built one of the first true funny cars using a Mercury Comet body, sister to the Fairlane. The car employed a full tube frame covered by a one-piece fiberglass body and a fuel-injected 427 Cammer. It had a tremendous impact on organized drag racing in the mid-sixties, becoming the number one match race car in the country. The car was called the Eliminator I and certainly lived up to its name by winning just about everything in 1966. The car's fastest quarter mile was a 7.94 second blast at 175-mph.

The 427 Fairlanes are extremely rare today, and because they are one of the sons of NASCAR, they are highly prized by muscle car collectors. Factory production figures for 1966 are reported at just 71 cars. It is not known exactly how many were produced in '67, but it is estimated at between 100 and 300. That makes these bruisers very rare machines indeed.

Formula-1 world driving champion and Indianapolis 500 winner Jimmy Clark ran one NASCAR race in this Holman-Moody 427 Fairlane at Rockingham, North Carolina, 1967.

1967 427 Yenko Camaro

Big block Camaros burst onto the muscle car scene in 1967 and became one of the most popular cars of the time. Chevrolet intended the Camaro to be a high-performance road handler second only to the Corvette. The 5-liter Z28 combined all the best. Yenko added the 427.

54 of these special edition 450-hp COPO Camaros were sold by Don Yenko in 1967. They were known as the Yenko Super Camaro and combined the heavy-duty hardware of the Z28 with big block performance. Many of these cars were drag raced and are still competitive in Super Stock classes today.

Both Plymouth and Dodge offered special edition drag race only cars in 1968, the Hemi 'Cuda and the Hemi Dart. This is probably the most successful of them all, Max Hurley's Hemi Dart. Max has won races with this car for 20 years and shut down all sorts of competitors to win 9 national championships.

Muscle Everywhere

What a year 1968! The momentum built during the previous five years had brought a more fantastic array of high-performance cars to new car showrooms than ever before. Once again, what was seen on the race tracks was what dealers offered. Super stocks were definitely "in", and you could go pick out your winner from any make you wished. Muscle was everywhere, showrooms, drag strips, stock car thunderdomes. There was also a new force in street machines. An extremely popular brand of road racing had developed for 5-liter sedans, and you guessed it, there were showroom models of these cars, too.

Muscle cars of the 400 cubic inch variety were the street bombers of the time. They were the cars that filled the staging lanes of Super Stock drag racing, and they came directly from the manufacturers. The rules for the cars required them to be unmodified from stock, except in some cases for safety, and that meant the manufacturers were still going heads up to beat the competition for the highly sought after publicity of winning. These were the cars that spectators could most identify with because they could go buy one.

By 1968, more high-performance hardware was pouring out of the Detroit manufacturers than ever seen. They were feeding the young buyer's urge for more power, to go faster, and to win. For a monthly payment, buyers could take their choice of many extremely quick cars. And whatever make was selected, there were several of them drag racing. It didn't matter that the drag cars were specially prepared, your daily driver was just like what you saw roaring down the quarter-mile, except... Spectators tended to identify the cars they drove with the drivers of similar drag racing cars. They became emotionally involved with their cars and the sport of drag racing, when "their" car went blasting down the 1320. Today, those same people look back nostalgically at the '60s cars they once owned, watched and raced, and fuel the rapidly escalating prices paid for these cars on the collector market.

What was Super Stock in 1968? These were American factory production vehicles. The class was subdivided into 12 separate brackets based on the power-to-weight ratio, using figures supplied by the manufacturers. Thus, sandbagging by underrating the output of an engine was a trick that placed cars into lower classes, those that they had good chances of winning. Each bracket was further subdivided into automatic and manual transmission categories. Just to win in class was tough enough, but to compete for top awards, Eliminator status, national acclaim and big bucks, class winners paired off to determine who was the overall winner, the Super Stock Eliminator. That title lasted for a year, until the same meet was run again the next year.

Super Stock rules allowed any size tire that would fit under stock fender wells, but altering the suspension was not allowed. By jacking up the rear of the car, a larger tire could be installed. More rubber on the ground meant lower ETs, just what every racer was after. Adding traction bars, and there were many varieties, improved traction and lowered elapsed times.

Engines specified by the manufacturer for that year and model car had to be installed for the car to be legal Super Stock. Any camshaft could be used, but stock size valves had to be retained, and combustion chambers could not be modified. Which manufacturer had the best parts was usually reflected in how successfully a car would run.

The 428 Cobra Jet engine was unveiled in these Mustangs mid-year 1968 at the NHRA Winternationals. Factory rated at 335-hp put the cars in SS/E class. The Super Stock Eliminator final was all Cobra Jet, Al Joniec vs Hubert Platt.

The Cobra Jet engine was the standard 428 Galaxie engine fitted with big valve low riser 427 heads and intake. Output was more like 410-hp than 335.

From the early days of Super Stock racing, drivers became identified with certain cars. By 1968, these drivers had become super stars. Don Garlits, Connie Kalitta and Pete Robinson in AA/Fuel Dragsters were known and admired nationwide. Super/Experimental Stock (finally recognized as Funny Cars) drivers such as Don Nicholson, Ed Schartman, Gas Ronda and Gene Snow put on thriller blasts in their 175-mph machines. And Super Stock had its own legion of super stars. Dick Landy, Bill "Grumpy" Jenkins, Ronnie Sox, and Hubert Platt are just four of many top caliber drivers in the sport that year.

After taking his SS/C Camaro to the top of Super Stock in 1967, Jenkins was the target of everyone else. Cigar chewer "Dandy" Dick Landy returned to Super Stock from Funny Car racing and was the leader of the "Dodge Rebellion". Super Stock racing got its start in southern drag racing, and one of the stars early on was Ronnie Sox from Burlington, North Carolina. He had been at the top of Super Stock since his first national championship in 1964. Back then, he drove a factory Comet. He was soon Plymouth's main hot shoe, and by '68 Sox had become one of the most recognized and respected names in drag racing. Platt was a Georgia boy from the same

southern mold of drag racing. He was Ford's main driver in '68, and teamed with many other top names to race Fords at various important meets. These drivers were only four among dozens of other well-known national caliber drivers, not to mention hundreds more local favorites who won lots of races, but didn't get national recognition.

One of the features of the Super Stock era was the clinics put on by top stars at dealerships around the country. Chrysler Corporation began the clinics in 1967 with Landy's Dodge and the Sox & Martin team of Plymouths. The next year, Ford was into clinics with Platt. Shirley Shahan representing Shahan motors was offering advice and encouragement to clinic attendees. The "Old Reliable" Dave Strickler was featured, and so was Jenkins, and many others. Films told of successful racing in the make the dealership offered, and of how to win in your own new Super Stock car. Clinics made good economic sense; they sold cars and made their speakers famous. They also attracted new drag racing enthusiasts who were introduced to the sport by the pros.

One of the not so glamorous features of Super Stock drag racing was caused by the indexing system used to classify cars. No longer was it heads up, quickest through the lights wins. Brackets had been set up based on current national figures, but if you had a legal car that could run under the index, you lost if you did. Quickest through the lights didn't matter anymore. That made for a lot of confusion. You buy a Super Stocker, build it to squeeze every ounce of power out of the engine, install every suspension trick you can think of to transfer the power to the ground, then jam on the brakes before going through the traps at the high end and hope you didn't break out. Then there were the teardowns. Every car had to be checked to insure that it was legal. Lots of talk circulated back then that the most sensible thing to do was classify cars on a weight per cubic inch basis and give wedge head engines a lower ratio to make them competitive with the MoPar hemi cars.

To get around the index brackets, many drivers agreed among themselves to run old southern style grudge races, now called match races. Without indexes, match racing was real drag racing, like drag racing once was. The best three out of five was the winner. Super Stock match racing was rekindled in '68 and became extremely popular.

Part of that popularity was because of the factory Super Stock cars anyone could buy. Chrysler produced a run of off-highway Hemi 'Cudas and Hemi Darts expressly for drag racing. National Sales Manager R. D. McLaughlin notified all Plymouth dealers in February 1968 that hemi-powered Barracudas were available in limited quantities. Body code B-029 and either transmission code 393 (4-speed) or 395 (automatic) fully specified the cars. These were no-option cars with lots of delete items not needed for competition, including finish coat paint and a back seat. List price: $5,495.00.

These were fiberglass front end cars that were completely legal in the 3200 pounds SS/B and SS/BA classes. To reduce weight, each one was fitted with thinner glass and the lightest

Ronnie Sox and Buddy Martin were Plymouth's big guns in drag racing for nearly a decade. The fleet of Sox & Martin drag cars of 1968 included a SS/D GTX (shown), SS/B Hemi 'Cuda, and a SS/C Belvedere. Later Pro Stock cars included a hemi SuperBird! This collection was on display at Riverside, January 1968.

components Plymouth had available. The engine? A 600-hp hemi with dual 4-bbl carbs on a cross-ram intake. These cars were similar in concept to Chrysler factory drag cars dating back to the '64 models. The Dodge version was the Hemi Dart and came as a package similar to the 'Cuda.

These factory cars were capable of running a full half-second under the index. With 10.30 second, 134-mph blasts on tap, the hemi MoPars practically owned SS/B.

Ford entered the fray with a new engine in fastback Mustangs. Putting the 427 low-riser heads and intake on the 428 cubic inch full size Galaxie and Thunderbird stump puller engine brought about the 428 Cobra Jet. A factory rating of 335 horsepower insured that these cars would be competitive in SS/E and SS/EA classes. When the Cobra Jets made their debut at Pomona for the Winternationals that year, NHRA did not know how to factor the cars, so their index of 12.02 seconds was the gauge. When the final run for Super Stock Eliminator pitted Al Joniec against Hubert Platt, both in factory Cobra Jet Mustangs, it was clear that Ford was sandbagging on horsepower rating. These cars were capable of 11.30 seconds at 120-mph!

Ronnie Sox and Buddy Martin answered Ford's bid to take Super Stock Eliminator at the Springnationals held at Englishtown, N.J. Both final round cars ran under the index, but Sox was under by the least amount. He won! It was his second Springnationals Super Stock Eliminator victory in a row. The previous year, his Sox & Martin Plymouth in SS/B took the title with an 11.34/123.45. His SS/D Hemi 'Cuda of '68 won turning 11.20/106.50. Look at the figures. Sox was heavy on the brakes to drop his top speed so much, and notice that the ET was lower for a car two classes lower in index. Yes, sandbagging was very much in force, and everyone was screaming at NHRA to clean up their act on sorting out rules.

NHRA changed the rules in time for the U.S. Nationals in September and allowed the Super Stock cars to run without indexes. The result was some of the best racing seen all year. Arlen Vanke piloted his SS/B Hemi 'Cuda to Super Stock Eliminator honors with an honest 10.89/118.11 win.

The final round for the year was the NHRA World Championships at Tulsa, and "Da Grump" couldn't have been in finer form. The year before, Ed Miller had taken the Super Stock World Championship title in his SS/A Plymouth (11.19/114.35), and the '68 round was loaded with hemi cars. Dave Strickler in Jenkins' SS/F Camaro won his class while Ed Hedrick took SS/D in Jenkins' Chevy II. As they worked their way through the maze of Super Stock class winners toward the World Championship, the final round came down to Strickler versus Hedrick. Jenkins had a 1-2 lock on the title, and Strickler took the crown on an 11.89/116.12 winning pass.

The year in stock car racing was not as eventful or dramatic as 1967 had been. The rules had been settled, and the manufacturers were much quieter in whatever disputes they had. Under the regulation that allowed intermediate size cars to run wedge type engines of 7-liter capacity (428 cubic inches) and two 4-bbls, Ford was back with a slick new fastback Fairlane and the hard-running 427 "tunnel port" engine. Fred Lorenzen had retired, and David Pearson was attracted away from Chrysler as Ford's top driver to drive for Holman-Moody. During the season of 20 Ford wins, Pearson took 16 and won the NASCAR Driver Championship. Mercury, with similar cars, added another 7 wins, six of them by Cale Yarborough. Ford took the Manufacturer's Championship.

Dan Gurney opened the season with Ford's 6th consecutive win at Riverside. Next, Yarborough drove the Wood brothers Mercury to victory in the Daytona 500, then made it two super-speedway wins in a row by taking the Atlanta 500. Cale's 6 wins and 12 top-five finishes made him the highest money winner in NASCAR history ($136,786). Buddy Baker scored Chrysler's only big four win of the season at Charlotte in a Dodge; then Pearson won the Southern 500 by setting a new record of 132.703-mph.

The hemi Plymouths took 16 wins in 1968, and all of them were by Richard Petty. Talk was increasing that the once glorious hemi had received no development and was no longer competitive. Ford had done nothing more than put its "tunnel port" 427 in a slippery aerodynamic Fairlane, and was now champion. Ford was not dead, after all. Chrysler en-

At the age of 17, John Elliot was the first Canadian to win major NHRA events and won both the Winternationals and the US Nationals in this A/Stock Automatic 427 Comet.

gineers went back to their tables to design a slippery new Dodge for '69, the Charger 500. The Ford men were also working on a few tricks; both a slicker car and a fantastic new powerplant, the Torino Talladega and BOSS 429 engine. Ford intended to win the championship again the next year, and by then people were saying the hemi was dead, even Richard Petty, who signed on to drive for Ford.

Ford's 427 had been around five years in 1968, and was still a winner in both drag racing and stock car racing. Note the cross-bolt main bearing caps that strengthened the lower end.

A. J. Foyt, shown here, was one of Ford's top NASCAR drivers in 1968. After Plymouth fans claimed "Ford is Dead" at the end of the controversial 1967 season, Ford returned in '68 with "tunnel port" 427 engines and a new aerodynamic body, the fastback Fairlane, and won the NASCAR Manufacturer's Championship. David Pearson won 16 of Ford's 20 wins and the driver's title.

GALLERY of FAST MUSCLE

America's Fastest Muscle Cars

The top-of-the-line Chevrolet in 1960 was the beautiful Impala with a 335-hp tri-power 348. The 348 W-series engine won a NASCAR championship that year (Rex White) and was about to spawn the legendary 409 that took the NASCAR crown in '61 (Ned Jarrett). Owner: Jim Wyatt.

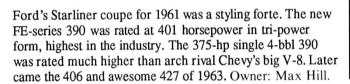

Ford's Starliner coupe for 1961 was a styling forte. The new FE-series 390 was rated at 401 horsepower in tri-power form, highest in the industry. The 375-hp single 4-bbl 390 was rated much higher than arch rival Chevy's big V-8. Later came the 406 and awesome 427 of 1963. Owner: Max Hill.

Studebaker's Hawk GT for 1961 was America's first Grand Touring car combining both high speed and luxury, features that later became muscle cars. The Hawk GT was in the mid-priced field and was the only U.S. production car offering good handling, a 4-speed transmission, full instrumentation, bucket seats and room for five. Owner: Bill Cheek.

Chevrolet's dual 4-bbl 409-hp, 409 cubic inch W-series big block of 1962 was a hard running Super Stock that captured the imaginations of drag racing fans everywhere.

Ramchargers Dodge with the cross-ram 426 wedge was a top Super Stock competitor in '63. Owner: Bill Blair.

The new RPO-Z11 engine of 1963 was not another 409. It was the NASCAR 427-cid, 425-hp W-engine.

Ford's mid-year 1963 425-hp, 427 FE engine was a larger displacement version of the cross-bolt main 406. The new Fords won the Daytona 500 that year 1-2-3-4-5. Owner: Clarence Haven.

The last gasp from Studebaker was the Raymond Loewy designed Avanti introduced in 1963. The marque was radical, more European than American in concept and the fastest production car built in this country. In supercharged form, Avanti was a true 150-mph car long before the advent of street muscle cars. Owner: Dan Miller.

Plymouth in 1963 received the increased displacement version of the 413, now upped to 426 cubic inches. This new cross-ram dual 4-bbl engine powered the "Color Me Gone" Super Stock Plymouth to many wins and fame. Owner: Rick Grape.

Recalling the early days of Super Stock and A/Factory Experimental drag racing, Bill Blair has restored and now races these legendary Pontiacs. The A/FX Tempest: a super car in its day. The lightweight Catalina: faster than anyone expected.

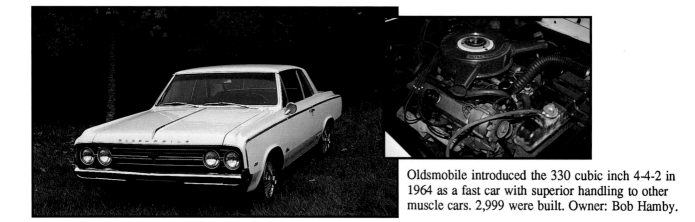

Oldsmobile introduced the 330 cubic inch 4-4-2 in 1964 as a fast car with superior handling to other muscle cars. 2,999 were built. Owner: Bob Hamby.

Studebaker's Challenger in supercharged R/2 or R/3 form was a very fast car in 1964. Horsepower figures were not advertised by the factory. Owner: Dan Miller.

Ford produced lightweight Galaxies in 1962, '63 and '64. In 427-cid form with dual quads, the '64 cars weighed 3450 pounds and produced 12 second, 118-mph 1/4-miles.

Pontiac introduced the GTO in 1964. With the legendary 389-cid engine dressed up with three 2-bbl carbs and producing 348-hp, the 4-speed GTO was an enthusiast's dream car. Owner: Cliff Ernst.

Plymouths for 1964 were as fast as they were beautiful. A top line Sport Fury with bucket seats, 4-speed and either a 426 wedge or 426 hemi made a high-style street fighter.

Chevrolet entered the muscle car field in 1965 with the 396 Chevelle. 200 were the special edition 375-hp RPO-Z16. The 327/300 small block Chevelle could hold its own, too!

A new 426-cid hemi engine for 1964 made street Plymouth and Dodge cars almost invincible. They ruled Super Stock automatic classes while the blown, injected Chargers that year gave Dodge a lot of exposure. Owner: Edgar Tutterow.

Fred Lorenzen raced this fastback for Holman-Moody in '65 and later won Daytona and Charlotte. Ford's 427 Galaxies totally dominated NASCAR stock car racing that year: 48 wins to Plymouth's 4 and 2 for Dodge. Ned Jarrett (Ford) won the championship with 13 wins. Owner: Kim Haynes.

Buick's entry into muscle cars was the Skylark Gran Sport of 1965. Standard was the 401 cubic inch, 325-hp single 4-bbl version. A dealer installed option was the dual quad intake system from the Riviera Gran Sport that bumped power up 13-hp. Owner: Byron Cooper.

Hemi Satellite, Plymouth's showroom dragster for 1966, could bang out 13-second quartermiles at near 120-mph, or top 135-mph in a 1/2-mile. On the highbanks, the hemi MoPars dominated NASCAR with 36 wins and set speed records that year. David Pearson (Dodge) won the NASCAR title with 15 wins. Owner: Chuck Irick.

Ultimate muscle cars were the 427 Cobra and 427 Corvette. These were fire-breathing 12-second cars straight off the showroom floor. Owners: Cobras, Bill Bradford and Al McLean. Corvette: Kim Haynes.

The fastest 5-place Chevrolet of 1967 was the new Camaro in 427-cid form from Don Yenko Chevrolet. These were COPO cars that any dealer could order. Owner: Jim Parks.

"If you've had it with Detroit compromise performance..." Baldwin Motion offered a complete line of "Street Racer's Specials" like this 427 Biscayne.
Owners: Bob & Kay Tangen.

Big block Camaros quickly became the rage of drag racing in the late '60s. Bill "Grumpy" Jenkins raced his SS/C Camaro to the '67 US Nationals Super Stock Eliminator title with a winning 11.55 second pass at 115.97-mph. Ben Wenzel took the Stock Eliminator title in his B/Stock Camaro with a 12.33/113.92. Camaros remain the most popular single type car in drag racing today.

The 1966 389-cid GTO was bigger than earlier GTOs. New for '67 was a larger displacement 400-cid engine with ram-air. '66 was the last year of tri-power, dropped in '67 in favor of the 360-hp single 4-bbl engine.
Owner: Byron Cooper.

Cousins to the Hemi 'Cudas built by Hurst were the Hurst prepared Hemi Darts of 1968. This one is still competitive in Super Stock. Max Hurley runs consistent 10.10 second quarter-miles with his over 20-year old Hemi Dart and has won 9 national events.

The "Gentleman's Express". Olds 4-4-2 of 1967: luxury, power and excellent handling, one of the best "Super Cars" of its time. Owner: Bill Watlington.

'67 Fairlane 427s were fast Fords from the Thunderbolt mold. They were quick Super Stock and NASCAR winners. At Daytona that year, Mario Andretti and Fred Lorenzen finished 1-2. Owner: Connie Moore.

Mercury Cougar, new in 1967, was the only American car of European styling in the luxury end of the ponycar market. Top cats in '68 could be ordered with the 390GT, like this XR-7, 427 or 428CJ. Owner: Bob Cowan.

Hot Rod magazine called the 1968 Cobra Jet Mustang "The fastest running pure stock in the history of man." 15 years later, Donnie Moore raced this hard to beat CJ to the IHRA Super Stock World Championship in 1983.

Shelby's first big block Mustang was the G.T.500 of 1967. With the new Cobra Jet 428 for '68, the G.T.500 became the G.T.500KR, King of the Road. High performance had met luxury with the KR, a true boulevard cruiser.
Owner: Jeff Murr.

Hurst made two versions of the SC/Rambler for AMC. All were 390 powered 14 second Q-ships. Owner: Mike Lewis.

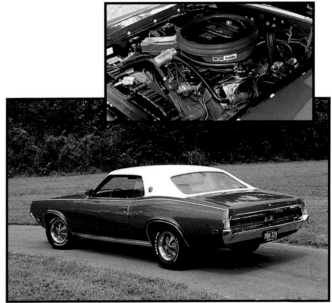

The top Cougar XR-7 for '69 was the ram-air 428 CJ with optional 4-speed, beauty and beast. Owner: Jamie Leonard.

Hurst built a number of special edition street bombers of high visual impact. One of the hairiest was the '69 H/O, the Hurst/Olds. Built on heavy-duty 4-4-2 hardware and fitted with a ram-air 455-cid big block, these bruisers looked mean and were mean. Owner: Jack Kerley.

Plymouth Satellite with a strong running 383 proved to be on target with young buyers in 1969 who wanted good performance on a modest budget.

Street version of the made-for-NASCAR fastback Fairlane Cobra for '69 was the Cobra Jet 428. A 4-speed and Drag Pack Cobra was vicious. Owner: Charles Alexander.

An aero-nose made the Cobra the Talladega, but only with an automatic. NASCAR versions with the BOSS 429 won the '69 Manufacturer's Championship. Owner: John Craft.

A few owners still race AMC cars. Herman Lewis and his IHRA World Record AMX won the 1981 Winston World Nationals Super Stock Eliminator title with a 10.42/131.00.

To meet NASCAR production requirements, Kar Kraft shoehorned the new semi-hemi 429 engine into Mustangs and created the BOSS 429 in 1969. Owner: Howard Murr.

The Six Pack became a Dodge "trademark" in the late '60s. The '70 Super Bee carried the system on the 440, an evolution of the earlier 426 wedge. Owner: Tim Fletcher.

Buick's GSX of 1970 combined grace and pace with phenomenal performance. With 455-cid, it was one of THE quickest muscle cars ever built. Owner: Hugh Richardson.

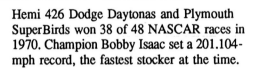

Hemi 426 Dodge Daytonas and Plymouth SuperBirds won 38 of 48 NASCAR races in 1970. Champion Bobby Isaac set a 201.104-mph record, the fastest stocker at the time.

The 1970 Cougar Eliminator was a car of high visual impact. Dual 4-bbl carbs were just one of many available dealer installed options from Ford's Muscle Parts program.

Hemi 'Cuda for 1970 was a thundering beauty that could rip out 13 second quartermiles. Owner: Cliff Ernst.

The hemi powered Motown Missile was Chrysler's drag racing development car and Pro Stock's quickest ride in 1971, 9.48/146.10.

The 450-hp, 454-cid LS6 was the hottest Chevelle ever offered by the factory. Owner: Cliff Ernst.

4-4-2 W-30 for 1970 was Oldsmobile's high class 13 second street bruiser. Owner: Keith Kibbe.

Pontiac Muscle: GTOs remain among the most exciting cars built in America.

The BOSS 351 Mustang of 1971 was the last of the BOSS line. With less than 400 cubic inches, it was by far the fastest small block of all time and one of the 10 best muscle cars ever built.

A few Dodge and Plymouth diehards are left in today's drag racing. Bob Reynolds gives fans a quick look at his 10 second "hot rod" Challenger down Bristol's Thunder Valley.

Pontiac's Trans-Am 400 of 1969 was a road handling Firebird with the Ram Air 400 HO engine. 697 were produced. Owner: Cliff Ernst.

BOSS 302 Mustangs and Cougars of 1970 were FoMoCo's 5-liter street warriors. 7,013 Mustangs and 450 Cougars were produced. BOSS Owner: Ralph Patterson.

Just 2,399 R/T Challengers were built in 1970. With the Six Pack, the 340-cid was tough to beat. Owner: Danny Cox.

The "runningest" Camaro ever built, the '69 Z28s sold 19,014. Owners: J.R. Johnson & "Satch" Conatser.

The first Chevrolet in Trans-Am road racing was this Roger Penske private entry Camaro driven by Mark Donohue. Jerry Titus in Mustangs won the '67 season chase. Owner: Pat Ryan.

Carroll Shelby's Trans-Am Mustangs ran under the Terlingua Racing Team banner in '67 and won the championship. '68s were the Shelby Racing Co. cars with dual 4-bbl carbs. Owner: Rick Nagel.

Penske went to AMC for the 1970 season after Donohue won two Trans-Am championships in Camaros. The Sunoco Javelins won the '71 championship. Owner: Brooke Mossgrove.

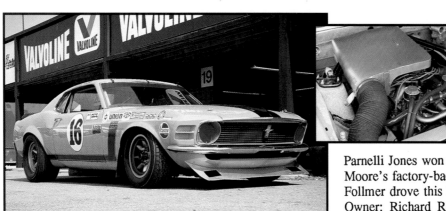

Parnelli Jones won the 1970 Trans-Am championship in Bud Moore's factory-backed BOSS 302 Mustangs. George Follmer drove this Bud Moore team car to third overall. Owner: Richard Rodeck.

After a super successful 1968 year, Bill "Grumpy" Jenkins entered the '69 season undefeated! He went full-time professional drag racing that year with this 427 Camaro and clocked the first 9 second pass in the new "heads up", no bracket Super Stock class that became known as Pro Stock. He swept the Super Stock Nationals that year with the only 9 second runs seen during the entire event. Gold Dust Classics photo.

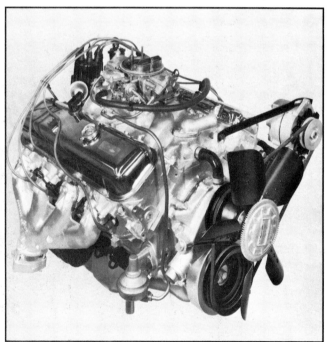

Chevrolet's heavy hitter, the Mk IV series L88, was rated at 430-hp with a single 4-bbl carburetor. In the real world, it proved to be closer to 530-hp. Chevrolet photo.

Richard Petty moved over to Ford in 1969 and won the Riverside season opener at record speed. He won 10 races that year and finished 2nd in the NASCAR points race. Here, Petty is running the World 600 at Charlotte in a BOSS 429-powered Talladega. Ford Motor Co. photo.

'68-'69

For the 1969 season, the Ford racing men put together the best team of drivers that had ever driven for a single manufacturer. The lineup was composed of David Pearson, Cale Yarborough, Richard Petty, LeeRoy Yarbrough and Donnie Allison. They were to drive new Fords with new engines, but the beginning of the season was run with year-old equipment because the new cars and engines were not quite complete. They were ready, anyway.

Chrysler Corporation had lost its top driver, Petty, and 1969 hopeful was Bobby Allison in a new Dodge, the special edition Charger 500. With Plymouth fortunes clearly not of the competitive sort, Petty had asked the corporate moguls to switch over to Dodge. With the new Charger 500 sure to be a step above the slopeback style Plymouth, there was little hope of making 1969 a Plymouth year. They told him that Plymouth was his ride, so Petty went off to join Ford and got both a new car and a new engine.

Richard told the media that he thought he had a better chance of winning the NASCAR championship in a Ford than in a Plymouth. He had not fared as well as hoped in '68 because of Ford's overwhelming involvement, the result of a "Total Performance" commitment to total victory. He almost made rumors of a switch to Ford a fact early that season, but remained with Plymouth instead. The new BOSS 429 hemi engine on the way was said to be more than a match for Chrysler's hemi, and the slick fastback '68 Torino body style had already proven itself. That was a lot to think about.

The new Dodge was an aerodynamic Charger with flush rear glass to improve smooth air flow, and flush grill and headlights for improved penetration to reduce front-end tur-

bulence. Just 500 of these cars were scheduled to be built, but only 382 were actually completed, and each was made expressly to qualify the line for NASCAR racing. By the numbers, the cars ran the season illegally. Like the 427 Fairlane of 1967, Charger 500s were another son of NASCAR, but rather than overlooking violations, as it had with the rather unenforceable rules of two years earlier, NASCAR tightened up the regulations considerably. Manufacturers were not only required to manufacture 500 cars, they also had to make 500 engines available to the public. Templates were now used to check body shape, and to have cars that would make the speeds that the new season promised, manufacturers had to actually build cars shaped the way they were raced. That made cars built for stock car racing available to the public. Engines, however, were a very different story.

The rules did not explicitly say that stock cars had to be built with the type of engine that was raced, and that produced three new cars for Ford buyers; the Talladega, the Mercury Cyclone Spoiler II and the BOSS 429 Mustang. Ford records show that 5 prototypes and 743 production Talladegas were built along with 519 Spoiler IIs. The showroom Talladegas came with just three color choices, white, maroon or dark blue. Each came with a matte black hood, and each one was built with a 428 CJ and a C-6 automatic. The only option was a radio. The Spoiler IIs came in special editions, the red and white Cale Yarborough Special and the blue and white Dan Gurney Special. Each of these cars received a 351 Windsor and an automatic.

However, note that an early run of similar Mercurys was built. These were called simply Cyclone Spoilers and were Torino-type cars without the aero-nose. They came with 428 CJ engines and autoshifters. The Talladegas and Cyclone

Ford's "Blue Crescent" BOSS 429 was new for 1969. It was a hemi head version of the 385 series big car engine introduced in 1968. BOSS 429 racing engines were champions. Street versions did not fare so well. Ford Motor Co. photo.

Spoiler IIs were Torinos with extended front sheet metal to house flush-mounted grillwork and headlight assemblies. This configuration was said to reduce aerodynamic drag by 10%. That translated into 4- or 5-mph higher speeds.

These cars were Ford's answer to the Charger 500. The Talladega was named after the new 2.66-mile highbank Alabama facility opened that year. Both the Talladegas and Spoiler IIs were built at Ford's Atlanta assembly plant, and both were mid-size cars in the Fairlane family. With the die cast in 1967, intermediates were the rule by 1969. These smaller cars were still favored for racing, although Ford officials wanted to race full-size cars, their biggest sellers.

By Riverside, production of the racers was behind schedule, and the Torino Cobra powered by 427 engines opened the season in California. Although the 427 was officially out of production in '69, NASCAR allowed the engine, but only with single carburetors. The famed 427 tunnel port intake and head system was replaced with a similar single 4-bbl carburetor setup.

The origin of the BOSS 429 Mustang was to meet homologation requirements for the new engine. Ford's Kar Kraft special production facility in Michigan was hurriedly stuffing the monster-size mill into Mustangs, but didn't complete the task to NASCAR's satisfaction until after Daytona. Consequently, long-nose Fords and Mercury's in that race were known as Torino Cobras and Cyclone Spoilers. It was spring before the aero-Fairlanes and BOSS 429 engines actually got together.

The racers went to Riverside for the season opener as usual, but the rains came. After back-to-back storms dumped nine straight days of driving rain, Governor Ronald Reagan petitioned President Richard Nixon for disaster funds and received $3 million for the state. The preliminary Permatex 200 had been called in mid-race, and for the next week, race teams and fans waited for the totally unexpected monsoon to pass. Some highways were washed out, and that postponed

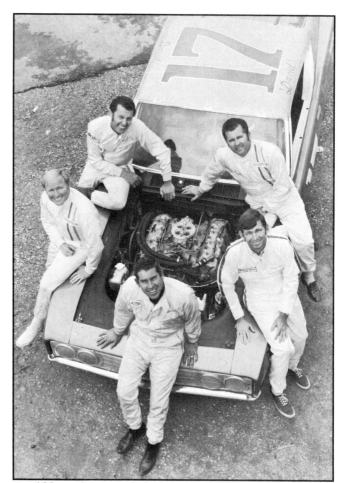

Ford Motor Co. not only had the best stock cars in 1969, they also had the best team of drivers. David Pearson in front, Cale Yarborough and Richard Petty (left), Donnie Allison and LeeRoy Yarbrough (right). Ford Motor Co. photo.

the race until February 1, just 20 days before Daytona. After the race, teams had to hurry across country to get in the desired amount of testing in Florida.

After the rain, A. J. Foyt set the pole at 110.366-mph in his Torino. Following him were LeeRoy Yarbrough in a Cyclone. Third position was Dan Gurney, heavy favorite, in a Wood brothers Cyclone. Richard Petty qualified 4th in a Torino Cobra. David Pearson, the '68 champion who was predicted to repeat in '69, took the 5th qualifying spot. Chrysler was in trouble. USAC driver Al Unser was on the third row with the highest qualifying MoPar, a '69 Charger. James Hylton was another MoPar driver further back on the grid, in a '67 Charger. There were no Holman-Moody-Stroppe cars entered in the Riverside 500.

The Dodge boys were having trouble of their own getting the Charger 500 ready for Daytona, and the opening round of the NASCAR season did not bode well for Plymouth and Dodge fans. Fifteen of the 44 entrants were Fords. The second highest number of entrants surprised everyone. Eight independent Chevrolets were entered (in the midst of the Division's "We Don't Race" period of close ties with the Roger Penske and Mark Donohue Trans-Am Camaro effort). Seven Plymouth entries and six Dodges totalled more MoPars than Fords, but there were also four Mercurys.

Mickey Thompson and Danny Ongias set over 200 new U.S. and World Class B records in a 1969 Mach I Mustang powered by a tunnel port 427. The car reached 190.951-mph. This was the fastest speed ever recorded up to that time by an American stock car. Bill Hielscher ran the "Mr. Bardahl" dual 4-bbl equipped 427 Camaro to 188.08-mph. Ford Motor Co. photo.

Petty opened the 1969 NASCAR season with a Ford flourish. The blue #43 Torino Cobra established a new Riverside record of 105.498-mph. After putting together the best team of drivers that had ever driven for a single manufacturer, the Ford "steam roller" was well built to win, and win it did. "Total Performance" had become "Total Domination".

The Daytona 500 was a LeeRoy Yarbrough affair. His Junior Johnson Ford rolled into the winner's circle after averaging 157.950-mph. It was a first win for the aero-nose style Torino. During the season, Yarbrough produced NASCAR's first "Grand Slam" year. He won on all 5 major southern tracks, adding the World 600 at Charlotte (averaging 134.361-mph) and Darlington's Southern 500 (105.612-mph). For such a spectacular individual season, he was voted American Driver of the Year, the first stock car driver to be awarded that distinction.

Cale Yarborough notched another major victory to the growing FoMoCo tally when he drove his Wood brothers Cyclone Spoiler II to victory in the Atlanta 500. A total of 26 Ford wins that year led all makes. Mercury added 4 more. Dodge drivers took 22 wins, including the first Talladega 500 won by Richard Brickhouse. Plymouth had scored just 2 wins. As predicted, David Pearson drove Holman-Moody Fords to the NASCAR driver championship that year. He was followed by Richard Petty. Pearson became the second driver to win three NASCAR championships. Lee Petty was the first. Had Richard won the title, the first two 3-time NASCAR champions would have been father and son. He won his third title in 1971, then added four more.

The NASCAR BOSS 429 had indeed proven to be superior to Chrysler's hemi. But now that both Ford and Chrysler had strong-running hemi engines, aerodynamics became the most important development factor. Chrysler engineers were hard at work designing and developing the most radical stockers to ever hit the oval tracks. They were the hemi 426-powered winged aero-Dodge Daytonas and SuperBird Plymouths that became the "steam rollers" of 1970. Combining for 38 victories (21 Plymouth and 17 Dodge) to Ford's paltry 6, ChryCo was back on track. And Petty was back with

Plymouth that year, but Bobby Isaac was the main man. He won the championship with Dodge. The MoPar drivers raced the fastest, most stable stock cars ever seen.

Like stock car racing, the top drawer cars of the 1969 drag racing season were also Fords and Chryslers. But in the straight line form of racing, Chevrolet was by far the most dominant considering all classes. While there were a few class winning Fords and MoPars, Chevrolet drivers claimed more than two dozen wins at national events throughout the country. Manufacturers' marketing strategies were different. Ford and Chrysler were after wins in the classes that got publicity, Super Stock and above. Chevrolet wasn't actively involved in racing as a factory, but Vince Piggins and his men kept the good parts available. Chevrolet sold far more high-performance hardware than either Ford or Chrysler and wasn't spending a dime on factory racing teams.

Bill Jenkins' fabulous 1968 Super Stock season pushed the intensity of drag racing rivalries even higher in '69. His were the cars everyone was shooting for, but it was a new year. If '68 can be called the year of Bill Jenkins and his Camaros, then 1969 can be called the year of Dick Landy and his MoPars. Landy's Dodge made its force felt at Pomona, opening round of the drag racing season. He brought his B/Modified Production "Flying Wedge" Charger R/T through to victory in class, then took on a host of Modified Production cars to take Street Eliminator with a thundering 10.80/128.20 pass.

MoPar drivers had a heyday at the Winternationals. Don Grotheer beat away a huge field of Super Stockers to win SS/BA class, then took his hemi 'Cuda to the winner's deck by grabbing Super Stock Eliminator on a spectacular 10.73/119.68 blast. Mark Coletti followed that with a winning 12.93/103.32 Stock Eliminator round in his '68 F/SA Plymouth. Of the three eliminator trophies available to cars classified as streetable, Landy's Dodge, and Grotheer's and Coletti's Plymouths made it a sweep for MoPar fans.

Modified Production classes corresponded with Super Stockers except that otherwise stock cars were fitted with factory equipment not available on production cars of similar type. Landy's ride was a dual-plug, dual distributor hemi car with twin 4-bbl carbs. This was the first time such exotic factory equipment was seen in drag racing. It showed, contrary to what some people thought, that Chrysler engineers were deep into high-performance parts development.

During NHRA's Springnationals, Landy had two cars, and each won its class, SS/EA and SS/F. Among 32 cars making up 5 rounds of Super Stock Eliminator competition, Landy's Dodges and Ronnie Sox' SS/B hemi 'Cuda thinned out the competition. Sox made it three Springnationals Super Stock championships in a row when he nailed S/S Eliminator with a winning pass of 10.63 seconds at 114.50-mph.

Don Nicholson had not retired as earlier announced, and followed his Cougar funny car of the year before with a Mustang running A/MP in '69. While Landy was doing battle in S/S during the Springnationals, Nicholson was Modified Production racing and added another string of wins, capped off by Street Eliminator, to his fantastic career record. He ran a winning 10.49/120.96 pass.

The American Hot Rod Association sponsored many national caliber drag races in those days, and their Spring Nationals attracted another huge turnout of the nation's finest machines. Landy was there with his SS/F Dodge. After notching another class win and wading through a tough field of class winners, the final round for Top Stock Eliminator was his.

For the US Nationals, he brought three cars and each one was class winner, SS/EA, SS/F and B/MP in "Flying Wedge". Along with Landy's "fleet" of drag racers were more MoPars than from any other manufacturer. And there was Sox again. He took his SS/B Hemi 'Cuda through the traps with a sensational 10.89/124.83 win.

NHRA held the Las Vegas Open, and once again the staging lanes were filled with the top cars and drivers in the country. Landy was there, too, with two cars. His 8-plug Dodge Charger was in the A/MP class this time, and once again he laid waste to the competition to win. Then running in SS/BA, he nailed down another class win on his way to the Mr. Stock Eliminator title.

The Super Stock show at the US Nationals of 1968 was one to remember. Akron, Ohio's Arlen Vanke in a '68 Hemi 'Cuda set a new SS/B ET record of 10.64 seconds against Wally Booth and his SS/E Camaro. Booth also set a new class ET record but lost to Vanke at the same time. His faster 121.45-mph to Vanke's 118.11 just didn't matter. And there was Dick Arons piloting his SS/EA '68 427 iron block Camaro to another NHRA national record.

There was also Bill Bagshaw's "Red Light Bandit" hemi Dart, the NHRA SS/B miles per hour national record holder at 133.72. And Ronnie "The Boss" Sox, always a threat, with several Sox & Martin Plymouths. Bill Jenkins, another perennial rival and winner of SS/C class, added to the field of tough cars to beat. There were lots more. All but Vanke lost on their way to Super Stock Eliminator. He took the title with stats of 10.64 seconds at 118.11-mph.

The Super Stock class winners that qualified to compete for Eliminator status consisted of 5 Plymouths and 4 Chevys. No Fords made it to final rounds. In fact, it was a very bad meet for Ford. In all 62 classes, only one was a Ford win. Thirty-nine were Chevys and MoPars took 18. Jenkins' class win continued his undefeated-in-class record in SS/C.

Stock Eliminator had the unlikely pairing of Larry

Chevrolet's fabled Mk IV ZL1 was an all-aluminum engine designed and produced solely for racers. A few made it into production cars through COPO orders. Chevrolet photo.

Lombardo's F/S '61 Corvette against Dave Duell's B/SA '63 Dodge wagon. All the newer stockers had been wasted by these old pieces. Lombardo took the title with a surprisingly quick pass for a small block, 12.73 seconds at 107.78-mph. Along with Lombardo's victorious Corvette was Sam Gianinno's 'Vette taking Street Eliminator (11.17/123.96). It was an excellent showing for Chevrolet, especially Corvette.

By the end of the 1969 drag racing season, the quickest cars built in this country proved to be SS/B class Hemi 'Cudas. Of the four top NHRA rounds, Winternationals, Springnationals, US Nationals and the World Finals, Ronnie Sox had gathered up three. Note that Grotheer's Winternationals SS/BA 'Cuda win was with a time (10.73 seconds) slower than two of Sox's wins (10.63 and 10.23 seconds). During this time, Sox's car was instrumented by factory engineers who were testing racing versions of the 727 Torqueflite transmission. He shifted a 4-speed faster than their best automatic!

Could there possibly be a better racing year than 1969? Yes, indeed, and 1970 came to be called the greatest year of drag racing on record. That was true in all forms of auto racing. Then the factories quit. Henry Ford II announced in August that his company was retiring from racing. Chrysler soon followed. GM had not been racing, so the change could only mean better times for the bowtie team. Racing had shown 10 years of progress, but suddenly it was over.

1968 427 Biscayne

If you saw this car sitting in a parking lot somewhere, you would no doubt think it was Granny's grocery getter, unless you happened to notice the little emblem on the front fenders. Rather inconspicuously, they read 427. If this was Granny's car, she no doubt must have been from Pasadena, where the song of a quartercentury ago spoke of a little old lady who took great pleasure in outrunning anything and anybody wanting to race. But, as the song goes, she did it in a super stock Dodge, not a lowly Chevrolet Biscayne.

It's obvious that this full-sized yellow bomber didn't come from any normal Chevrolet dealer. It was special ordered. Now you are probably asking, "From the factory?" No, not quite. This car came from a special dealer located in New York, the famed Baldwin Motion, father of the "Motion Commotion". Baldwin's cars were built to the purchaser's specifications ranging from kick-ass street cars to full-tilt drag racers. In general, the muscle cars bought from showrooms were compromise machines intended by their manufacturer's to be good all-around high-performance cars. Not so with Baldwin Motion.

"If you've had it with Detroit's compromise of performance and styling..." said Baldwin's advertisements,"...you can outfit any car purchased from us with any of the SS-427 Special Performance Options..." Their Street Racer's Special was such a car. On the 2-door Biscayne sedan body, you could order any of three 427 cubic inch engines; the L88 with aluminum heads and compression ratio of 12:1, the L89 with 11:1 or the all-aluminum ZL1 full-spec racing engine. Option prices were $750, $500 and $3,000 respectively. Thirty-three other pure performance options were available from Baldwin for their Street Racer's Special. The base price? A bargain basement $2,998!

Baldwin's options list included no useless items like air

conditioning or power steering but instead offered speed equipment that would make any street racer smile. There were special ignitions, racing cams, heavy-duty clutches, racing flywheels and NHRA-approved scatter shields on the list. The legendary Muncie M22 "Rockcrusher" close-ratio 4-speed along with a Hurst competition shifter made a winning combination. (The "Rockcrusher", heavy-duty clutches and gears, and other powertrain hardware was the work of Chevrolet engineer Gib Hufstader.) A modified 3-speed Turbo-Hydramatic autoshifter was also on the option list. Headers, traction bars, a choice of racing tires, cast alloy wheels, special gauge package, and special suspension set-ups could also be yours. What's even better is that all the above wasn't all that expensive. Except for the engines, most options ranged from $29.95 for a special gear drive injector kit for the Holley 3- or 4-bbl carb to Corvette-type side pipes at $275. Things really have changed.

From the factory, the Turbo-Jet 427 engine came in six forms in 1968. All were 4.251 x 3.76 inch bore and stroke, but output varied as follows:

385-hp @ 5200 rpm	460 lb-ft @ 3400 rpm	1 4-bbl
390-hp @ 5400 rpm	460 lb-ft @ 3600 rpm	1 4-bbl
400-hp @ 5400 rpm	460 lb-ft @ 3600 rpm	3 2-bbl
425-hp @ 5600 rpm	460 lb-ft @ 4000 rpm	1 4-bbl
430-hp @ 5200 rpm	450 lb-ft @ 4400 rpm	1 4-bbl
435-hp @ 5800 rpm	460 lb-ft @ 4000 rpm	3 2-bbl

From the factory came the rather mundane Super Sport Chevrolet with the 385 horsepower 427-cid engine. Transmission choices were limited to the M13 three-speed, the M20 4-speed, and the M40 Turbo-Hydramatic. Rear-end ratios ranged from 2.73:1 to 3.73:1.

According to the owner, this 1968 Street Racer's Special is one of around 1,600 built by Baldwin and is a 425-hp 427

425 horsepower with 460 ft-lb of torque gave the Baldwin Biscaynes 13 second quartermile capability.

"Sleepers" have always been satisfying cars. Cruise around without attracting attention, then pull the plug on 427 cubic inches when the other guy needs dusting off. That's the story of the Baldwin Motion "Street Racer's Special", a dirt cheap 425-hp, 427 Biscayne.

Biscayne with 4.88:1 positraction gears. On a wheelbase of 119 inches, the full-size Biscayne weighed around 3,650 pounds in production form. That's not bad for a large car with the torque of a Rat engine to draw upon. This car has turned quartermile times to the tune of 14.04 seconds at 98.9-mph. Looking over some old stats, the 427 Biscayne of '68 with 4.56 gears holds down a set of healthy performance figures, 13.65 at 105 as recorded by *Super Stock & Drag Illustrated* magazine.

For 1969, Baldwin advertised the same Street Racer's Special with the 427 engine turning up 450 horsepower. Since the L88 was the same for both years, it is probable that the '68 cars were also of that figure, but recall that all power figures of the time were underestimates. Insurance companies tended to believe factory figures, and that saved buyers a lot of hassles and cost of coverage.

As an example of what Chevrolet's 427 engine was

capable of, the ZL1 mentioned above was in top racing form when run by McLaren Racing in their M8 cars of 1968. These full-bore racing cars were built in England for the Canadian-American Challenge Series in North America. Two of the factory cars took four wins in six starts and earned three seconds. And one of these monsters could be ordered for your Street Racer's Special! Power figures for this engine were not widely published, but it is known that in full racing trim they produced a whopping 620-630 horsepower at 7000 rpm. Later development took them to 740-hp with fuel injection and racing octane gasoline.

That should tell you something of the tremendous performance potential of the Mk IV 427 engine. Chevrolet advertised 425 - 435 horses, yet offered a multitude of racing equipment to go well beyond those figures. In their *Chevy Power* manual, Chevrolet's racing development engineers showed how to build the engines, gave part numbers and details on several engines for several different applications, and gave instructions showing how to prepare entire cars for racing.

Whether it was drag racing, street racing or road racing, Chevrolet had the parts and the know-how. Although the factory maintained its "no racing" policy, dealers like Baldwin Motion brought Chevy's fastest hardware to the people. The Street Racer's Special was one.

1968 Shelby Mustang G.T.500KR

During the late 1960s, at the height of the muscle car era, Carroll Shelby's G.T.500KR Mustang rolled across America. The KR brought a new twist to the Shelby marque.

The earlier G.T.500 Mustang was introduced by Shelby in 1967. Basically, the 500 was the small block G.T.350 with a 360-hp, 428-cid version of Ford's Police Interceptor 428 with 410 horsepower heads. But, depending on what was handy, both 390- and 427-cid engines found their way into the cars at times. The few G.T.500s that received the 427 NASCAR-based engine, which was conservatively rated at 400 horsepower, were advertised to be the ultimate Grand Touring Mustangs. A magazine test of an early 427 G.T.500 returned quartermile stats of 14.2 seconds at 100-mph. Not at all bad for a bone stock stoplight cruiser that weighed 3,480 pounds.

Ford introduced a new engine halfway through the 1968 model year, the 428 Cobra Jet. At the Pomona Winternationals, the new Cobra Jet grabbed Super Stock Eliminator honors, and *Hot Rod* magazine called it "... the fastest running Pure Stock in the history of man." That engine was the heart of a KR.

Rumor had it that GM was about to introduce a new big block Camaro to be called the "King of the Road", but Carroll Shelby moved to deftly apply the needle to the Chevy guys by formally offering his mid-year G.T.500KR, his own "King of the Road", and once again stumped GM before they really got moving.

Through 1967, Shelby had manufactured the cars bearing his name, but that ended with the '68s. Shelby chose not to emasculate his cars according to the new federal anti-pollution mandates and stopped production of his race-bred champions. But Ford wanted the Shelby image to continue and moved the assembly of the Shelby cars from the Los Angeles airport facility to A. O. Smith, a FoMoCo contractor in Ionia, Michigan. This firm built upon the GT performance image of the '67 Shelby Mustangs, producing the super-sophisticated '68s. These cars still carried the Shelby name as well as the G.T.350 and G.T.500 nameplates. The G.T.500KR was added at mid-year and coincided with the release of the 428 Cobra Jet Mustang as a new model. For the first time, excluding the six G.T.350 convertibles built in 1966, there were ragtop Shelbys. The KRs came in both fastback and convertible forms.

The KR Shelbys were ram-air 428 Cobra Jets advertised to produce 335-hp at 5400 rpm and to deliver a whopping 440 ft-lb of torque. In reality, power was around 410 purebred horses. Ford intentionally underrated the cars in an effort to sandbag in drag racing, but the ploy didn't fool NHRA for a minute, and KRs were bumped up in classification. On the other hand, insurance companies took Ford's word for it and thus saved Shelby buyers a bundle on premiums.

Outwardly, the most obvious changes that made a KR were the rocker panel side stripes that read, "G.T.500KR", and the 428 Cobra Jet and "snake" emblems. Inside on the dash on the rider's side was a raised gold "snake" emblem reading "Cobra Jet". There was also a Cobra Jet emblem on the steering wheel, and another one on the gas cap. Underneath the car were many more changes.

The engine, the CJ, was the 428 with big port 427 medium riser heads and intake manifold with a single 735-cfm Holley four-barrel carb. The KRs also came with additional chassis beefing; for instance, the lower edge of the front shock towers received a 1/4-inch thick plate wrapped around and welded in place. KRs built with 4-speed transmissions received staggered rear shocks to control axle wind-up. The cars that

One of the many homes for Ford's 428 Cobra Jet engine was the G.T.500KR Shelby, a luxury cruiser by 1968.

Tilt wheel, air conditioning, power options and controls to monitor a muscular engine, the KR was a beautiful ride.

received automatics got a transmission oil cooler. The KRs also were built with wider rear brake shoes and drums, and received heavy-duty wheel cylinders and brake line fittings which were not interchangeable with other '68 Shelbys. KRs also got a larger diameter, less restrictive exhaust system.

Their Ford Vehicle Identification Number (VIN) plates read 8 (1968 model year), T (manufactured in Metuchen, New Jersey), 02 or 03 (for fastback or convertible respectively), R (engine code for the Cobra Jet), then came a 6-digit Ford consecutive serial number followed by a dash and a unique Shelby five digit serial number beginning with -00001 and ending with -04450.

That was the G.T.500KR Mustang; a high-performing luxury cruiser available only as a 1968-1/2 model.

1969 Hurst/Olds

For the man looking for street high performance of 1969, George Hurst provided the answer, his 4-4-2 based Hurst/Olds. Hurst was the founder of one of the nation's most respected transmission shifter and speed equipment manufacturers. He recognized the potential of Olds' 455-cid full-size car engine by using simple logic; more cubic inches mean more power and torque. Couple that with a lightweight, good handling, intermediate-size car, and you have a formidable street bomber. Selling Olds' bean counters on the idea proved to be a bit tricky. For the business suit types, Oldsmobiles were already fast enough. Lee Kelley set the C/Production speed record at Bonneville at 169.133-mph in

The Olds 4-4-2 Ram-Air engine had cold air pickup points under the front bumper. Oldsmobile photo.

By 1969, rear-mounted wings were the fashion on muscle cars. Almost all the top cars had them.

a '68 4-4-2. How much faster could you want to go?

Simple logic; in the world of muscle cars, more is better. Hurst took a '68 4-4-2 with the 360-hp W-30 400-cid engine and built his idea of a real muscle car. First, he discarded the "small" 400 incher for a hotted-up stump-pulling 455. Then he added a conspicuous paint job and went tooling around town embarrassing people. It wasn't long before a deal was struck with Demmer Engineering to build replicas of his car.

The heart of the '68 Hurst/Olds was the engine. Hurst started with a stock 455-cid plant and added his performance magic. In place of the factory heads went the W-30 big valve, 10.5:1 compression ratio heads. The factory cam was changed to a radical .474-inch lift, 308-degree duration hydraulic stick. The factory distributor was recurved, and the big Rochester Quadrajet was rejetted. Olds' forced air induction system, which rammed cooler, denser air from under the the front bumper into long flexible tubes connected to the air cleaner's dual snorkels, was retained to boost top-end power. To carry away burnt fuel, a 2.25 inch diameter, free-flowing, dual exhaust system was employed. The entire package produced 390 gross horsepower.

Demand for these "Go-Mobiles" with quartermile ETs in the high 13-second range at speeds over 100-mph was so high that there weren't enough produced to fill the orders. A total of 515 cars were built before '68 production ended; 451 of them were 4-4-2 Holiday coupes and 64 were 4-4-2 pillared coupes. The marketability and cash in hand orders for the '68s assured that there would be a '69 Hurst/Olds.

Olds released the specifications for the '69 4-4-2s early in the year. Again, the top engine option would be the "W-30" 400. Oldsmobile also announced that 700 Hurst/Olds Holiday coupes would be built. The cars began arriving in April, and many were sold sight unseen to people who wanted an H/O but couldn't get one of the '68s.

For '69, the heart of the Hurst/Olds was once again the 455-cid Rocket V-8, although it had been slightly revised. The horsepower had been rolled back a little to 380 at 5000 rpm. The torque was an incredible 500 ft-lb at 3200 rpm. The cold air induction system was also changed for the '69 cars. Instead of having the cold air pickup under the front bumpers, Hurst installed huge "mailbox" hood scoops which fed directly into a pressure box/air cleaner assembly.

Early literature showed the only transmission available to be the Turbo-Hydramatic, but later advertisements listed a 4-speed. And both were, of course, fitted with Hurst shifters. The rear-end was an anti-spin differential with standard 3.42:1 gears. Optional 3.91:1 was available on non-air conditioned cars while 3.23:1 was mandatory for refrigerated cars.

The real change for the '69 cars was exterior. Where the '68 cars, painted silver with black trim, had been rather sedate looking, the '69s were head turners. The Cameo white exteriors were trimmed in Fire Frost Gold, the Hurst trademark. On the rear deck was a negative lift spoiler designed from a Cessna aerofoil. The rear wing was reported to give 15 pounds of downward force at 60-mph and 64 pounds at 120-mph. Hurst included Goodyear F60x15 Polyglas tires mounted on beautiful Super Stock II wheels. Dual racing mirrors imported from Europe further graced the exterior.

The advertisement for the '69s pretty well summed up the car. "Awesome is the word for it. You roll up to the light next to the cocky looking guy in the supercar. He gives you a couple of blips...then looks you over. And you watch the creeping horror of realization hit him. 'That's more than a 4-4-2...it's a '69 Hurst/Olds!' Guys do funny things then. Some start looking for something under the seat. Some blow their noses 'til the light changes. Most just look out the other window and try to pretend they never really blipped at all. That's half the fun of owning a Hurst/Olds. The other half is the joy of punching that big Hurst Dual/Gate Shifter up through the gears...feeling those 455 cubic inches grab you...all to the genteel accompaniment of the silkiest snarl you ever heard. That, sir, is awesome!"

For only $4,180, the '69 H/O had plenty of go to match its show. The cars, off the showroom floor, were capable of running in the high 13 to low 14 second range at about 100-mph in the quartermile. They were quite a car.

The H/O was the pinnacle of the Hurst/Olds connection, more refined and streetable than the '68s and offered much more image appeal. Hurst production figures show that 912 hardtops and 2 convertibles were built. Olds records show 906. The difference was in prototypes and promo cars.

For 1970, Oldsmobile lifted its ban on 400+ cubic inch engines in intermediates and installed the 455 in the 4-4-2 as a new option. The '69 H/Os truly represent the last of a breed.

1969 BOSS 429 Mustang

BOSS-9! That's what some people call them. This was the Mustang carrying FoMoCo's biggest, baddest, most awesome NASCAR-based engine ever produced, the "Blue Crescent 429". Today, those engines are back in all-aluminum form via AR Inc. of Ventura, California, and are stronger than ever. Most people know them by another name, the BOSS 429, Ford's canted-valve, semi-hemispherical combustion chamber big blocks that were first shoehorned into Mustangs back in 1969. Not just any Mustang, mind you, but hand-built special Mustangs classified by Ford as "Special Performance Vehicles."

Their origin goes back to the sixties, that famous era of one-up-manship, when Ford countered Chrysler's hemi with one of its own. Following Ford's highly successful SOHC 427 engine of the mid-60s, a true hemi, the BOSS 429 was introduced in 1969 as its replacement. The engine was a hemi head conversion of the 385 series big block that Ford offered first in 1968 in heavy cars, Lincoln and Thunderbird. Its origin was simple: the engines had to be sold in enough cars (500) to make them legal in the eyes of NASCAR as a stock car engine. How to do it gave rise to the BOSS 429 Mustang.

Ford's arch-rival on the highbanks was Plymouth and Dodge. When Plymouth, meaning Richard Petty, blew Ford out of the point race in 1967, FoMoCo engineers went to work on the tunnel port 427 for '68 and produced another Ford championship year. And a new engine was in the works. A 2-pronged attack against Chrysler was begun; convert the big wedge head 429 to a hemi and put it into a slicker car. By early in the '69 season, the plan came together, and Chrysler racers didn't have a chance against the BOSS 429 powered aerodynamic Talladegas and Mercury Cyclone Spoiler IIs.

NASCAR rules required at least 500 units of both cars and engines, but didn't stipulate that the car had to have the engine. As events unfolded, the cars went into production before the engines. To get the cars on the highbanks, Ford chose to market the Talladegas and Spoiler IIs with other engines instead of BOSS 429s. The Talladegas received Ford's high torque 428 CJ The Spoiler II got the meek 351W. Ford was forced to install the BOSS 429 in another line of cars when they became available. The Mustang, Ford's youth market car, got the nod for the monster mill, and the BOSS 429 Mustang was born for the sole purpose of homologating the engine for NASCAR. This car and engine combination sold more than enough to qualify the engine for NASCAR racing.

On paper, Ford originally sold bare-bones, stripped down 428-cid Mach 1s to Shelby American, Inc., but in reality shipped them to their own racing shop, Kar Kraft of Brighton, Michigan. Once finished, the cars were re-invoiced to dealers with only the engine code in the serial number changed; Z replaced Q. Thus, the cars are the product of Kar Kraft, Ford's racing organization at the time.

The BOSS 429 engine, not to be confused with Ford's passenger engine of the same displacement, was designed solely for NASCAR racing. For production purposes, the engine had to be de-tuned, and that required considerable re-thinking as the engines were meant to race, not be "docile" on the street.

But rules were rules, and Kar Kraft began production of streetable BOSS 429 Mustangs on January 15, 1969, and completed the first 100 cars by the following March. End of year production for 1969 accounted for 857 Mustangs with Kar Kraft serial numbers 1201 through 2059 (except 1684 and 1685 which were Cougars). In 1970, production totalled 499 cars with serial numbers 2060 through 2558. Total BOSS 429 Mustang production was 1,356. (Note should be made that the two Cougars mentioned were Kar Kraft built with BOSS 429 power and bring Kar Kraft's total BOSS 429 car production to 1,358.)

The racing BOSS 429 engine was designed and built to be bullet-proof. Inside it boasted 4-bolt mains, forged steel crank,

The only showroom car available with the BOSS 429 engine was the BOSS 429 Mustang of 1969 and '70. The powerplant filled the engine bay.

Kar Kraft finished building BOSS 429 Mustangs with a great deal of hand work. To fit the engine, shock tower spacing was widened and the front suspension was lowered, which also lowered the top shock absorber lockdown point, the most obvious sheet metal change under the hood. The A-arms were lowered as well, and the front suspension was beefed up. The cars sat about 1 inch lower than Ford's production line Mustangs, and because of the wider tires, they had a meaner stance.

Additional welding was required in several places, and special inner fender panels and front fenders were installed. The inner lips of all four fenders were "re-rolled" to provide additional tire clearance, and the hood was modified for that huge hand-operated ram-air hood scoop, the most distinctive visual feature of BOSS 429 Mustangs. A manual choke cable was also fitted, and both the scoop and choke cables were mounted onto a small plate located at the bottom of dash to the right of the steering column. This was another of the special features of the cars.

The "29 Group" extraheavy-duty battery (a BOSS 429 only item) was mounted in the trunk and required special brackets and venting. The front spoiler of black plastic was placed in the car with taped-on instructions for dealer installation. The radio was also dealer installed, and Kar Kraft applied their serial number plates to the driver's doors. They read KK 429 NASCAR #1201 through KK 429 NASCAR #2558 including the two BOSS 429 Cougars.

The Vehicle Identification Numbers read 9F02Zxxxxxx for '69s and 0F02Zxxxxxx for '70s as shown on the VIN plate located on the driver's door. Matching numbers were also stamped into the engine block, transmission case, inner fenders and chassis. All numbers should match on an original car.

forged rods, forged aluminum pop-up pistons and forged rocker arms. In racing fashion, the aluminum heads were precision dry-decked to the block. Everything else was heavy-duty with lots of tricks learned from Ford's extensive racing efforts. A single 735-cfm Holley double-pumper on an aluminum high-rise intake fueled those 429 cubes through huge ports and canted valves. The crescent-shaped combustion chambers, the source of the "Blue Crescent 429" name, came close to being hemispherical and provided a 10.5:1 compression ratio. Special cast iron exhaust manifolds vented leftovers into dual exhausts.

The BOSS 429 engines fitted into Mustangs came in two varieties; the 820S and 820T. The S engine is considered the heavier duty of the two and was intended primarily as a competition engine. The first 279 engines were of this type and received cast magnesium valve covers, a hydraulic cam, special rods with floating pins and 1/2-inch rod bolts with 12-point nuts.

The T engines had different rods with pressed pins and 3/8-inch rod bolts. Early T engines also got magnesium valve covers and a hydraulic cam, but later engines were fitted with cast aluminum valve covers and mechanical cams. Both S and T engines gave similar torque and horsepower - advertised by Ford to be 375, "and that's understating it considerably" they said. Estimates run as high as 500 horsepower cranked out by a good running mechanical cam BOSS 429. These were strong big blocks. The proof of that was that output was rated at 6500 rpm, high for a big block engine.

BOSS 429 Mustangs were built from the SportsRoof design with top-of-the-line Mach 1 interiors and numerous performance options. Transmissions were heavy-duty 4-speed top loaders that fed power to 3.9-to-1 Daytona type locker rear-ends. Heavy-duty axles drove 7-inch wide chrome plated Magnum 500 wheels fitted with wide F60x15 Polyglas performance tires. Suspensions consisted of high-rate springs and shocks with heavy-duty anti-roll bars fore and aft. The cars also had staggered rear shocks to reduce axle wind-up produced by torque from the big BOSS engine.

For a list price of around $5,000, Ford lost a bundle on each car, but BOSS 429s showed up at selected dealers anyway. Because the cars were first invoiced to Shelby American, the losses looked like Shelby American losses, and that was the straw that broke the Carroll Shelby/Ford relationship. When Ford accounting showed his highly successful company taking heavy losses, Shelby ended his near-decade-long association with Ford.

BOSS 429 colors for 1969 were Royal Maroon, Raven Black, Candyapple Red, Wimbledon White, and Black Jade. For 1970, colors were Grabber Orange and Calypso Coral, Grabber Blue and Pastel Blue, and Grabber Green. All '69s received black interiors, while '70s got either black or white.

The NASCAR connection and low production quantity of the BOSS 429 Mustang, because of hand fitting their engines, make them rare and a favorite in the high-performance Ford family. Although the cars themselves earned little acclaim in racing, and were generally not among the top running street machines, family ties beyond the production line gave them a unique legacy.

1969 427 Yenko Camaro

When Chevrolet finally got around to introducing a ponycar of its own, the 1967 Camaro, it was an instant success. But there were other cars competing in the same market sector. Camaro production reached 310,636 from its introduction through the end of the 1967 calendar year. During that time, 1966 and '67, 975,249 Mustangs were sold. The new Mercury Cougar, also released in the fall of 1966, reached 179,756 buyers. Most of these cars were small engine versions, but a few were big block powered and were among the upward spiral toward larger and more powerful engines as the decade progressed toward the '70s.

This was the era of the muscle car, and each manufacturer had its own version of 400 or more cubic inch engines. Performance cars had improved dramatically over the temperamental street Super Stockers of the early sixties. The packages were well integrated with better handling suspensions, larger and improved tires, heavy-duty brakes including new disc brake packages, and attention-grabbing exterior graphics to compliment increased performance.

The 1967 Camaro benefitted from all of these. When the car was designed, computers laid out the suspension and calculated optimum geometry to control roll angles and improve the handling. As the car progressed in the design stages, the track was widened to further improve the handling characteristics and to allow easy placement of a big block engine. Chevrolet engineers intended from the beginning to fit the cars with big block engines. Camaro exterior styling reflected European lines with the long hood and short rear deck theme.

Performance option packages for the Camaro were designed to fit nearly every budget. For economical, basic everyday transportation, there were the 140-hp, 230 cubic inch and the 155-hp, 250 cubic inch inline 6-cylinder engines. For those interested in more performance, all sorts of V-8s were optional. In '67, two were 327 options, the 210-hp base

and the 275-hp L30. Later came the 295-hp L48 350, and two 396s, the 325-hp L35 and the radical solid lifter cam 375-hp L78.

At the time, one of the least known and very underrated options was the Z28. This package netted a heavy-duty racing type suspension, mandatory power front disk brakes, and mandatory floor-mounted 4-speed transmission. There was only one engine available, Chevrolet's new 302, which came from using a special 283 crank in a 327 block. The 302 internals were designed strictly for high winding with a forged steel crank, radical solid lifter cam, and forged 11.0:1 compression ratio pistons. With an aluminum intake manifold topped off by a 780-cfm Holley 4-barrel and low restriction exhaust manifolds, the engine was rated at just 290 horsepower. They were purebred horses.

As impressive as the performance options list was for the Camaro, several performance enthusiasts asked, "Only 396 cubes?" Enter Don Yenko and his better idea for the Camaro.

Yenko ran Yenko Chevrolet located in Canonsburg, Pennsylvania, and made a specialty out of offering muscle Chevrolets that did not show up on the option lists. Yenko got his start in the early sixties when he began modifying Corvairs into Stingers. Though the cars received a great deal of national publicity, they failed to find a niche in the power hungry market. Yenko subscribed to the philosophy that too much is just right, and as soon as the Camaro hit the market, he conceived the idea of switching the engines around. His idea was basically simple: pull out the 396, and drop in a L72 Corvette 427. Later, he could do that through the factory as a Central Office Production Order (COPO), and to the outside world, it looked like he was building the cars at his dealership.

The L72 was rated by Yenko at 450 horsepower, which was what NHRA rated the engine for classification purposes. Chevrolet put a 425-hp label on it. The internals of the engine

Camaro for 1969 offered very sporting accommodations for five. Don Yenko went even further, the Super Camaro.

Introduced in 1965, Chevy's big block has survived all competitors. Here in 450-hp form, the 427 was the heart of 12-second Yenko Camaros, among the quickest ever built.

were clearly designed with performance and hard driving in mind. Forged, 11.0:1 compression ratio pistons, forged steel connecting rods, and forged steel cranks were just some of the internal goodies. On top was an 800-cfm Holley 4-barrel carb on an aluminum highrise intake manifold. The large 2.19-inch intake and 1.725-inch exhaust valves were actuated by a radical .520-inch lift, 316-degree duration camshaft. Fire was handled by a dual point distributor and exhaust by low restriction manifolds or an optional set of Doug Thorley headers. Two transmissions were available, a heavy-duty Turbo-Hydramatic shifted by a Hurst dual gate shifter or a Muncie M21 4-speed also with Hurst shift linkage.

Yenko made the engine switch through 1967 and 1968, producing 54 cars the first year and 64 the second, but in '69 he was able to get them from Chevrolet with the 427. By specially ordering the cars through COPO and specifying code 9561, the Camaro came with the L78. Also in '69,

Yenko's cars got eye-catching exterior graphics which were not present on the earlier cars. Strips and spoilers graced the body panels of the car, and billboard letters boldly read YENKO/SC, SC standing for Super Car or Sports Car. The SC has also been interpreted to mean Super Camaro, but this cannot be since the Yenko Novas also carried YENKO/SC lettering. The '69 cars came with all the best; the Z28 suspension and disk brakes and a 427. The cars were handles and straight line bullets.

And go they would! In 1969, *Super Stock and Drag Illustrated* magazine tested one of Yenko's creations. The car was driven by noted drag racer, Ed Hedrick. In full street tune running on F70x15 street tires, the car ran an incredible 12.80 seconds at 108.56-mph bone stock! Then in a effort to see just what the car would do with drag legal preparations, the headers were uncapped and a set of six inch extensions was added to improve exhaust scavageing, the air cleaner was removed, the timing was bumped 2 degrees, and a set of M & H Racemaster slicks were added. After a few practice runs, Hedrick brought the Camaro through the traps to an unbelievable 11.94 seconds at 114.50-mph! For any production car to drop under the 12 second mark was phenomenal. Neither a magazine tested stock 427 Cobra nor 427 Corvette ran that quick, and they are considered ultimates of the '60s. The Yenko Camaro shown here is that car.

1969 proved to be the biggest year for the Yenko Camaro, 201 sales. Of the few that were made, it is not certain how many remain today. Because of their ultrahigh-performance, many turned up at race tracks around the country, and that makes it almost certain that few remain intact today. But those that have survived are lasting testimony to the competitive spirit of Don Yenko, who was tragically killed in a private plane crash on March 5, 1987.

1969 Torino Cobra

When the word "Cobra" is mentioned around car enthusiasts, visions instantly appear of a roadster with two seats and two doors and a huge engine giving very high speeds. They see bulged fenders surrounding gigantic tires and long chrome side pipes that emit a ground-shaking roar every time the throttle is romped. The whole idea of comparing the hairiest of sports cars to a Fairlane was just what Ford product planners had in mind.

During the early and middle sixties, the muscle car market blossomed, and nearly every major American auto manufacturer had a car that came with an engine displacing 400 cubes or more. Advertisements were aimed at young people who went to the drags every weekend and talked in terms of horsepower, ETs and top speed. But the early sixties muscle cars were expensive and were priced out of the so called "youth market". In 1968 a new type of muscle car appeared, one aimed squarely at the youth market. The idea was to offer high-performance engines and equipment in less expensive bodies, thus allowing sticker prices to remain low. The Plymouth Road Runner and the '68 Chevrolet Chevelle are two examples of youth market muscle cars.

Not to be left out, Ford introduced the newly restyled '68 Fairlane with a new model name, Torino. The Torino could be ordered in several trim packages and engine combinations depending upon how much money a buyer wanted to spend. There were also three body styles available, the formal roof (or notchback), the sports roof (or fastback), and the convertible.

The 1968 GT trim package was the top exterior option and provided for several trim pieces to dress up the basic Fairlane body. The grill could be ordered matted out, hoods with NASCAR-style tiedown pins were optional, and chrome wheel well moldings were available. For GT versions, there was a stripe package that resembled the long reversed "C"

worn by the Mark IV Fords that won Le Mans in 1967.

There were enough engine options to fit every budget. On the economical end of the scale was the 302-cid 2-barrel Windsor with 210 horsepower and the 390 cubic inch 2-barrel with 265 horsepower. For more romp, the 390 GT bearing engine marking "S" developed 325 horsepower and 427 ft-lb of torque. In mid-1968, Ford unleashed the 428 Cobra Jet which replaced the 427 side oiler as the top performance engine. The new Cobra Jet, or CJ, engine was rated at a low 335 horsepower and 440 ft-lb of torque. For the '69 model year, little changed externally on the Fairlane and Torino. There was, however, a new exterior trim and performance package available called the Torino Cobra. The new package added Cobra decals, which were later replaced by chrome-plated emblems of a coiled snake ready to strike. These were installed on the front fenders and rear panel. The package also included a standard 4-speed gear box and F70x14 inch white wall tires.

The engine lineup for '69 saw the addition of several new engines. The 351 Windsor and 351 Cleveland were two new small blocks. The 351 Windsor, an outgrowth of the 302 Windsor, came with a 2-barrel carb and offered more power while maintaining economy. The 351 Cleveland, on the other hand, was Ford's new high-performance small block. With a single 4-barrel producing an underrated 290 horsepower, it was a highly respectable performer. Also new for '69 was the 428 Super Cobra Jet, a ram-air version of the Cobra Jet with beefed-up internals.

The Super Cobra Jet, or SCJ, was built under higher quality control specifications than the CJ and was stronger internally. The SCJ option included a functional hood scoop and a special air cleaner box. Ford conservatively rated the horsepower of the SCJ at 335-hp and torque at 440 ft-lbs. These figures were identical to those of the CJ engine. It has

Torino Cobra ram-air 428 Cobra Jet was a true street bomber for 1969. Its rating of 335-hp was a laugh. Perhaps 420.

Interiors were spartan in the low-buck muscle cars, just the essentials, gauges and a 4-speed mattered.

been estimated that the CJ engines actually produced 410 horsepower, and that suggests that the SCJ was even higher, perhaps more than 420.

When the Torino Cobra was ordered with the SCJ engine, F70x14 Wide-Oval belted tires were required. A Select-Shift Cruise-O-Matic could be opted instead of the standard 4-speed. Other options included a tach, power front disc brakes, bucket front seats, and Traction-Loc rear end. A heavy-duty competition suspension was standard, and on 4-speed cars, staggered rear shocks were employed to control axle wind up and wheel hop.

In a 1969 test conducted by *Car and Driver* magazine, a Torino Cobra equipped with a 428 SCJ, four-speed trans, and 3.50:1 locking rear ran a 14.04 quarter at 100-mph. Compared to other cars in its market segment, only the Plymouth Road Runner equipped with an optional 426 hemi was quicker, and a 383 Magnum equipped Super Bee could tie it. *Car&Driver* also tested a CJ equipped Cobra against a SCJ Cobra to see if the ram-air option, costing $133.44, actually added to the performance of the car. They found that the option knocked two-tenths of a second off quartermile times. Two-tenths translates into about 40 more horsepower. With the Drag Pak or Super Drag Pak options, the Torino Cobra was indeed a healthy muscle car.

Carroll Shelby's famous Cobra roadster was no longer in production in 1968, and the Torino Cobra continued the prestige of the Cobra namesake. There was, of course, considerable difference in cost. The Torino Cobra offered young people a muscular, sporty-looking high-performance car that they could afford.

1969 SC/Rambler

The Rambler Rogue all grown up to be a genuine muscle car became the SC/Rambler. These were exciting low-buck cars.

AMC's largest displacement engine was the 390-inch form of the 343. For the weight of the SC/Rambler, the 390 could go.

American Motors has been defunct for several years now and is an all but forgotten marque. When drag racing and muscle cars are mentioned, there is almost never any association with American Motors. Few people realize that a few cars from red, white and blue were actually heavy-duty street pounders.

When AMC and George Hurst got together in 1969 to produce a special-edition performance machine, the SC/Rambler, there was almost no doubt that it would end up being a supercar. The basic idea was to take a small, lightweight car and drop a big cubic inch engine into it. The car that was chosen was the Rambler Rogue. To many people, that seemed an unlikely choice since the car was the only acknowledged U. S. competition for the VW Beetle. With its standard 199-cid, 128-hp straight six and a single 1-barrel carb, the little Rogue didn't communicate what muscle power potential lay hidden within. That is where an ambitious design staff and Hurst came into the picture.

The puny little six was trashed and a 390-cid, 315-hp big block was selected. Add a 4-speed gear box and front disc brakes, then put a performance-tuned suspension under it, and you've got a truly balanced machine. But there was something lacking: visual appeal. To solve this problem, the SC/Rambler received one of the most eye-catching paint schemes ever seen on a factory car.

Red, white and blue fashionably emblazoned in two patterns, wild and wilder, insured that no SC/Rambler would ever be passed unnoticed. The cars were painted overall in white, itself not too exciting, but from there it got interesting. On the sides extending about three-quarters of the way down the doors was painted a huge American red panel, with black pinstriping, running the entire length of the car. On the hood was placed a large, fully functional hood scoop with a 12-inch wide American blue arrow, interrupted by the figures 390 CU.IN in red, pointing down its throat. To be sure that nobody would mistake the function of the scoop, AIR was painted on its top in four-inch-high red letters. In European tradition, the grille and rear light panel were finished in matte black. Other exterior appointments included racing-style hood tiedown pins with cables, dual teardrop racing mirrors, and SC/Rambler-Hurst emblems on each front fender and the rear panel.

With all of the exterior treatment, American Motors had to ensure that there was enough go to match the show. To provide the go-power, the 390 cubic inch engine was chosen. It was the largest engine offered in the American Motors line. That engine was basically a punched-out version of the 343-cid block with the pan rails stiffened. Internally it had a forged steel crank and rods, special lightweight pistons, and tri-metal main and rod bearings. With a single Carter 4-barrel carb on top, factory-rated power was 315 horsepower at 4600 rpm. Torque was rated at a very respectable 425 ft-lb. Though the engine was redlined by the factory at 5000 rpm, it would pull strongly well past that to about 5800 rpm where the valves would begin to float.

Road Test magazine had this to say about the engine combination. "This is one of the best performing hot engines we have ever encountered. It starts with a jump even after sitting outside on a winter night and quickly settles down to a smooth 1200 rpm idle."

A hot engine is only the first part in designing a good high-performance package. Backing up the engine was a heavy-duty 10.5-inch diameter dry plate clutch which transmitted torque to the 4-speed gearbox. Gear ratios were set at 2.23, 1.77, 1.35, and 1.00:1. The Hurst "T" handle shifter, which *Road Test* magazine described as "one of the smoothest operating units we have ever encountered", made rowing through the gears quite a pleasure. To complete the powertrain, a 3.54:1 Twin-Grip differential transmitted the power to the ground.

It would be fair to assume that changing out the little six for a huge V-8 would cause the car to handle poorly, but American Motors thought of that potential problem. Underneath, a carefully developed suspension borrowed from the AMX came standard. Up front there were high-mounted coil springs, tube shocks with swinging arms and an anti-sway bar. The rear suspension was equipped with long leaf springs with tube shocks and a pair of radius arms mounted above the rear axle and attached to a reinforced section of the chassis. This combination was quite effective at preventing dreaded axle wind-up and wheel hop on acceleration. To aid in traction, Goodyear E70x14 Polyglas Wide-Tread tires were mounted at all four corners on special mag-styled 14-inch by 6-inch wheels. Each of the wheels had a blue stripe to accent the exterior color scheme.

The whole point of a muscle car is to go fast, and the SC/Rambler was no exception. *Road Test* magazine took one out to Orange County International Raceway to see what it could do. The numbers it generated were impressive. The best time that it recorded was 14.14 seconds and the best top speed was 100.44-mph. The magazine reported that "On the strip the whole car works like a charm - engine, clutch, and the Hurst shifted transmission." All-out top end runs were performed at Riverside International Raceway. The top speed was reported at 109-mph, but the car was hampered by the gearing and the shortness of the straights. Estimated top speed was given as between 115- to 120-mph.

With this sort of performance and the wild exterior graphics, why haven't more of these cars been seen? The answer is, only about 500 SC/Ramblers were built, probably fewer than one per American Motors dealer. Those that remain are few and very far between, and as the muscle car collector market continues to climb, they will become even more scarce.

Stock, Super Stock and Street Eliminators, NHRA 1968-69

Winternationals:

1968	Super Stock	Al Joniec	'68 Mustang CJ SS/E	12.50/97.93
	Street	Bo Laws	Corvette D/SP	11.70/117.95
	Stock	John Barkley	'57 Chevrolet M/SA	14.59/89.64
1969	Super Stock	Don Grotheer	'68 Cuda SS/BA	10.73/119.68
	Street	Dick Landy	'69 Charger B/MP	10.80/128.20
	Stock	Mark Coletti	'68 Plymouth F/SA	12.93/103.32

Springnationals:

1968	Super Stock	Ronnie Sox	'67 Cuda SS/B	11.20/106.50
	Street	Bo Laws	'67 Corvette D/SP	11.66/119.04
	Stock	Ron Garey	'63 Oldsmobile E/S	12.78/98.57
1969	Super Stock	Ronnie Sox	'69 Cuda SS/B	10.63/114.50
	Street	Don Nicholson	'69 Mustang A/MP	10.49/120.96
	Stock	Max Sterling, Jr.	'62 Pontiac D/S	12.24/102.50

US Nationals:

1968	Super Stock	Arlen Vanke	'68 Cuda SS/B	10.64/118.11
	Street	Sam Fianinno	Corvette D/G	11.17/123.96
	Stock	Larry Lombardo	'61 Corvette F/S	12.73/107.78
1969	Super Stock	Ronnie Sox	'68 Cuda SS/B	10.89/124.83
	Street	Glen Self	Camaro F/MP	12.33/109.89
	Stock	Bill Morgan	'63 Plymouth C/SA	12.01/115.80

World Finals:

1968	Super Stock	Dave Strickler	'68 Camaro SS/F	11.89/116.12
	Street	Fred Hurst	Cuda F/G	9.45/149.59
	Stock	Dave Boertman	'56 Chevrolet P/S	15.10/88.49
1969	Super Stock	Ronnie Sox	'68 Cuda SS/B	10.23/101.58
	Street	Mike Fons	Chevrolet A/MP	10.52/110.58
	Stock	Robert Burkitt	'62 Dodge G/SA	13.17/65.12

Most Wins: Ronnie Sox - 4, 'Cuda SS/B

Quickest Super Stock: Ronnie Sox - 10.23 seconds, 1969 World Finals

The winged Dodge Charger 500 was introduced at Talladega in 1969. Top line drivers walked away from the cars, saying they were too fast for the bumpy track. The race went on anyway, and Richard Brickhouse won in one of the cars. Here, Buddy Baker is on his way to setting a world closed course speed record at Talladega, 200.447-mph. Later, NASCAR champion Bobby Isaac raised the record to 201.104. Ford Motor Co. photo.

Final Thunder

Beginning the 1970 season, Plymouth advertised with 2-page layouts saying "The obvious reason Richard Petty came back" was the new SuperBird. These 426 hemi powered NASCAR machines promised to be so superior to Ford's Talladegas that Petty had no doubt which one would make a NASCAR champion. Richard commented, saying "The Pettys and Plymouth are like, well, like family." The 1970 season began Petty's 12th year with Plymouth. By then, he had won 2 championships and earned the most total money paid to a NASCAR driver. His 101 wins, 92 in Plymouths, account for the "family" ties. The new year would add 18 more wins to his already phenomenal record, but not another championship.

The winged wonders from Chrysler's Chelsea proving grounds rolled up a fantastic new racing machine. The Dodge Daytona was the development car, and the Plymouth version was derived from what was learned by the Dodge boys. The cars were designed for the fast circuits, the big tracks where speed, and consequently aerodynamics, was important. A. J. Foyt had taken his Talladega around the Riverside road course to victory to begin the season. The Ford/MoPar rivalry picked up right where it left off the year before.

Then came the Daytona 500 and debut of the winged machines. Pete Hamilton rolled his Plymouth into the winner's circle after averaging 149.601-mph. Everyone was talking about the new Chryslers, and for the remainder of the season, another win didn't matter so much. But more were to come. Hamilton went on to win both rounds of the fastest of them all, the Talladega races, by setting new race records each

time, 158.517-mph and 152.321-mph, both in Plymouths. Both rounds of the Atlanta features were also MoPar showcases. Bobby Allison took the first 500 while establishing a new record, 139.554-mph, and Petty notched his only major win in the second round with a new race record of 142.712-mph.

The two races at Charlotte were Ford shows, Donnie Allison (Ford) in the World 600 and LeeRoy Yarbrough (Mercury) in the fall 500. By mid-season, it was becoming clear that the SuperBirds and Daytonas were the best of the year-old Ford Talladegas. Buddy Baker became the first man over 200-mph on a closed course on March 24 when he set the world closed course speed record at Talladega, 200.447-mph. Then in September, he won the Southern 500 in a winged Dodge, leading Bobby Isaac's Dodge and Hamilton's Plymouth across the finish line, a 1-2-3 sweep for the winged machines. Later on November 24, Isaac raised the record to 201.104-mph, in another aero-Dodge.

A final tally for the '70 season shows that Chrysler aerodynamics worked. Out of ten super-speedway races, Plymouth won 4 and Dodge took 2. Ford gathered in 3 victories and Mercury 1. During the season, Isaac entered 47 of 48 races, capturing 20 poles, and won 17 races. Petty added 18 Plymouth wins. The two makes combined for 38 races won, compared to Ford's 6 and Mercury's 4. Add in the records and comments by drivers that the aero-MoPars were the most stable stockers they had ever raced, and that should drive the last nail into Ford's NASCAR coffin of 1970.

The factory battles had reached new ground. But Henry Ford II was about to stop his machine in its tracks. Whether or not the NASCAR-derived cars were well received by the public was not an issue. They were all sales busts, but they were required to meet the regulations written by Bill France. The question had been asked before, who was running America's automotive manufacturers? In stock car racing, it was France who played the tune while the factories danced. Now the government was calling some tunes of its own, and the Detroit big three were in for heavy changes.

The Daytonas and SuperBirds were super-speedway cars while smaller Road Runners were the short tracks cars. (The Road Runner caricature for these cars was used on contract from Warner Brothers-Seven Arts, Inc.) Plymouth claimed to have the most comprehensive high-performance program in the country and called it "The Rapid Transit System". The scope of the factory's efforts encompassed cars such as the Road Runner and SuperBird with an illustrious supporting cast of GTX, 'Cuda, Sport-Fury and a host of smaller engine cars, along with tuning manuals and high performance parts to cover Trans-Am racing, Super Stockers and AA/Fuel dragsters. If you wanted it, Plymouth had it. Manuals loaded with factory go-fast tips covered the 426 hemi, 440 and 383 engines, 340, 318 and 273, and lowbrow 6s.

At a time when Chrysler racers were making lots of noises about blowing Fords into trackside weeds, Henry Ford II announced in December 1969 that a $7.5 million research facility aimed at reducing exhaust pollutants was under construction. At the same time, he announced that Ford's racing program was being cut. First it was, $3.5 million. Within 60 days, another $3.5 million was cut. That left only $3.5 million where there had been $10.50 million just months before. It was a stunning blow to the well-entrenched Ford racing teams and supporting factory design and development engineers, who were reassigned within the company or moved on.

Over at Chevrolet early in 1970, Jim Musser resigned. At 35, he had been in charge of all high-performance development programs but found that further upward mobility within the company was difficult because he was an engineer rather than an accountant. It was rumored that he and famed stylist Larry Shinoda were launching a firm of their own involving recreational vehicles.

During that time, Musser was instrumental in developing the 465-hp, 454 cubic inch LS7 big block engine. This was a true racing powerplant, unlike the LS6, and was the 454 version of the L88 427. The factory planned to place the LS7 in production cars with a warranty, but increasing emission requirements killed the engine. It never made it to the as-

The fastest, most stable high speed cars of the '60s era were the Dodge Daytonas and Plymouth SuperBirds. These were Chrysler's ultimate machines of post-war American stock car racing. Ford Motor Co. photo.

The hemi powered SuperBird Road Runner was a direct result of Plymouth's entry into the NASCAR aero-war of 1969 and '70. It remains a very rare bird.

sembly line, although parts were fully developed and offered to bowtie racers over-the-counter.

Just when Henry was tightening up on racing funds, Ford of Canada announced that it would be sponsoring an expanded racing program centered on a 4-car team with Vic Beleny and AA/FD pilot Scott Wilson touring the country giving performance clinics. Wilson's duties involved driving an SOHC 427-powered Pro Stock Mustang and a SS/HA 428 CJ Mustang. Beleny's chores were to compete with a G/SA Mercury Cyclone and an H/S 428 Cougar.

During 1970, racing was still very big on all fronts, and no one quite realized the impact of Ford's end-of-the-year pullout. With the rapid decline of the fast-paced blue oval machines, Chevrolet received a great boost in converts. If you wanted to race and didn't mind staying in the sportsman ranks that gathered very little publicity, the bowtie brand was tough to beat and cost a lot less than other makes.

With the demise of factory Fords, drivers such as Dickie "Mr. Chevrolet" Harrell became serious threats. His credits already included AHRA Driver of the Year in 1969, and the distinction of being the first driver over 200-mph in a Chevy

Dale Young and this SS/HA, 11.84 second 428 CJ Cougar ran every 1970 AHRA event and won both the Grand-Am and All American Championships. Ford Motor Co. photo.

Ohio legend Eddie Schartman ran this 10.36 second Pro Stock BOSS 429 Cougar for the factory during 1970. Only 2 of these Cougars were built. Ford Motor Co. photo.

powered Funny Car. He and Don Madden of Howard Cams were involved in developing 4-valve per cylinder hemi heads cast of aluminum for the big block Chevy. They were attempting to break the domination of the Chrysler hemi, but little came of the project without considerable factory involvement.

The drag racing season opened without a hint of future doom. Some 675 entries made the pilgrimage to Pomona for the 10th annual running of NHRA's Winternationals. It was the best turnout on record, and began what has been called the greatest year of drag racing ever seen. To the delight of the huge crowd, the new Pro Stock category brought 16 qualifiers, including the finest drivers in the country. Ford drivers Don Nicholson, Sam Auxier and Dick Loehr demonstrated that Ford had some catching up to do when they lost in the first round. Camaro men Bill Jenkins, Wally Booth, Bill Blanding, Rich Miracki and Bill Hielscher looked tough, especially when Jenkins turned the only sub-10 second passes during the entire meet. MoPar pilots included Don Carlton in the '69 Sox & Martin 'Cuda while Ronnie shifted the cogs in a new '70 'Cuda that proved to be faster. Dick Landy in a Hemi Dart and Arlen Vanke in another 'Cuda made Pro Stock a well-tuned field of MoPars.

Sox was No. 1 qualifier with a 10.00 flat followed by Jenkins at 10.08, Booth at 10.09 and Landy's 16-plug hemi turning 10.11. Bill Hielscher put a hole shot on "Grump" in round 1, and to beat the Texan, Jenkins turned up the wick running a sensational 9.98/138.46 to squeak by. With the Fords no contest, the semi-final round had Booth almost beating Sox, but he lost at the lights in another squeaker. The finals? Sox and Jenkins. The crowd loved the Pro Stock shootout. The 426 Hemi 'Cuda and 427 wedge Camaro came out of the hole side-by-side. Jenkins pulled a little in 1st, then more in 2nd and was away in 3rd. Chevy fans went berserk when the Pennsylvanian went through the traps on a 9.99/139.53 blast that was well ahead of Sox's 10.12/138.46.

With the Pro Stockers putting on a thrilling show, Super Stock drivers added another dimension. Class winners were 7 Fords (4 of them factory cars), 4 Plymouths and 4 Dodges making up the Super Stock Eliminator field. No GM cars got that far. Sox was in a SS/A 'Cuda along with Don Grotheer in a similar SS/AA entry. Because of Sox's Pro Stock commitment, Don Carlton drove the S&M 'Cuda and fouled on the

second pass to Bill Allis in a 428 CJ Mustang. John Teddar's '69 SS/EA hemi car fell to Barrie Poole's Sandy Elliot sponsored CJ from Chatham, Ontario, Canada.

Final round for Super Stock pitted two CJ Mustangs, Canadian Poole in a SS/H car against American Allis in a SS/HA machine. Poole laid down a come-from-behind victory of 11.26/117.34 to Allis' 11.52/120.16. The all-Mustang Super Stock final regained a significant measure of what was lost in the drubbing in Pro Stock. It was Poole's first major US victory with more to come.

Stock Eliminator saw Keith Berg's ancient V/S Oldsmobile lumber off to a 3.5 second start on Dick Charbonneau's 427-powered E/S Ford Fairlane wagon. Leaving the line with a smoker, the Ford pulled out the win and gave Ford two of the coveted Eliminator titles that year, and Charbonneau added another trophy to his 1969 World Points Championship.

In Modified Eliminator, Dick Landy's '69 victory made him reigning Winternationals champion, and he defended his title in a Hemi Dart instead of a hemi Charger like the year before. He set a new B/Modified Production ET record against a hot rod Anglia that broke on the line.

To illustrate the amount of drag racing going on in 1970, NHRA held 6 national events, AHRA had 10 and UDRA ran a full schedule in the mid-west. Throw in *Super Stock and Drag Illustrated* magazine's Super Stock Nationals on the east coast, the *Popular Hot Rodding* magazine feature on the west coast and all sorts of other feature meets along with match racing throughout the nation, and that should provide a convincing idea of what the sport had become. Racing was going on everywhere.

While the Chrysler men were relishing another spectacular year of racing, the Corporation was experiencing a downward spiral in sales. With more models than ever to choose from, manufacturing and inventory costs had grown higher than ever. Total 1968 production was 1,585,591 but dropped 12.2% in '69, then another 8.6% in 1970. Rather than improving sales, the wide variety of cars offered was accruing more cost than profits.

Ford Motor Co. experienced the same down turn. From 2,396,924 cars produced in 1968, '69 produced a 9.8% drop followed by another 6.4% in 1970. Henry Ford's realignment

Canadian John Elliot took this SS/F 428 CJ Mustang to the 1970 NHRA Springnationals class win (11.15/109.62), then went on to shut down Bob Lambeck in Dick Landy's SS/EA Dodge Charger to take the Super Stock Eliminator crown with a winning 11.29/110.97 blast.

of funds toward satisfying tighter air quality standards was undertaken in a climate of revenues some $1.5 billion below 1968, itself a so-so year.

General Motors had held up well under industry-wide declining sales in 1969, down just 3.7% from 1968's 4,592,114 cars produced. But in 1970, the General took a beating, down 32.6% and approximately $5.6 billion.

The combination of a very active year of racing in 1970 and massive spectator turnouts indicates that America was perhaps spending more on entertainment than on new cars. Another factor was that the "baby boomers" were creating a baby boom of their own, and rising costs of living precluded super stock cars in the driveway. The econobox era was just

around the corner. Also by 1970, the public conscience was becoming alarmed by the US Government's posture on Viet Nam. The southeast Asia "war" was exacting a moral price on the country, and it was showing up in declining confidence in anything the government said or did.

Muscle cars were legislated out of existence. To meet increasingly more stringent emissions requirements, their big engines were emasculated even more after 1971, and that left a once-vibrant automotive culture wondering where the fast cars had gone. With rising costs of everything, small and economical Japanese imports began filling the void created by a rapidly changing world. It had taken 10 years to get there, but the great era of muscle cars came to a close in one year.

Ford's top Mustang for 1971 was the BOSS 351. It was the quickest showroom stock small block car ever built and was faster than many over-400 inch big block cars. Motor Trend tested one to a 13.8/104-mph quartermile, faster and quicker than their 13.9/101 440 Charger R/T test car.

Ronnie Sox was "the man" in top Pro Stock drag racing of 1970 and '71 (see page 120). He was the winningest driver with 6 Eliminator titles and set both the quickest and fastest stats of any Pro Stocker during NHRA national events. This was in Hemi 'Cuda "Lil Boss II". Chrysler photo.

1970 Buick GSX

Does the name Buick conjure up neck-snapping, spine-tingling, tire-burning performance? No? Well, it should, especially when talking about the 1970 GSX.

The cars from GM's "quiet" division most likely evoke images of land barges, though luxurious to be sure. And that picture would not be complete without a row of fake "exhaust" outlets along the trailing portions of the front fenders or the hood, the treatment the '50s Buicks received. These "portholes" were accepted styling, and everyone knew that styling and luxury were about all the Buick line offered.

Buicks were automobiles of status. They were, traditionally of course, big and heavy cars well known for comfortable traveling. The Roadmaster is an example. What it and other Buicks offered buyers was not excitement, but the solid-citizen, "I've made it in the financial world" sort of image that never attracted young buyers until the yuppie movement of the '80s.

To think of a Buick on the line at a drag strip, with smoke boiling from its rear tires, and then rocketing to a 12 second quartermile is a study in contrasts. Buicks just didn't do that sort of thing. At best, they were supposed to be in the parking lot, perhaps Dad's barge spirited away by teenage son and friends out to watch other cars that showed true performance.

A Buick with spoilers, hood scoops, a rear wing, fat high-speed tires, blindingly bright colors, yellow for instance, a tachometer, 4-speed transmission and an engine delivering neck-snapping performance to the tune of basso profundo howls of power from under the hood is a different sort of Buick indeed.

Geritol generation Buicks! Quarters in 12.30 seconds at 110.97-mph was the tune that one line of Buicks could dance to, the GSX. And if you know anything about drag racing, such performance was literally awesome for a production car of Buick's size and weight, even if it was a sports coupe for five passengers.

Few people know that Buick built a few hairy-chested bombers capable of quietly getting groceries, then blasting a few other "image" cars on the way home, cars like street hemi Chargers and the semi-hemi BOSS 429 Mustangs included. If Dad bought one of these Buicks, teenage son would have it on the strip, not hidden in the parking lot!

The Buick image usually didn't convey "elephant engine" supercars, but 455 cubes in the Gran Sport with the "X" twist definitely was. As a mid-year 1970 entree with absolutely stunning graphics on your choice of Saturn Yellow or Apollo White, the GSX was the wildest Buick in the Wildcat tradition of high-performing machines. Those Buicks, the Wildcat of 1964 for instance, were the last vestiges of the high-powered land barge philosophy. By the time of the GSX, big car performance had given way to the more youthful idea of smaller and lighter cars with even higher powered engines.

The transition was made with the likes of the Skylark Gran Sport of 1966 with the Wildcat 401 engine and heavy-duty suspension. The year 1967 saw the 340 horse Gran Sport 400, another hot stuff Buick with some youth appeal. But these cars still were not known for much more than being high-speed cruisers for the sports-minded executive, Buick's time honored place in the marketplace.

Then, in 1969, the 400 gave way to the monster motor 455 cubic inch engine rated at 360-hp in Stage 1 form. These Buicks quickly became sleepers that teenage son could do some Saturday night stoplight cruising in and have the satisfaction of embarrassing the drivers of a lot of other cars. The 455s were real haulers, and Dad probably never knew that son was getting the reputation of being the stoplight racing champ. These cars built a quiet respect among other drivers who had learned that there were some Buicks you didn't pick on. If it was a GSX, you'd best leave it alone. Instead of being laughed at for driving a Buick, young drivers in this sort of Buick found themselves talked about as driving one the fastest

455 cubic inches of ram-air Buick. That was the heart of the Stage 1 GSX. If you wanted more, there was more.

Inside, the GSX was among the best appointed of the grand touring type 5-passenger cars of 1970.

cars around

The Stage 1 offered buyers a special high-lift cam (.490-inch lift for both intake and exhaust valves), special valve springs, larger diameter Stellite valves, forged steel connecting rods, a crankshaft with oversize journals and extra large oil pump pickup. The engine block was cast for larger oil passages to improve high-speed oiling. Heads had larger intake and exhaust ports for the "tunnel ram" effect that increased volumetric efficiency. A special distributor was also part of the Stage 1 option, which included low-restriction dual exhausts, a high-rpm valve train and a limited-slip rear axle. A higher shift-point M40 Turbo-Hydramatic 3-speed automatic was optional as was a Hurst shifter on a Muncie M22 "Rockcrusher" 4-speed manual (for $184.80), the same as used in racing Corvettes.

The GSX list of options goes on to include a heavy-duty Hayes clutch and lots of other goodies meant for one thing, winning its class in drag racing! The Stage 1 option cost $199.05, a terrific bargain, and gave buyers one of the best all-around street/strip machines of its time.

But that was just Stage 1! Stage 2 brought up a higher lift, longer duration cam, an Edelbrock aluminum high-rise intake manifold under an 850-cfm Holley 4-bbl and lots more. Like Webers! Yes indeed. Stage 2 development saw Mickey Thompson doing some work for Buick toward four dual-throat Webers on another aluminum manifold. But it would be unfair to say they were options since only two manifolds were reportedly built.

Just what was the X-tra in GSX? First, it was a look like no Buick before or since. Here was a car that combined high quality, luxury and performance with superb roadability in quiet driving comfort. They were racy with ram-air induction through a scooped hood topped with ultra-wide black stripes, a wing and air dam, stripes and fat tires. But power steering, power front disc brakes, electric seats, electric windows and electric door locks didn't slow this Buick down a bit. Compared to contemporary cars, the '70 GS Stage 1 could hold its own very well at 13.38 ET at 105.50-mph, certainly in the top 10 quickest muscle cars ever built. *Motor Trend* seemed to think so in their January 1970 road test.

The GSX option ($1,195) was really the Stage 1 in a new guise, and with suitable preparation beyond the norm for street use using Stage 2 goodies, a GSX clocked the quarter mile in 11.85 seconds at 117-mph. In another road test, a pure stock GSX shot the traps at 13.95 seconds at 100.5-mph, not at all bad for a 3,900 pound car. Such rapid acceleration came from the 455's massive torque, 510 ft-lb. Standard rear gearing was 3.64:1 but 2.93:1 to 4.76:1 final drive ratio gears were available providing a range of applications, strip or road work.

Such tire-smoking go came at a costly price by today's standards, around 10 miles per gallon back when gas was real gas. But then, base price was just $3,283 and fully optioned, a GSX came in at around $5,000. The GSX was more than simply image. These cars rank among America's ultimate supercars in five passenger, sports coupe form. Reportedly, Buick lost money on pricing GSX options low to attract young buyers. Whether or not the gambit worked can be surmised from the fact that the GSX was a one-year-only car.

In total, 678 cars were built in four guises, Stage 1 with either 4-speed (199) or automatic (289) and the 455 with either 4-speed (79) or automatic (120). Stage 2 options were generally dealer installed equipment and are quite rare.

Just one peak at a GSX and there's no doubt that Buick did not build a Geritol generation car in this model. One stab at the peddle says the car is definitely not for the faint-of-heart. If anything, the GSX rivals anything from anywhere for shear go-fast appeal. It was a very well appointed car that proved to be an excellent design exercise in both styling and performance, one that remains, without doubt, the most potent Buick of the muscle car era.

1970 440 SIX PACK Super Bee

Without a doubt, Dodge built some of the best performing muscle cars on the street during the '60s, and the factory supported their fans with the Dodge Scat Pack club begun late in the decade, so fans had a direct connection to what was going on. But before 1968, Dodge lacked a youth market muscle car, a car with exterior graphics that matched performance capabilities and came at a reasonable price. All that changed when the Super Bee was introduced that year. It was the Dodge answer to the Plymouth Road Runner, an example of the inter-divisional rivalry that existed between the two marques. The Super Bee became a big hit.

The base engine for the '68 Bee was the 383 Magnum, the same as the Road Runner. It came with a single Carter AVS four-barrel carburetor, 10:1 compression, and a .476-inch lift, 276 degree duration camshaft. To handle the exhaust, the cast iron exhaust manifolds were connected to 2.25-inch diameter dual exhaust pipes. Horsepower was factory rated at just 335 at 5200 rpm. Torque was listed at a healthy 425 ft-lb at 3500 rpm. The standard transmission was the New Process A-833 four-speed manual with inline linkage and shifter. To transfer the power was a single dry plate Borg and Beck 11-inch clutch and final drive gearing of 3.23 with optional ratios available.

The Bee also received heavy duty suspension components and heavy-duty 11-inch diameter drum brakes. The interior came standard with the Coronet 440 trim and Charger rally instrumentation. The exterior had special trim to identify the car as a Super Bee. There was the bulged performance hood, Scat Pack matte black sports grill, and red line tires.

The entire package made for a good performing car with quartermile times posted at 15 seconds flat. But, if the Magnum engine wasn't enough to light your fire, Dodge offered the awesome street 426 hemi as an option. With this monster mill under the hood, you were just about ensured the status of "king of the hill". A Super Bee equipped with the hemi was capable of running the quartermile in the mid-13 second range with speeds exceeding 100-mph, and that was in showroom rather than drag racing preparation.

For the 1969 model year, the Super Bee was basically unchanged externally, the most noticeable difference being the bumblebee stripe. The inline shifter and linkage was dropped in favor of better shifting Hurst units. The standard four-on-the-floor with full synchronization came with a 2.66 first gear, 1.91 second, 1.39 third, and 1.00 fourth. The excellent Chrysler TorqueFlite automatic was retained as an option and could be gotten with either a tree or a floor-mounted shifter.

All new for '69 was the matte black fiberglass hood with an integral hood scoop. The new hood, called the Ram-Charger fresh air package, was held down by four NASCAR type fasteners and certainly let the intent of this car be known to all the other drivers on the road.

In mid-1969, Dodge added more kindling to the muscle car fire when the new 440 cubic inch "high block" B-series wedge with multiple carburetion was introduced. The new engine was designed in line with the MoPar muscle car marketing strategy of maximum performance per dollar and was intended to be an intermediate between the high-performance 440 4-barrel engine and the hemi. The three 2-barrel 440 engine, or "Six Pack" as it became known, was offered in many performance cars, including the Super Bee. The engine offered incredible performance and was much more affordable than the street hemi. In stock form the 440 Six Pack was rated at 390 horsepower at 4700 rpm and delivered 480 ft-lb of torque at 3600 rpm.

The three 2-barrel carburetion on the early cars was mated to an aluminum high-rise intake manufactured by Edelbrock. Later cars came with manifolds produced by Chrysler. Carburetion was provided by three in-line, high-flow, series 2300 Holley 2-barrel carbs. The primary carb had

Another illustrious home for the "high block" 440 in tri-power form was the hard-running Super Bee. 390-hp at 4700 rpm.

Interior trim was typical of Chrysler products of the late-'60s, well equipped. The Super Bee speedo went past 140-mph.

1.5-inch throttle bores and the two secondaries had 1.75-inch bores. The front and rear 2-barrels were operated by vacuum while the center 2-barrel was mechanically operated by the throttle. This provided for reasonable economy while just tooling around, and tremendous acceleration when the go pedal was used as intended.

To generate such ground-pounding power, the internals of the standard 440 engines were modified to handle the additional stresses. The pistons were redesigned using moly-faced top rings and high-tension oil rings, giving a 10.5:1 compression ratio. For increased strength and durability, new connecting rods with heavier cross sections were used. The valve train was also modified for more strength. To prevent scuffing, the camshaft was given a "lubrite" treatment. Also, low-taper camshaft lobes and flat-faced hydraulic tappets were used to reduce stresses. The valve springs were the same as those used in the 426 hemi. Rocker arms were specially selected for high quality. Chrome plated valve stems and hardened tips reduced wear. Spark was controlled by a double breaker high-performance distributor.

Test reports of the 1969 Super Bee show that it was a very strong performer. Equipped with the bulletproof Chrysler 4-speed and Hurst T-handle shifter, 3.55:1 Sure-Grip rear end, and Goodyear Polyglas tires, the '69 Bee was able to run quarters in the mid-14 second range. 0-to-60 times were around 6.5 seconds. The little Polyglas tires were unable to harness the power produced by such a responsive engine and hindered the performance stats.

1969 was the first year that the Super Bee became its own model. Factory production figures show that 27,846 were produced that model year. Throughout the industry the next year, production took a dive, and that was reflected in the declining numbers of muscle cars produced. The Super Bees netted just 3,966 buyers of coupes and 11,540 hardtop coupes. These cars were options on the 117-inch wheelbase Coronet line during the 1969 and '70 model years. In 1971, the Super Bee option was shifted over to the 115 inch wheelbase Charger, and even fewer were built, 5,054. Horsepower was scaled back that year; from 390 for the '70 models, the '71s were rated 385 for the Six Pack. Still, a lot of go.

1970 454 LS6 Chevelle

Spacious and well-appointed interiors were one Chevelle feature. A 4-speed and an awesome LS6 engine were others.

The most powerful production engine Chevrolet offered in the Chevelle was the 450-hp LS6. LS7s were dealer installed.

When Pontiac shoehorned the full-size car 389-cid engine into the intermediate size Tempest/LeMans, creating the GTO in 1964, the automotive world was taken by surprise. The long-brewing youth performance market boiled over with enthusiasm, and the GTO became an instant sensation. Seeing the enormous market of over 32,000 GTOs sold before the end of the year, other divisions of GM rushed to put together comparable combinations of their own.

Chevrolet was quick to introduce the Chevelle Super Sport in 1964, a catch up attempt. But the standard 220-hp, 283-cid small block appeared anemic beside the 325-hp standard 389 in the GTO and downright wimpy compared to the 348-hp high-performance version. This called for action.

In late 1965, Chevy dropped the big one, the new "semi-hemi" 396 cubic inch engine, into the Chevelle. The new engine was the Mk IV big block that evolved from the infamous Mk IIS "Mystery" engine of 1963. The 427 cubic inch Mk IIS was Chevrolet's secret all-out racing engine designed by Dick Keinath. It was officially canned after Daytona of 1963 by GM's top brass, then was reborn, considerably changed, as the Mk IV big blocks that came in 1965.

The new package for the Chevelle was coded RPO-Z16 and offered performance that equaled or surpassed that of other high-performance intermediates. The chassis was modified to handle the added horsepower of the big engine's 375-hp. As incredible as these cars were, just 201 were built.

For the model years that followed, the 396 was the top performance option for the Super Sport Chevelles, excluding the COPO cars. But as the '60s progressed, so did Chevrolet's competitors. Pontiac GTO and Olds 442 went to 400 cubic inch engines. Ford made the 427 side oiler available in the Fairlane. Each year brought more cars that left public reaction to the Chevelle as "only 396 cubes?" It became obvious to GM that something had to be done to be competitive, so in mid-1970 the 400 cubic inch engine limit on intermediate-size cars was lifted. GM divisions were now allowed engines displacing 455 cubes. The 454, which had been sold in Corvettes and full-size Chevrolets, was now dropped into Chevelles.

The 1970 Chevelle was a restyled version of the 1968 platform. Contained under a new roofline were new body flanks, revised back pillars, and a completely changed grill and rear panel treatment. The new sheet metal, with slightly bulged fenders and domed hood, gave a strikingly purposeful, muscular appearance. The Super Sport models got blacked-out grills and prominent SS emblems on the front, rear, and both sides. Also for added flair, there was the special ZL2 hood option, which made use of the low-pressure region just at the base of the windshield, otherwise known as cowl induction. Whether it worked or not is of little consequence compared to the image it added to the car.

The big news for the '70 SS Chevelle was under the hood. There was a choice of four engines, 2 versions of the 396 and a pair of bruiser 454s. The two 396s were basically carryovers from '68. There was the base 350-hp engine featuring oval port cylinder heads, cast iron intake and a single Rochester four-barrel. This engine came with a relatively sedate compression ratio of 10.25:1. The second 396 was the RPO-L78 rated at 375-hp. It had rectangular port heads, 11.0:1 compression, solid lifter cam, and a single Holley four-barrel mounted on a low-rise aluminum intake.

Then came the option that made the earth move. The base 454 was the RPO-LS5. It had a two-bolt main bearing block with a forged steel, 4.00-inch stroke crank and forged steel connecting rods. Heads were closed chamber with oval ports and the pistons were of the 10.25 compression cast aluminum variety. With a lone Quadrajet mounted on a cast iron dual plane intake and a high-performance hydraulic cam the engine was certainly under-rated at 360-hp at 5400 rpm. Torque was a tremendous 500 ft-lb at 3200 rpm.

Then there was the RPO-LS6. If there ever was a Chevrolet production engine of the King Kong sort, this was it. The LS6 was based on the 4.250-inch bore, 4-bolt main block. The internals were designed strictly for high-performance with a forged steel crank, forged steel connecting rods, and forged aluminum 11.0:1 TRW pistons. The heads were closed chamber jobs featuring large ports and 2.19-inch diameter intake and 1.88-inch exhaust valves. Carburetion was handled by a single 800-cfm Holley 4-barrel riding on a low-rise, dual plane aluminum intake. Horsepower was rated at an incredible 450 at 5600 rpm. Torque was still pegged at 500 ft-lb though bumped to 3600 rpm. Both figures were no doubt under-rated for insurance purposes.

Only two transmissions offered with the LS6 option, the famous Muncie M22 "Rockcrusher" and the heavy-duty M40

Chevrolet's largest displacement production engine, the 454, meant tremendous power - 450+.

Turbo-Hydramatic autoshifter. Rear-end ratios ranged from 3.31:1 to 4.10:1.

The performance potential of the LS6 can best be described as awesome. In their November 1969 issue, *Car Craft* magazine tested a 4-speed LS6 and turned a fantastic 13.12/107.01 quartermile. In *Muscle Car Review* magazine's list of the all-time fastest fifty muscle cars, the LS6 Chevelle placed a remarkable 5th. If you rule out the 427 Cobra and 427 Corvette as muscle cars of the same genre, then the LS6 ranks 3rd overall. However, the car was fitted with 3.55:1 rear cogs. With 4.10:1 gears, the LS6 was probably one of the very

few production cars capable of 12 second quarters, perhaps the quickest ever built.

The LS6 Chevelles, among many big-inch muscle cars of their time, are considered by many enthusiasts to be the height of the supercar era. Had the movement lasted another year or two, Chevrolet would have released the LS7, the 454 L88. While this is arguable, one thing is for certain, the '71 season brought drastic changes to the automotive world. From then on, the norm was wimp engines with low compression, open chamber heads, meek cams, and emission controls. The days of the earth movers, the days of the LS6, were over.

1970 Hemi SuperBird

Early in the 1966 NASCAR season, Chrysler engineers began to notice problems with the shape of the new Dodge Charger body. Its fastback roof aided in top speed but caused

the back end to lift at high speed, and that made the cars very tricky to drive. The new problem was called aerodynamic lift, the same difference in forces that allows airplanes to become

Still rated at just 425-hp in 1970, Chrysler's legendary 426 cubic inch hemi had awesome potential. Chrysler photo.

A winged Dodge Daytona in action; Richard Brickhouse on his way to winning at Talladega, 1969. Ford Motor Co. photo.

airborne, was solved by a rear spoiler. That suggested to the R&D men that aerodynamics was more important than previously recognized.

During that year, development began on the second generation Charger, a car that would take into account the lessons learned on the high banks. Bill Brownlee, then chief of Dodge Design Studio, set before his group the task of designing a car that was "extremely aerodynamic in image and function, something that looked like it had just come off the track at Daytona." The design penned by Richard Sias was chosen. The car had hidden headlamps, a recessed grill, and a forty-five degree sloped back glass. The latter two proved to be troublesome on the track.

In 1968 when the cars were tested on the high banks, they were indeed fast and ran around 183- to 184-mph. But the Mercurys and Fords were four to five miles-per-hour faster. Again the problem was inherent aerodynamic problems due to the body design of the cars. At high speeds, there was very dangerous front end lift which kept the speeds low. So, once again it was back to the drawing boards.

Chrysler's Special Vehicles and Product Planning Groups got together to come up with design modifications on the existing Charger to keep from having to develop an entire new car. The resulting sketches of the Charger showed the car with a flush mounted grill and back glass. These modifications alone were calculated to boost top speeds by a healthy five miles-per-hour.

Bob McCurry, Vice-president and General Manager of Dodge, gave the go-ahead to proceed with the modifications. The grill was borrowed from the Coronet but the flush mounted back glass was more difficult. A custom rear window as well as a plug to go under it had to be specially made. Also the slope of the back glass was changed from approximately 45 degrees to about 22 degrees, carrying its trailing edge further aft into the trunk lid area. This meant that a new trunk lid had to be produced. After all the modifications were made, wind tunnel and track tests proved it to be a success. The Charger 500 was born. The 500 number was selected on the basis of Bill France's NASCAR production requirements, and 505 were eventually produced.

Yet again Ford stole Chrysler's thunder by beating them to the punch. Early in 1969, Ford introduced its droop nosed, fastback Talladega Torino and Mercury Cyclone Spoiler II. These cars were slightly more aerodynamic than the Charger 500, and that put them ahead. Chrysler was once again playing catch-up.

With data acquired from testing a Charger 500 in the Locheed-Georgia and Wichita State University wind tunnels, another shape was formulated for the Charger. Aerodynamicists John Pointer and Bob Marcel teamed together to come up with sketches for the new car. The resulting drawings showed the Charger with a streamlined fairing on the nose instead of the normal grill and bumper. The sketches, as yet, showed no rear wing.

There was very little opposition to the project from within Dodge, as it was to be treated as a public relations project to get Chrysler back on top of Ford. The goal was a fifteen percent reduction in drag over the Charger 500 and again work was carried out in conjunction with the Lockheed-Georgia and Wichita State wind tunnels.

Various shapes and sizes for the nose cone were tested. extensions between 9- and 18-inches long. Initially, the 9-in. nose showed the greatest reduction in front-end lift but further testing with the addition of a front spoiler to the 18-inch cone proved even better. The optimum placement for the spoiler was found to be 13-inches behind the leading edge of the nose. This combination reduced front axle lift dramatically and reduced the tendency for the front end to "push" into turns.

As the shape of the nose cone was nailed down, work began on a full-size mock-up at Chrysler's proving grounds at Chelsea. The car used as the mule was Bobby Isaac's 1968 Firecracker 400 car. Early testing with the car showed that the nose totally upset the balance of the car; rear-end lift was pronounced. NASCAR rules allowed for the use of rear lip spoilers to control rear axle lift, but wind tunnel tests proved that a rear deck spoiler would have to be huge to have any effect. Attention was then turned to the use of a wing, or inverted aerofoil. The final design was a 58-inch long, 7.5-inch wide wing placed on 23.5-inch high struts over the rear edge of the trunk.

Further wind tunnel testing showed an advantage in dropping the front end over its suspension. This initiated an unforeseen problem: when run at high speeds the front tires rubbed against the top, inside surface of the front fenders. To remedy this problem, holes were cut into the tops of the fenders and covered by backward facing scoops.

What resulted from the wind tunnel testing was one of the wildest cars ever to run on America's highways or a NASCAR track, the Dodge Daytona. The complete package proved to be extremely competitive. From the wind tunnel, it was found that the combined effect of all the aerodynamic add-ons made for a zero or slightly negative total lift. This effect actually helped to hold the Daytona on the track at high speeds and made it one of the most stable cars ever to run the highbanks.

Buddy Baker had this to say about the car: "The car is so stable you can't believe it at first. Normally, when you try to go under someone in a corner, the draft starts to pull the back end of your car around. Most people think that drafting is just the slingshot action when the rear car zips past the first. They ought to ride in a race and find out. When you're drafting, you get quite a ride in a regular car. But the Daytona is just as stable in a draft as it is when it's all by itself on the track..."

Early track testing resulted in speeds of 194-mph with engine problems holding the car back. Later, problem-free testing resulted in speeds over 204-mph.

To make the cars NASCAR legal, Chrysler contracted with Creative Industries to fulfill the 500 units demanded. In 1970, after seeing the success of the Daytona, Plymouth developed its SuperBird, and more construction was undertaken. Though the two cars looked very similar, there were actually many differences in the cars, such as the rear wing, nose cone and back glass shape.

The 1970 NASCAR season proved to be one of the most illustrious Chrysler has ever had: Dodge took 17 wins, Plymouth 21. Ford and Mercury combined for 10 wins, 6 and 4 respectively. At the end of the '70 season, Bill France once again changed the rules and placed limitations on all aerodynamically enhanced cars. It was a move designed to make the aero-MoPars noncompetitive.

By then, it became very clear that the NASCAR game playing was to "outlaw" the season winner for the coming season despite Detroit's conformance to the previous rules. Because the rules changed from year-to-year, new models appeared regularly on the muscle car market. The winged Daytona and SuperBirds were the wildest ever.

The 1970 NASCAR season brought to a close the era of factory aero-wars. It marked the end of the droop-nose fastbacks from Ford and Mercury, and the winged things from Chrysler. They had become the pinnacle of a great age of American cars and culminated an exciting decade, one that can never be again. When the doldrums of the '70s passed well into the '80s, muscle car fans looked back at a golden age of muscle cars and recognized that "ultimates" had lived, the hemi-powered Daytona and SuperBird.

1970 Cougar Eliminator

In closing out the '60s decade of "Total Performance", Ford opted for a new slogan, "The Sizzlin' 70s". Performance was still the word at the beginning of the 1970s, but that changed when "Bunkie" Knudsen left as head of Ford. Ford's philosophy under new management took the sizzle out of Ford performance, and federal mandates made the '70s the decade of legislated mediocrity for all cars.

The legacy of "Total Performance" was that an American marque was, for the first time, on par with or more competitive than the European automakers that had continually scoffed American cars. Ford had beaten everybody in every form of automotive competition and became the world's premier racing marque. No other American manufacturer has ever won a world championship. Ford won several. The

Cougar Eliminator interiors offered wood-grained luxury from door-to-door, a 4-speed and full instrumentation, too.

Ford's Muscle Parts through dealers included dual 4-bbl carbs and all sorts of HiPo equipment for any FE engine.

"Total Performance" commitment produced a wide variety of FoMoCo high performers. Many are known and appreciated far and wide, while others have been forgotten. Because only a few were made and even fewer have survived, some muscle cars are largely unknown. Most of the hot Mercurys fall into this category. This is the story of one of those, the muscular Cougar Eliminator.

Mercury had been among the hottest tickets going throughout the '60s decade. "Dyno Don" Nicholson and Jack Chrisman put Comet Cyclones into drag racing record books throughout America. Nicholson and Ed Schartman put Cougar fear into drag racers throughout the country. On NASCAR's highbanks, the big Mercurys were always a threat to anything and took many wins in the hands of top drivers. On the Trans-Am circuit, Mercury fielded 5-liter Cougars, and in NASCAR's Baby Grand GTC races, Cougars won the 1968 championship.

The foundation had been laid for Mercury to display its muscle image in addition to the refined class displayed in its high-style Cougars. That came about when the Eliminator entered the market as a 1969-1/2 model. Nicholson's drag racers by that name matured into a showroom model.

To test the public's interest, Mercury first showed a prototype Eliminator at the Los Angeles Auto Show on October 24, 1968. The response was so favorable that Matt McLaughlin, Lincoln-Mercury General Manager, proclaimed the Eliminator to be "...the most distinctive entry in the mushrooming musclecar market." The idea for the Eliminator was to offer the Cougar's luxury, styling and class with proven FoMoCo handling and performance. Rather than market their Eliminator as a single type car like the BOSS 302 or BOSS 429 Mustangs, Mercury management chose to offer 5 engine options in their first models, then dropped back to 4 for the 1970 models, the last of the Eliminator line.

With a range of performance from sedate to awesome combined with a vast array of options, Eliminators were a true roll-your-own personalized performance car. Their rear wing and front spoiler, bright colors, bold hood scoop and stripes, were sure eye-catchers. Eliminator was unquestionably a muscle Mercury and very possibly the most distinctive Mercury ever built.

Other than front grill treatment, the '69-1/2 and '70 Eliminators were very similar cars. Both came in only a small range of colors. The '70s, for instance, were white, yellow, orange or blue. The earlier cars came with engines ranging from the base 351W to the BOSS 302, the 390GT, the 428 CJ (Cobra Jet) or the Ram-Air 428 CJ. For 1970, the 351W and 390GT were dropped and replaced by Ford's canted valve 351C-4V. Horsepower ranged from 290 for both the 351W and BOSS 302 (although there were great differences in the performance of those horses), to the 300-hp 351C and the 428 CJ advertised to produce 335-hp, a very conservative figure that kept insurance companies at bay. The Ram-Air CJ was the only option with a fully functional hood scoop for cold air ram induction. It gave real horsepower well into the 400 range. Although the Ram-Air CJ came with a competition suspension system, a Drag Pak option offered still more goodies.

The Eliminator project team planned its cars on the sedate end to give buyers good all-around motoring performance. For the road racing buff, the BOSS 302 package came with all the trick stuff for full-tilt road handling, which included the "CJ-Type Suspension" but with even stiffer rear springs. This package included high rate front springs, .85-inch diameter front anti-sway bar and rear anti-sway bar, heavy duty shocks front and rear, and a special staggered rear shock placement to prevent rear axle wind-up. The BOSS 302 cars also got a mandatory 4-speed transmission, power assisted front disc brakes and an engine rev-limiter mounted on the driver's side front fender inner panel.

For drag racing buffs, the 428 CJ and Ram-Air CJ were astounding tire burners. With just a little tuning beyond showroom condition, the Ram-Air turned in 13.91 second quarters at 103.92-mph in magazine track tests. The BOSS 302 Cougar ran 14.92s at 98 flat while the 351W Eliminator claimed respectable 15 second quarters at 90-mph.

Both close- and wide-ratio manual transmissions with Hurst shifters were available, and final drive gearing ranged from open 3.25 types to 4.30 Traction-Lok differentials. Thus, performance was about anything you wanted and made the

Cougar Eliminator fairly close to being all things to all performance car buyers.

Options included all sorts of power assisted features, steering and brakes for instance, including front disc brakes. Many other options were on Mercury's long list; air conditioning, sports consoles, Polyglas F70x14 Belted tires, decor and lighting groups, Cougar only sport wheels and with hound's tooth cloth insert upholstery.

Standard features included concealed front headlights with blacked-out vacuum-operated doors, sequential rear turn signals, Ford's styled steel wheels, high-back bucket seats, and the Cougar image. For a rather heavy Grand Touring style car in the European tradition of personal luxury, the Eliminator was an excellent package: beauty, comfort and thrilling performance.

Sliding into the interior of an Eliminator brought before the driver a full set of needle type gauges, a clock and padded wood-grain luxury all around. Comfortable form-fitting bucket seats and a bench rear seat gave space for 5 passengers. Ample space in the trunk for traveling made the Eliminator a well thought out, yet eye-catching highway cruiser. But the wing and spoiler were not just for looks. Mercury engineers claimed they achieved a 10% reduction in drag at high speed.

Their appeal was worth a lot more.

At a base price of $3499.50, a Cougar Eliminator was quite a car. For a list of $4526.30, a heavily performance optioned BOSS 302 Eliminator was a lot of car, and for about the same price a Ram-Air 428 CJ Eliminator was downright wicked.

Regardless of engine or transmission combination, Cougar Eliminators were meant to handle. With their competition-derived suspensions and neutral steering, roll angles through curves varied only slightly. They were, simply put, Mercury's road huggers. They could take the turns that made other cars squirm with discomfort, and a touch of big cube V-8 power brought on great pleasures in driving through twisty bits and satisfying admiration from the performance set, who knew at a glance that the Eliminator was something special.

So far, production breakdown by engine has not been fully determined. But any engine combination must be rare because there were only 2,411 '69-1/2 Eliminators and 2,200 '70 models built. It is known that 450 BOSS 302 cars were produced, and Kar Kraft built 2 with the BOSS 429 engines before the decision was made to rule out that option. Those two became drag racers, naturally.

1970 4-4-2 Oldsmobile W-30

From its rather unsure beginning, the 4-4-2 emerged as one of the most successful of all the youth-oriented muscle cars. In 1965 Olds increased the engine size to 400 cubes in order to gain a displacement and power advantage over the GTO. The legendary W-30 option first became available in 1967. It included fresh air pickups between the headlights feeding into a single 4-barrel carb and special engine mods designed to improve power and overall performance.

1968 marked the beginning of the Hurst involvement with Olds which created some of the meanest street rockets yet

seen. That year was also the introduction of a new, smaller body size that lasted through 1972. The Hurst/Olds, with a monstrous 455 cubic inch V-8, defined what the executive muscle car should be, a luxurious boulevard cruiser capable of full-tilt take-off when provoked. There was also a Hurst/Olds in 1969, one of the most flamboyant cars ever to drive America's highways. The Hurst Oldsmobiles paved the way for factory-produced 455-inch cars in 1970.

For the first time, Oldsmobile offered the 455 as the base engine in the 4-4-2. Although there were no Hurst cars that

For 1970, the top Olds performer was the 455-cid W-30. Advertised at just 370-hp, this ram-air engine went higher.

The most imaginative advertising of the muscle car era was Dr. Oldsmobile and his Youngmobiles. Oldsmobile photos.

year, there was a car that offered everything the H/O did. The 1970 4-4-2 equipped with the W-30 455 has been called the best Olds performance machine ever built. The W-30 option called for Oldsmobile's "select fit" program for the engine. What this meant was that the engines were built using higher quality control, selecting the best internal components to ensure extra strength and reliability. The engines were factory rated at just 370 horsepower, another underrating ploy. The most outstanding aspect of the W-30 engine was the huge amount of torque it generated. Rated at 500 ft-lb at 3600 rpm, it could literally melt rear tires.

Benefitting from the "select fit" process, to begin with, the W-30 engine option included many other goodies. The engine was topped off with a lightweight, cast aluminum intake manifold with a large Rochester 4-barrel with 1.375-inch diameter primaries and 2.25-inch secondaries. Feeding the huge carb with fresh, cool outside air was the W-25, all-fiberglass hood with dual integral hood scoops. Just under the scoops was a special air cleaner box with a vacuum-operated flapper valve to direct the air into the carburetor when the go-pedal was romped.

The engines were cammed relative to the type of transmissions ordered in the cars. The M-21 close-ratio four-speed equipped cars came with a 328 degree duration, .472-inch lift high-performance stick. Because the cam was such that the engine produced minimal vacuum, the four-speed cars came with manual front disc/rear drum brakes. When the M-40 Turbo-Hydramatic was optioned, the cars came with a milder .472-inch lift 285/287 dual pattern cam. With automatics the cars came standard with power front discs and rear drums.

An optional center console could be ordered for between the front bucket seats. With it, the automatic's standard column shifter was replaced by a floor-mounted Hurst Dual Gate unit. With the Dual Gate, drivers had the option of either leaving the tranny in drive or manually going through the gears. In the manual gate, there was a spring-loaded lockout to prevent an accidental shift into neutral.

True to the 4-4-2's heritage, the 1970 W-30 package was well integrated and balanced. The 4-4-2s had a longstanding reputation for being extremely good handling cars for their

size and weight. Oldsmobile's engineers realized that the added mass of the huge 455-cid engine meant the suspension had to be beefed up. To control body roll under hard cornering, .937-inch diameter front and .875-inch diameter rear anti-sway bars reduced body roll. The rear anti-sway bar used boxed lower control arms to add stability. The cars also came with G70x14 inch tires for better traction.

The W-30 option included many dress-up and styling features. There was no mistaking the hood paint scheme and bold stripes running along the car's lower belt line. A W-30 emblem resided on each front fender. The standard W-25 hood had wide stripes along the tops of its coops and a set of chrome, twist-down hood locks. On the doors were racing-style mirrors. The driver's side was remote controlled. In an effort to reduce weight, red fiberglass front inner-fender liners were used and the amount of body sound deadener was reduced. The interiors reflected Oldsmobile's luxury status in GM's product line. Standard was a set of high-backed bucket seats, simulated burled walnut trim, and door-to-door nylon twist carpet.

In the area of performance the '70 4-4-2 W-30 was a force to be taken seriously. Standard fare was a 3.42:1 limited-slip rear-end with optional units ranging up to 3.91:1. Dealer installed ratios were available up to 5.00:1. The cars were definitely a roll your own performance machine. A *Hot Rod* magazine test report showed that a completely showroom stock '70 W-30 was capable of running the quarter in 13.98 seconds at 100.78-mph. Olds engineers put together specifications for all sorts of high-performance applications that could lower ETs by more than a half-second. That made the cars extremely competitive, so much so that in 1971, the "W-Machines" won NHRA's Manufacturer's Cup.

The '70 Olds W-30 is a perfect example of the zenith of the muscle car age. For 1971, performance took a nose-dive as compression ratios were cut, cams became milder, and emission controls became the norm. The vigor and youth of the '60s peaked in 1970 and began to die when the '71 models were introduced in the fall of that year. By '72, the muscle car rage was all but gone. Perhaps better than any other manufacturer, Oldmobile factory advertisements showing "Dr. Oldsmobile and his Youngmobiles" describe the temper of the time.

1970 Pontiac GTO Judge

By 1970, popularity of the Pontiac GTO had waned considerably. Sales of the Tempest/LeMans/GTO line were less than half the volume of 1968. The GTO had been restyled several times and had gotten bigger and put on weight through the '68 models. When each GM division inherited the new corporate-wide body style with the '68 models, the GTO/4-4-2/Grand Sport types of cars were set through the mid-'70s. At Pontiac, the GTO was no longer the top muscle car in America. Its performance and popularity, as well as sales, were on the skids. One factor affecting the popularity of the GTO was the lack of a racing heritage. Racing during the '60s was going on everywhere and was a good way to improve cars and keep them in the public eye. By then, there were plenty of muscle cars to choose from and many had bigger engines, better performance, and lower cost than the GTO. It was clear that something had to be done to bolster Pontiac's performance image.

In mid-1968, Pontiac conceived the idea of developing a GTO super performance car which would be named The Judge. The car was first announced in the summer of 1968 and was advertised month after month in high-performance magazines, even though it was not to be available to the public until the following year. The car was introduced to the press along with the new Firebird in December of 1968 at Riverside International Raceway in California and was presented to the public on March 8, 1969 at the Chicago Autoshow.

The Judge came with many performance options that stirred lots of interest. Some examples are the 400-4V (High Output) engine which was designated the Ram Air III, functional ram-air hood scoops, heavy-duty 3-speed gearbox, dual exhausts, and a wild exterior graphics scheme that was sure to be an eye-catcher. Pontiac listed performance options that would be available on the car to include the 400-4V Ram Air IV engine, a close-ratio 4-speed trans with a Hurst shifter, a hood-mounted tach, and power front disc brakes.

The cars began arriving at Pontiac dealers a month after the Chicago show in what Pontiac called Day-Glo colors, a fitting description. The first few thousand cars were painted in a cross between yellow and orange, and looked as if they could indeed glow at night. Over each wheel well arch were green, yellow, and white striped decals that resembled eyebrows. On the rear deck was a prominent wing which was useless for performance at normal driving speeds but made the car look as if it was doing 150-mph while sitting still. The tach was mounted on the hood enclosed in a small bubble and was well within the driver's peripheral vision. Also on the hood was a set of small scoops, with decals reading "Ram Air" on the sides. These ducted fresh air to the engine.

Aside from the eye-popping exterior, there was another wild element to the car. It was under the hood. Both engine options were 400 cubic inch mills. When *Motorcade* magazine tested a Judge equipped with the Ram Air III engine and a 4-speed gearbox, they found it to be quite a performer. They related to readers: "The first time you really drop the hammer you are in for a shock. If the needle on the hood-mounted tach is anywhere above 3500 rpm here is what happens: The back of the seat kicks you smartly in the shoulders and the steering wheel tries to move away. At the same time your ears are being assaulted by a piercing shriek and the back end of the car begins to move slowly but steadily around toward the left." *Motorcade*'s test drivers were able to ring a respectable 14.59 second 99.44-mph quartermile pass out of the car. It had more potential but was held back by poor quality tires which spun instead of hooking up with the track. Another factor was excessive weight that had to be set into motion. That slowed low-end acceleration. The Judge, at 3,960 pounds, had put on quite a bit of tonnage since the first GTO back in 1964.

The Judge was a well-balanced muscle car. In addition to offering excellent performance it could also be mild mannered. *Motorcade* called it "an almost perfect balance be-

Pontiac's quick-winding Ram Air III or Ram Air IV engines were the heart of the Judge.

Beautiful and fast, the GTO Judge continued the theme of the first GTO but failed to capture the public's imagination.

ego and practicality." To accomplish this feat, the engineers at Pontiac chose a relatively mild cam rather than one that would jar your fillings out every time the engine turned over. This meant that the Judge would be extremely tractable at low speeds to make in-town driving no problem. Another benefit of the mild camming was high gas mileage, rated at 15-mpg on the open highway, good for the time. Remember that good, high octane gasoline was available back then for about 35 cents a gallon!

The GTO Judge sold relatively well for a mid-year entry. Pontiac records show that a total of 6,833 units were sold in 1969. This was enough to justify carrying the Judge over to the 1970 model year, but while the car generated great interest and some controversy, it failed to achieve its primary goal: to boost Pontiac's performance image into the front ranks of the muscle car sales arena. But there were so many muscle cars on the market during the late sixties that no car could have the same impact as the first GTO. Though the car was lost in a sea of muscle during the late '60s, it has emerged as a highly sought after collector car by today's GTO enthusiasts.

1970 Hemi 'Cuda

The 1970 and '71 Plymouth Hemi 'Cuda has been called the pinnacle of the muscle car era. While this is an arguable

The "Shaker" air scoop was attached to the engine and shook with it, thus the name. 426 cubic inches, 425-hp.

Functional simplicity at its best, but 150+ on the speedo was a reminder. This is a Hemi 'Cuda.

point, one thing is for certain, they were one of the "baddest" factory-built street machines ever seen, not just in the muscle car era, but of all time.

The Barracuda nameplate had been used since 1965. The marque was Plymouth's entry into the ponycar arena. Although the early cars were reasonably good performers with small block 273s and 318s, they failed to capture the enthusiasm that the Mustangs and later Camaros did. One reason was that their styling did not generate the appeal in the youth market as did the Ford and Chevrolet products. When the Barracuda line was totally redesigned for the 1970 model year, it became a styling hit with the long hood, short deck theme, but industry-wide sales were in a slump and so were 'Cuda sales. The following year was even worse.

The 1970 and '71 Barracudas came in several packages ranging from high-style grocery getters to ground-pounding super stock winners. The cars could be ordered to do just about anything a performance car buyer could want. For the road race enthusiast who saw himself zipping around tight hairpin turns like Dan Gurney, there was the AAR 'Cuda. These cars were Gurney's special edition All American Racing ponycars, and were Plymouth's answer to the Ford BOSS 302 Mustang and Chevrolet Z28 Camaro. Then there was the straight-liner, the awesome 426 hemi-motivated 'Cuda, a legend among legends. These cars were meant for the drag racing enthusiast who pictured himself blasting down the quartermile like Ronnie Sox.

The hemi had been redesigned for the 1966 model year in order to make it a more streetable engine. The "Street Hemi" was first used in B-body cars consisting of the Coronet, Charger, Belvedere, and Satellite models. It was this engine that went on to power the 'Cuda. The later street engines differed in many ways from the early, race-bred hemi. Chrysler chose to change the cam timing and valve train to improve low-end torque and longevity. Mechanical lifters were retained, but the cam was changed to a milder .460-inch lift, 276-degree duration stick. The compression ratio was dropped from 12.5:1 to 10.5:1 so that the engines would run on premium pump gas rather than require racing fuel. In an effort to reduce engine noise, steel tube headers were replaced by a set of cast iron units. The dual 4-barrel aluminum intake manifold was redesigned to include an exhaust heat chamber to improve

cold weather starts and driveability. The last major change was to the carburetor set-up and linkage. Instead of using two fours on a cross-ram intake, the carbs were placed inline with a new progressive linkage to improve fuel economy.

With all their changes, the engines were still excellent performers and used many of the race engine's bulletproof bottom-end components. The forged steel crank and cross-bolt main bearings were retained, as were the chromium alloy steel valves, beefier connecting rods, and roller timing chain. The engines were still rated at 425 horsepower at 5000 rpm and 490 ft-lb of torque at 4000 rpm.

The car's driveline also received a great deal of attention to ensure that it could stand up to the engine's brutal power. There was a choice of transmissions that included the excellent 3-speed 727 Torqueflite automatic and the A-833 4-speed manual box. While the automatic, when equipped with the optional Slick Shift, was a pleasure, any fun from rowing through the 4-speed box was canceled out by the balky shifter linkage. Final drive gears were by Dana and came in many different available ratios.

The performance potential of the Hemi 'Cuda placed it right at the top of every muscle car built. *Car Craft* magazine tested one of the cars in 1969 and ran a scalding 13.10 seconds at 107.12-mph! And that was with a not-so-inspiring 3.54:1 rear-end ratio. With a 4.10, it would certainly have dipped into the 12 second range. Which muscle car is chosen to be THE fastest showroom stock vehicle continues to be hotly debated among enthusiasts, but pick three, and the Hemi 'Cuda has to be one of them.

Not only did the cars offer tremendous performance, they also offered beautiful styling with nicely appointed interiors. Driver convenience was one of the car's themes. Instruments were mounted in a hooded panel that contained four pods. If the optional Rallye Cluster was specified, an ammeter, fuel gauge, temperature gauge, tachometer and clock were included. Comfortable and attractive high-back bucket seats were accented by an optional center console that was tilted toward the driver. While most Hemi 'Cudas came with floor-mounted shifters, a few were delivered with column-mounted shifts.

Outside, there was a myriad of wild and crazy colors ranging from Lemon Twist Yellow to Hemi Orange. Other options included a sinister-looking, fully functional, shaker hood scoop, rear deck mounted wing, and a variety of stripe packages. The cars also came in coupe and convertible body styles with sharp-looking Rallye wheels and wide rubber at all four corners.

The Hemi 'Cudas were produced in very low numbers, which has contributed to today's high collector interest. In 1970, there were only 652 hardtops built, 284 equipped with 4-speeds and 368 with Torqueflites. For the 1971 model year,

there were even fewer. Just 108 hardtops, 60 4-speeds and 48 Torqueflites. Seven were convertibles, 2 with 4-speeds and 5 with Torqueflites.

1971 marked the end of the muscle car era. With tighter emission controls came lower compression ratios and mild cams. De-tuning the once mighty big blocks became the new charter. Smog pumps and exhaust recirculaters emasculated the power that muscle cars could produce. Even the legendary hemi could not survive that.

1971 Hemi Challenger "Motown Missile"

The hemi 'Cudas practically owned Super Stock Eliminator and Pro Stock drag racing classes from 1968 through '72. Ronnie Sox won more class and eliminator titles than any other driver, all in Hemi 'Cudas. His toughest competition was Don Carlton in the "Motown Missile" Dodge Challenger and Bill "Grumpy" Jenkins and his Camaro. By 1971, the MoPars basically competed against themselves in Pro Stock. The quickest of them all that year was the Missile.

That car was a Dodge Division test vehicle whose story began back in 1970. The invoice for the car, dated 01-28-70, read to ship it to Chrysler's Product Planning Garage and bill it to Chrysler Motors Corporation, Open Account. The Manufacturer's Statement of Origin of that date shows that the car was the property of Chrysler Corporation, and the Car Order form stated:

"To be used as basis for building the Dept. 1277 automatic transmission test and development car - Ted Spehar."

From the Product Planning Garage, the Invoice-Shipper read to assign the car to Drag Programs & Drag Liaison, Dept. #1277 CWO-73004, and it was shipped to Spehar Performance in Royal Oak, Michigan.

The invoice description of the car was: Challenger R/T - 2HT Serial #JS23-ROB-242444 followed by the same "test car" notation given on the Car Order form.

Factory drag racing cars are extremely difficult to trace, but determining the origin of the Motown Missile is an example of what it takes to establish the authenticity of such a car. What can be concluded is that it was a one-of-a-kind drag/development car originating deep in the heart of Chrysler Corporation.

Although the serial number does not identify it as a factory Super Stock car, it is a factory hemi car as given by the "R" in the VIN code. Development of the car into a Pro Stock drag racer had been assigned to Spehar Performance, a captive competition development firm to Chrysler. Ted Spehar was the man responsible for developing the car into the legend it became.

The car originally came in "body-in-white" and went through extensive modification to become the black Motown Missile. Along with the latest of everything, it was fitted with a full roll cage, a full-house hemi engine and an automatic transmission, at first. Lightweight body panels and fiberglass front-end components and rear deck lid helped reduce weight as did

One of the premier drag racers of the classic era of Pro Stock, the factory days of 1969 through '71, was Ted Spehar's Motown Missile. Driven by Don Carlton, it was the quickest of them all.

By the late-'60s, Pro Stock and Modified Production hemi MoPars were running dual-plug heads. Single plugs are shown here. Output was said to be well over 700-hp for duals.

others, one of the main features of the Motown Missile was its set of twin-plug heads. Two giant 4-bbl carbs on a tunnel-ram intake surrounded by sixteen spark plug wires was an uncommon sight. Likable Don Carlton from Lenoir, North Carolina, who had driven for the Sox & Martin team, was signed on by Spehar to race the car. Comparing the cars and the drivers shows that Carlton was the quickest Pro Stock driver in the country in '71. He set an all-time low ET of 9.48 seconds at 146.10-mph.

Carlton won Super Stock Eliminator at the AHRA Grand American in Palm Beach, Florida. (April 16-18, 1971) with a time of 9.71 and 141.50-mph. Although Ronnie Sox in the Sox & Martin 'Cuda won five of a possible six NHRA Pro Stock titles by being cool and fast behind the wheel, his car posted a best time of 9.58 (at 142.85-mph) during the NHRA Nationals in Indianapolis (Sept. 2-6, 1971) where he won. Carlton and the Missile ran a 9.55 but lost in a mix-up among the lights on the 'tree that gave Sox a head start. By this time, the Missile had been fitted with a 4-speed manual.

It was at the NHRA Grandnationals in Quebec (August 13-15, 1971) that Carlton set the lowest ET, 9.48 seconds for the quartermile. The best a non-MoPar could do that season was "Dyno Don" Nicholson's Maverick that took the NHRA Summernationals at Englishtown, NJ (July 16-18, 1971) where he won Pro Stock Eliminator with a 9.63 at 141.73-mph. There just wasn't much left by the Chrysler hemis.

Ted Spehar and company did the Motown Missile right. Its 426 hemi with aluminum heads was machined by Diamond Racing Engines, and surprisingly enough, quite a few of its internals were stock factory items, although probably not the sort the average guy could buy unless he knew the numbers of the special quality hardware. When Ronnie Sox protested the Missile's low ETs at Indianapolis, it checked out legal, much to his embarrassment, and proved that the black Dodge Challenger could trip the lights quicker than his red, white, and blue Plymouth 'Cuda.

While looking over the NHRA Pro Stock results from 1970 and '71 (page 120), note that of 12 top events, hemi-powered Dodges or Plymouths took 9. Of those, Ronnie "Mr. Cool" Sox put on quite a show taking 6! Those were the great days of Plymouth and Dodge hemi cars at the drag strip.

an aluminum hood and custom-fabricated engine compartment sheet metal. From time-to-time, the car was heavily instrumented to determine what went on during drag tests, stresses, loads and such, and two Chrysler engineers were assigned to the car. Folklore has it that the factory spent around $100,000 on the car before it was sold in 1971 for $20,000.

Like other top hemi cars, those driven by Sox, Landy and

Super Stock class winners, NHRA 1970

Winternationals: Pomona, CA Jan. 30 - Feb. 1

SS/A	Ronnie Sox	'68 Hemi 'Cuda	10.44/117.03
SS/B	Jim Johnson	'69 AMX	11.02/123.00
SS/C	Ken Dondero	'67 Ford	11.22/122.61
SS/D	Disqualified		
SS/E	Dick Landy	'69 Dodge	11.15/122.00
SS/F	Geno Redd	'68 Mustang CJ	11.30/122.61
SS/G	Ken McLellan	'69 Mustang CJ	12.31/115.23
SS/H	Barrie Poole	'68 Mustang CJ	11.46/99.33
SS/AA	Don Grotheer	'68 Hemi 'Cuda	10.62/114.79
SS/BA	Jim Clark	'65 Hemi Dodge	11.07/125.17
SS/CA	Jim Morton	'67 Ford	11.35/122.95
SS/DA	Lee Cameron	'67 Dodge	11.41/109.35
SS/EA	John Teddar	'69 Plymouth	11.96/105.63
SS/FA	Disqualifed		
SS/GA	Bill Allis	'69 Mustang CJ	11.63/114.79
SS/HA	Ken Myers	'68 Mustang CJ	11.34/117.34

Springnationals: Dallas, TX June 12 - 14

SS/A	Ed Hedrick	'68 Hemi 'Cuda	10.75/132.93
SS/B	No Entries		
SS/C	No Entries		
SS/D	George Warren	'70 AMX	11.07/106.63
SS/E	Dave Van Luke	'67 Ford	11.70/118.42
SS/F	John Elliot	'68 Mustang CJ	11.15/109.62
SS/G	Ken McLellan	'69 Mustang CJ	11.35/99.00
SS/H	Barrie Poole	'69 Mustang CJ	10.55/98.79
SS/AA	Judy Lilly	'68 Hemi 'Cuda	10.34/131.77
SS/BA	Tom Crutchfield	'65 Hemi Dodge	10.95/124.48
SS/CA	No Entries		
SS/DA	Ed Ward	'67 Plymouth	11.28/120.80
SS/EA	Bob Lambeck	'70 Dodge	11.68/111.80
SS/FA	Stacy Shields	'78 Mustang CJ	11.46/120.00
SS/GA	Bill Allis	'69 Mustang CJ	12.06/115.08
SS/HA	Bob Glidden	'69 Mustang CJ	11.87/116.12

US Nationals: Indianapolis, IN Sept. 3 - 7

SS/A	Jim Wick	'69 Hemi 'Cuda	10.55/131.19
SS/B	Ken Barnhart	'69 Camaro	11.16/121.13
SS/C	Ed Capullo	'67 Camaro	11.39/122.44
SS/D	Lorin Downing	'69 AMX	10.79/126.05
SS/E	Ernie Musser	'69 Chevrolet	11.43/121.72
SS/F	John Elliot	'68 Mustang CJ	11.17/114.64
SS/G	Ken McLellan	'69 Mustang CJ	11.15/122.78
SS/H	Barrie Poole	'69 Mustang CJ	11.26/113.06
SS/AA	Ron Mancini	'68 Hemi Dodge	10.41/110.15
SS/BA	Tom Crutchfield	'65 Hemi Dodge	10.80/127.11
SS/CA	Jim Morton	'69 Ford	12.37/113.03
SS/DA	Gary Ostrich	'70 'Cuda	11.22/113.63
SS/EA	Ray Allen	'70 Chevrolet	11.37/119.68
SS/FA	Dave Morgan	'68 Mustang CJ	11.60/120.32
SS/GA	Bill Allis	'69 Mustang CJ	11.70/104.52
SS/HA	Hubert Platt	'69 Mustang CJ	11.88/115.08

Super Stock, Stock and Pro Stock Eliminators, NHRA 1970-71

Winternationals:

1970	Super Stock	Barrie Poole	'68 Mustang CJ SS/H	11.26/117.34
	Stock	Dick Charbonneau	'67 Ford E/S wagon	12.06/117.03
	Pro Stock	Bill Jenkins	'69 Camaro	9.98/138.67
1971	Super Stock	Barrie Poole	'69 Mustang CJ SS/H	11.28/121.62
	Stock	Dave Boertman	'71 Dodge L/SA	(NA) (NA)
	Pro Stock	Ronnie Sox	'71 Hemi 'Cuda	9.86/141.20

Gatornationals:

1970	Super Stock	Ed Hedrick	'69 Camaro SS/DA	11.28/111.94
	Stock	Tom Callahan	'67 Plymouth F/SA	12.56/92.61
	Pro Stock	Bill Jenkins	'69 Camaro	9.90/138.46
1971	Super Stock	Carroll Fink	'71 Plymouth SS/DA	12.01/84.50
	Stock	Dave Boertman	'71 Dodge J/SA	12.74/73.56
	Pro Stock	Ronnie Sox	'71 Hemi 'Cuda	9.60/141.95

Springnationals:

1970	Super Stock	John Elliot	'68 Mustang CJ SS/F	11.29/110.97
	Stock	Marvin Ripes	'57 Chevy M/SA	13.42/101.23
	Pro Stock	Ronnie Sox	'70 Hemi 'Cuda	10.02/136.77
1971	Super Stock	Carroll Fink	'71 Plymouth SS/DA	11.19/112.50
	Stock	Bobby Warren	'69 Chevrolet K/S	12.32/110.97
	Pro Stock	Ronnie Sox	'71 Hemi 'Cuda	9.70/143.08

Summernationals:

1970	Super Stock	Ron Mancini	'68 Hemi Dodge SS/AA	11.14/131.19
	Stock	Dave Boertman	'69 Chevrolet N/SA	13.60/81.22
	Pro Stock	Dick Landy	'70 Hemi Dodge	10.38/130.43
1971	Super Stock	Ken Montgomery	'69 Hemi 'Cuda SS/BA	10.88/107.85
	Stock	Judi Boertman	Dodge L/SA	13.98/71.37
	Pro Stock	Don Nicholson	'70 Maverick	9.63/141.73

US Nationals:

1970	Super Stock	Ron Mancini	'68 Hemi Dodge SS/AA	10.33/131.77
	Stock	Dave Boertman	'69 Chevrolet N/SA	13.48/100.67
	Pro Stock	Herb McCandless	'70 Plymouth	9.98/138.03
1971	Super Stock	Greg Charney	'65 Hemi Dodge SS/B	11.01/106.88
	Stock	Al Corda	'64 Plymouth E/SA	11.73/117.18
	Pro Stock	Ronnie Sox	'70 Hemi 'Cuda	9.58/142.85

World Finals:

1970	Super Stock	Ray Allen	'70 Chevrolet SS/EA	12.37/74.50
	Stock	Bobby Warren	'69 Chevrolet J/S	12.21/111.30
	Pro Stock	Ronnie Sox	'70 Hemi 'Cuda	10.00/136.36
1971	Super Stock	Ken McLellan	'69 Mustang CJ SS/G	11.56/117.95
	Stock	Dave Boertman	'71 Dodge	12.91/95.84
	Pro Stock	Mike Fons	'71 Challenger	10.05/135.95

Trans-Am battles among 5-liter ponycars became war between the manufacturers in 1967. New that year were Cougars and Camaros. Mark Donohue ran Roger Penske's private entry Sunoco Camaro. Old pros were '66 champs Jerry Titus in Carroll Shelby's Terlingua Racing Team Mustangs. Ford Motor Co. photo.

Trans-Am Warriors

The origin of Trans-Am (Trans-American Sedan Championship) was simply nothing more than another kind of racing to do. The series grew out of an opener for the 1966 12-Hours of Sebring. The late Alec Ulmann, Sebring promoter, was a great champion of automotive competition and used pre-race attractions to draw more entrants and spectators. In 1966, he presented the public with a series designed to pit small but powerful European 2-liter sedans against larger American 5-liter cars. Of the 44 starters, only 9 were American, and almost nobody cared.

Almost nobody. Well-known driver, Dr. Dick Thompson, the "flying dentist" from Washington, D.C., was the first entrant in the 4-Hour Governor's Cup Race for Sedans. His car was a maroon notchback Mustang that set the fastest lap at over 88-mph. Bob Tullius entered a Dodge Dart. A couple of Corvairs promised little, but A. J. came to race, and that said a lot. The other 39 cars were European, and one of the factory Alfa Romeo GTAs went on to win. Tullius finished second, and Thompson was last.

The fact that Indy 500 winner A. J. Foyt was in the sedan race gave it instant credibility. Press people converged on the personable Foyt, and their coverage began spreading the word to America that a new racing series had begun. For the Trans-Am series, SCCA had adopted international regulations set down in FIA Groups 1 and 2 specifications.

It was a slow start that first year, but it grew. The main attraction was that the American sedans were loud and fast, they could outrun the European cars, and more importantly, they were nothing more than stripped-down factory-built cars. Here was road racing that enthusiasts could do on modest budgets.

The rules were simple, but would "stock car" racing with the little sedans fit into the Sports Car Club of America's idea of road racing? Ulmann's single race feature was one thing, but a full-blown series? That would require sufficient response from racers to make it a real thing.

Until the early '60s, SCCA had not been interested in professional racing and always cast its lot with amateur sportsmen who raced for the thrill of it on weekends, then went back to work on Mondays. The gentlemen racers of that time had an admiring audience, America's "baby boomers", who were reaching driving age. Things changed rapidly. Enthusiasm for racing during that time grew into an atmosphere of high technical competence from factories supported by a rapidly growing cadre of excellent drivers who were paid for their services. Not only did racing attract potential customers to new car showrooms, it also attracted spirited young men who aspired to be professional racing drivers.

In this country, Ford was leading the way with its "Total Performance" commitment to challenge and beat Ferrari in world class endurance racing. Corvette had long been a favorite road racer, led by Dr. Thompson's 5 SCCA national championships in them, but Carroll Shelby sent the 'Vettes down a side track when he introduced the small block Ford-powered Cobra in 1963. Chrysler Corporation had nothing similar, but bought into England's Rootes Group and acquired the Sunbeam Tiger in 1965. All that completed the loop; kids wanted to race and go to races, the factories wanted to see their cars win races and to sell more new cars. The Trans-Am sedan series was born in this environment. It was bound to succeed. Part of the reason that success was assured was Ford's new youth-oriented Mustang that was introduced in the spring of 1964. They were a big part of Trans-Am racing right from the beginning.

America's high-performance enthusiasts were primed for sedan road racing. With cars that came directly from the factories, like drag racing, here was another way for the kids to brag about "their" cars. And that sold more cars. They especially loved the small Mustang and made the new car a

After 2 years of winning road races, Shelby's T-A Mustangs were the best developed. Titus won the title again in '67.

Bob Tullius and his Group 44 Dodge Dart were hard to beat at Daytona in the early years of 5-liter racing.

market sensation when a total of 303,408 were produced by the end of the year. In 1965, another 580,187 rolled out of Ford factories. The following year, just in time for the first Trans-Am season, another 580,767 of the first ponycars were produced. By the end of '65, 556,721 Dodge Darts had been built along with 104,965 Plymouth Barracudas, and each of these cars had high-performance models in showrooms. Trans-Am was the showcase for these cars.

Many other small cars were on the highways. Ford's Falcon soared past 2.3 million by then, and Chevy's Corvair, Ralph Nader's nightmare, had topped 1.6 million. 710,317 of the small Buick Special and another 752,096 Olds F-85s, some V-8 powered, added to the growth of small cars produced in this country. The Trans-Am was a place they could be raced. Four Mustangs on the starting grid for the Sebring 4-Hour that year was no mistake. It was the sign of great things to come.

The crowds of spectators grew that first year and watched Mustang and Barracuda go into the 7th and final round tied for the championship. That race was at Riverside, 135 laps around the 2.6-mile desert raceway. When the fans looked up, they saw Cobra World Champion Carroll Shelby's rig roll in. With Ford's top road racing team there, Trans-Am had become big time. *Sports Car Graphic* editor Jerry Titus, who was one of Shelby's top B/Production G.T.350 Mustang team drivers, rolled up to the line in what must have been the most sophisticated American car seen that year in the Trans-Am. He proceeded to set a new lap record (91.85-mph) to win the pole position, then flooded the car's engine at the start and left some 30 positions down. Within a few laps of blasting around the little cars, he was near the front. Then an attempted pass in a curve sent him over a corner marker that broke the car's oil filter. After a pit stop for repairs, he was back with such aggressive driving that he broke his own record with a 92.58-mph lap during the race.

And he won! And Ford won the first Trans-Am Manufacturer's Championship. Not only were the Shelby G.T.350 Mustangs racing winners, fans had seen that the "regular" factory cars were also winners. What they didn't know, but could easily have guessed, was that the cars were the same underneath. Soon, Shelby American was advertising made-to-order, complete Trans-Am prepared cars for sale.

Points were scored for cars finishing as low as 9th, so not only were wins important, finishing was also. There were more Mustangs than any other make, and points added up. The Tullius Dart won big victories at Daytona and at Marlboro, Maryland. With more Darts in the series, Dodge might have been a real threat to win the championship, but the factory men were too busy with stock car racing and hemis to pay attention to the little guys road racing. Ford didn't see it that way; Trans-Am championships were important enough to send the best.

In January 1967, George Wintersteen, a Roger Penske associate, picked up the 12th Z28 Camaro built from the factory and drove it back to Penske's shops in Reading, Pennsylvania. They had just three weeks to prepare it for the Daytona-300 Trans-Am (Feb. 3, drivers Mark Donohue and Wintersteen) and the Daytona Continental 24-Hour (Feb. 4-5, drivers Wintersteen and Joe Welch). This car, #36, raced under the dual banner of Roger Penske Chevrolet and Wintersteen Racing, Inc.

With little experience with such cars, no one was sure how to set it up. Mechanic "Murph" Mayberry and Donohue "guessed" what it would take to produce a sedan that could handle the infield road course and highbanks at Daytona. Their selection of 1200 lb/inch front springs and 400 lb/inch rears made for rock-solid, if not atrocious handling. It was a beginning.

The battle heated up considerably in that year. New in showrooms were the Camaro and Mercury's Cougar. Chevrolet was still "We Don't Race", but Penske and Donohue saw the opportunity presented by the Trans-Am. So did Mercury. Bud Moore of Spartanburg, South Carolina, was contracted to run a 3-car team of Cougars for no less than Dan Gurney, Parnelli Jones and accomplished sports car driver Ed Leslie. Mercury was serious about winning the series, too, and the parent firm was as much a rival as were the Penske Camaros.

Daytona in 1967 was SCCA's first Trans-Am race of the season. It was also the first showing of a Camaro in road racing competition. Four were there. Among the Mustang teams, Shelby was back with "Terlingua Racing Team" Mustangs for Titus and Thompson. So was Bob Tullius in a lone Dodge Dart. They were all there to begin the 9-race points championship schedule. Tullius was to win the enduro, the make's last.

Development of the new Z28 Camaro into a winning road racer took some time. Without Mark Donohue, they would not have been competitive.

Mark Donohue, August 8, 1967. Marlboro, Md.

Mercury aimed for the Trans-Am championship in '67 when they formed Team Cougar with Gurney and Jones as lead drivers.

All the big guns had troubles.

With his boyish good looks, Donohue had also received the moniker of "Captain Nice". He looked like a teenager, but he was fast becoming a seasoned and aggressive professional and was certainly a tough competitor. He followed his first national title with two more in the seats of a Lotus 23B and a Shelby G.T.350 Mustang. He received SCCA's highest award in 1965, the Kimberly Cup for outstanding driving, and was also named "Amateur Driver of the Year" by the *New York Times*. If not already, he was sure to be tough.

SCCA had production rules specifying a minimum of 1,000 cars and limited engine displacement to 5-liters (305-cid). Although Camaro was offered with the RPO-Z28 package (602 were built in '67), they did not technically qualify. Because Chevrolet's presence intensified the long and heated Ford versus Chevy rivalry, and sure to enhance spectator turnouts, officials bent their own rules and allowed the Camaro 350 (larger than 305) with the 302-cid Z28 option to qualify for production status. Ford and Mercury raced cars

that they actually built in sufficient numbers, cars with 289-cid engines, and were understandably not pleased with SCCA's action.

Gurney and Jones won the front two starting positions in Cougars with identical 104.86-mph lap average speeds around the 3.81-mile circuit. The Daytona 300 looked to be a Cougar affair. During the race, Donohue put his Camaro in the lead for a time, and so did Titus and the Mustang, but 79 laps proved too grueling. Tullius came through, and few cared. Chrysler didn't.

The 12-Hours of Sebring was the second race, and 13 Camaros showed up! The Z28 was a natural road handler. However, the 4-Hour was a Titus show. His Mustang won the pole, set the race record and led all but a few laps. Donohue was 2nd, always within striking distance, and was followed by two more Mustangs and the sole surviving Cougar in 5th.

The Cougars finished 1-2 at Green Valley in Texas. Dick Thompson was 3rd and Donohue 4th. The season was heating up. While Jones and Gurney were off running the Indy 500, Mercury brought in Peter Revson, of the Revlon fortune, for the Lime Rock, Connecticut, Trans-Am, and he gave Cougar its second win in a row. Donohue, still winless, was 2nd followed by Titus. Cougar had a clear lead, but there was more to come.

During the season, an estimated 100,000 paid spectators saw the series come down to a Cougar versus Mustang finish at Kent, Washington. Donohue had finally dialed in his Camaro and was on the pole. Cougar would win if either Gurney and Jones won the race, or at least finish ahead of Titus if Donohue won. Both were gridded ahead of the Shelby Mustang of Titus, but luck favored Titus. With Donohue's Camaro running the strongest it had all year, Jones' Cougar failed to restart after a routine pit stop, and Ronnie Bucknum in the second Shelby Mustang got by Gurney. Camaro won the race, and Mustang won the 1967 Trans-Am by 2 points.

The early Trans-Am races were confined to Friday events preceding main features. By 1967, they became feature events

USAC star Parnelli Jones was Bud Moore's lead driver of Ford's team of factory-backed BOSS 302 Mustangs of '69. They led arch-rival Donohue and his Camaros early in the season. Then a crash sidelined 3 team cars.

of their own. "Race on Sunday, sell on Monday" was working better than ever. The ponycar wars had heated up to become another factory war, but Chrysler was out of it. 'Cudas and Challengers were yet to make a mark.

Chevrolet had a winner in the Camaro. Although '67 was a tough year on the Trans-Am circuit, the make was selected as the official pace car of the Indy 500 in its first year. Both coupes and convertibles were built, but only coupes were raced in the Trans-Am series. It all contributed to 310,636 Camaros produced by the end of that year. The Z28 was offered only on the Sport Coupe. This option cost $400.25 and included a 327 cylinder block with a special 283 crankshaft to produce 302.4 cubic inches. That was off-the-shelf hardware that just happened to fit within the 305-cid limit imposed by SCCA. At a production curb weight of 3355 pounds, the Z28 was not a lightweight, but they were able to post top speeds over 130-mph at 7100 rpm in stock form. That made their price of $4435 a lot of car for the money.

George Follmer teamed with Jones in the Bud Moore BOSS Mustangs of 1970 to win the Trans-Am championship.

Mustang did not have a comparable package to the Z28. The 289 High Performance of 1965 and '66 were rivals in spirit, but by '67, both lines of cars were offered with small block and big block engines, and the HiPo 289 lost its significance. The Barracuda S package was the hottest of the line, and along with the Dart GT, both were home for Chrysler's 273-inch small block.

Although not part of the Trans-Am, one of the main features of 5-liter racing in 1967 was the grueling Daytona Continental 24-Hour. Three Camaros were on the starting grid along with 5 Mustangs, two Shelby G.T.350 Mustangs, a Dart and a Ford Falcon. Not one of the Camaros finished. It was an embarrassing showing of the new cars, especially since Paul Richards and Ray Cuomo brought their Mustang in 11th overall, averaging 83.50-mph for 2004.06 miles of twice around the clock racing to lead the American sedan finishers. They won the Grand Touring Over 2-liter class, and the lowly Ford Falcon was 12th overall, followed by the Brock Yates Dodge Dart in at 15th. Another Mustang was 16th and still another finished 20th.

Donohue was driving a Ford GT-40 and of the three Camaros, the George Wintersteen team set a qualifying record over the 3.81-mile course (2:10.60 minutes at 105.022-mph). That was 9.5 seconds a lap behind the record-setting Ford GT-40 in the Sports Car class and 15.5 seconds behind the Prototype record set by the Gurney/Foyt MK II Ford.

The final tally of the '68 Trans-Am season was just what Donohue had planned for in Penske's Newtown Square, PA shops. Jerry Titus drove Shelby's Mustangs to a series of defeats. The Cougars were gone that year as a factory supported team, and although a new team of AMC Javelins was there to do Trans-Am battle, the crown was to be between Camaro and Mustang. Donohue and Camaro won so convincingly that it clearly showed the Z28 had a great advantage over the Mustangs. Why wasn't so clear.

The Trans-Am had become such a heated series that rule

Dan Gurney's AAR 'Cuda. With more development time, these cars might have become a real Trans-Am threat.

Developed from the 340-cid engine, the Trans-Am AAR 'Cuda had plenty of potential.

bending was rampant. Penske was good friends with John DeLorean, Chevrolet General Manager. Perhaps that accounts for how a run of thinner body panels got made. Other teams simply acid dipped the cars to lighten them. New rules allowed engines to be taken up to a max of 5-liters (305-cid), minimum weight was set at 2,800 pounds, wheel width was increased to 8-inches, and anything that could be gotten by tech inspectors was part of the game.

Like the year before, both Camaros and Mustangs ran 302 cubic inch engines. Chevrolet continued with its small block, as did Ford until Bridgehampton when a new tunnel port 302 engine was introduced. It was far stronger than the small block Windsor line, which included the HiPo 289 and standard 302. The new block had 4-bolt main bearing caps on the 2, 3 and 4 journals, and heads were smaller versions of the highly successful tunnel port design. The engine showed great promise in dyno tests, but later on, problems of various sorts arose, including the engines, that hand handed Titus and other drivers of the Shelby Racing Co. Mustangs an overwhelming defeat.

Overall, it was a thrilling year of racing with all sorts of unexpected events. After recovering his lightweight Camaro from a ravine it fell into on the way to California, Donohue rebuilt the car as the backup car for Craig Fisher. A new Camaro was under construction in the winter of '67, and the Penske-Sunoco team was to run two cars in a major effort to win both the Daytona and Sebring endurance races of 1968, and follow that with the Trans-Am title. The new Camaro was built as the long-distance car and incorporated everything that had been learned during '67. One thing was just how many engines were required to be a front runner. Bill Preston, Sunoco PR man and constant ally in the pits, confirmed that the Sunoco team bought about 50 Traco-built engines during each season.

During the winter, Titus and his crew at Shelby's place in California honed their Mustangs into shape. After three years of intense endurance racing worldwide, there was no doubt that this team had the most ability and was the best prepared. Thorough development and top preparation usually means top finishes, and Shelby's win record proved that point. Donohue intended to prove his team was better.

When he and Penske firmed up plans for the February 2nd Daytona 24-Hour, Donohue contacted Smokey Yunick to inquire if his place could be used as a base of operations. Smokey agreed, but he was also building a Camaro to run the race, and it was off limits. Smokey let them use a shed between his main buildings. Once there, the casual and noisy atmosphere at Smokey's place was a big change from Donohue's normally precise and quiet surroundings. Working long hours, both Donohue and Yunick got their cars finished. Then Donohue took his Camaro to the track down the road a few miles to do a 24-hour test before the race.

He and Fisher did the driving chores by trading off each pit stop. Hour after hour they ran the car. The engine lost a little oil pressure, then a head cracked and was changed, and all the little things that should break or go wrong in testing did. The test session was doing its job of showing up weaknesses.

One piece of equipment that went through the testing was a cross-flow, staggered, dual 4-bbl intake manifold that Chevrolet engineer Fred Frincke designed and development engineer Bill Howell tweaked to perfection. It ran extremely well. With it, Donohue had another "unfair advantage".

About halfway through the test, Smokey rolled in with his beautiful gold and black Camaro. The factory engineers happed along about then. Without a driver, Smokey talked Donohue and Fisher into taking his car out. They concluded that their Sunoco car was a better handler but Smokey's was faster.

During qualifying for the 24-Hour, Donohue was fastest among the Trans-Am entries and was gridded 12th, two Trans-Am spots in front of Titus' Mustang in the 22nd starting position. Smokey's Camaro qualified second. After completely rebuilding the new car for the race, once underway, Donohue and Fisher were hampered with another cracked head. It cracked in the same place, across a valve seat. (Over the years, for engines fully stressed in racing applications, that has come to be recognized as one weaknesses in the small block Chevrolet design.) Changing the head dropped the Sunoco team well down at the finish, to 12th overall. Lengthy stops to change brake pads was another area needing improvement.

Penske and Sunoco shifted to the AMC Javelin factory team in 1970, but couldn't beat the BOSS Mustangs.

Jim Hall teamed with Chevrolet to run the Chaparral Camaros of 1970. The effort was not enough to win.

At the finish, Titus and Bucknum rolled in a triumphant 4th overall. 4th in a Mustang?! That was unheard of. Among 67 entries, the finest racing cars in the world, their Trans-Am Mustang had beaten most of them. Fans loved it. Titus and Bucknum ran 2,396.49 miles averaging 99.85-mph, and crossed the finish line behind 3 prototype Porsches. It was a superb showing for Detroit iron.

With healthier cars and a trick for quick brake pad changes, the Sunoco team rallied to victory in the March 23rd Sebring 12-Hour. Another trick was getting the second car inspected. It was the old acid-dipped car that SCCA had warned Penske about, it was not legal and would not be allowed to race. Donohue, always clever, rigged the number circles on the cars so that they could be interchanged. He then took the new #15 car to inspection first. Once it was approved, the car was taken back to the garage where the numbers were switched. Then the same Camaro with #6 on it went back through inspection. Both Camaros were in!

Sebring was a Camaro success. After 12-hours of racing around the flat and rough ex-World War II bomber base, the Penske-Sunoco cars rolled in 3rd and 4th overall (car #15 followed by #6). Like Daytona, Detroit iron was proving to be tougher than most of the world's top "real" racing cars. After two years of high finishes, T-A cars were not part of '69 and '70 races. If they should win over Ferrari...well.

With the long distance races evenly split between Mustang and Camaro, (but Camaro leading 16 to 14 points), the season's shorter length Trans-Am races unfolded into a 11-event series. Donohue won 10 races and the championship.

Ford Motor Company had won the first two titles at a cost of millions. Chevrolet received its trophy in 1968 for practically nothing. "We don't race" was still the corporate edict, and with the Trans-Am title handed to Chevrolet, it was more of an embarrassment than a coveted award. It really belonged to Donohue, not Chevrolet.

The '69 season opened with all new BOSS 302 Mustangs against restyled Z28s. The BOSS 302 was conceived as a low production, high-performance package with a special engine and suspension. It was made to fit Trans-Am rules.

Two official factory teams campaigned the new cars, Shelby American in California and Bud Moore in South Carolina. With two highly competitive teams, Ford was

serious about winning the series.

The new BOSS engine was nothing more than the tunnel port block with Ford's new canted valve 351 Cleveland heads. (Remember those two "Mystery" engines that Bill France forced Chevrolet to sell to Ford in order to run the Daytona 500 in '63? Chevrolet engineer Dick Keinath patented the canted valve "porcupine" design back then.) Although the Ford engines were not called "porcupines" like the big block Chevys, their similar canted valve train, huge ports and large valves made a high winding performer capable of over 480-hp in Trans-Am form. Suddenly, the Z28 had a new and tougher adversary.

Although there were Firebirds, Javelins and growing numbers of competing Camaros, the Trans-Am for 1969 was another Chevy versus Ford shootout. When a mid-season crash took out 3 of the 4 team Mustangs, Donohue raced on to his second championship in a row.

SCCA opened its 11-race Trans-Am season of 1970 at Laguna Seca. Old rivals, Donohue and Parnelli Jones fought round after round throughout the year, but the Sunoco cars were now factory-backed AMC Javelins. This time it was a Mustang year. The BOSS Mustangs won 6 races. Jones paced Donohue by 1 point, 142 to 141, to take the title.

Without Penske, racing superstar Jim Hall was brought on to handle two new-generation Camaros that year, and that brought out-spoken ties between Chevrolet and his Chaparral team. The cars turned out to be less of a threat than expected.

Plymouth moved into Trans-Am racing with a 2-car team run by Dan Gurney, his AAR 'Cudas. Although there were no MoPar 5-liter engines, the 340 could be de-stroked to conform to T-A regulations. Swede Savage was Gurney's driver for the second car. Dodge Division looked for a Trans-Am team and settled on Sam Posey to campaign a single car effort. Neither MoPar was successful. SCCA rules required at least 2,500 production cars to qualify, and that put the AAR 'Cuda, Challenger T/A, and BOSS 302 in dealer showrooms.

1970 is considered the best year of Trans-Am racing until the '80s. When the factories pulled out, the Trans-Am died. For '71, the Sunoco Javelins were the only factory-backed team, and Donohue won against Follmer in a lone Bud Moore Mustang among sportsman teams. Big drops in new car sales signalled that bad times had arrived.

Index